TWENTYSOMETHING

ESSAYS

BY

TWENTYSOMETHING

WRITERS

CALIFORNIA THE WALTZ THE MUSTACHE
RACE SEX AND THE SICKBED TRICYCLE
PRIME-TIME YOU BACKLASH THINK
OUTSIDE THE BOX BUT STAY INSIDE THE
GRID FINDING THE BEAT YOU SHALL GO
OUT WITH JOY AND BE LED FORTH WITH
PEACE THE IDIOT'S GUIDE TO YOUR PALM
SHEER DOMINANCE LIVE NUDE GIRL AN
EVENING IN APRIL CLICHÉ RAPE STORY
ROCK MY NETWORK GOODBYE TO ALL THAT
ALL THE RIGHT ANSWERS WHY I HAD TO
LEAVE IN-BETWEEN PLACES A RED SPOON
FOR THE NAMELESS MY LITTLE COMMA
FIGHT ME THE SECRET LIVES OF MY
PARENTS MY ROARING TWENTIES IN, FROM
THE OUTSIDE THE MYSTERIES OF LIFE . . .
REVEALED! SO YOU SAY YOU WANT A
REVOLUTION WORKING AT WENDY'S JESS
LACHER MARY BETH ELLIS BRONSON
LEMER JENNIFER GLASER RACHEL KEMPF
JOHN FISCHER SHAHNAZ HABIB EMMA
BLACK ELI JAMES KYLE MINOR COLLEEN
KINDER CHRISTOPHER POLING KATHLEEN
ROONEY RADHIYAH AYOBAMI MARISA
McCARTHY THEODORA STITES EULA BISS
BRENDAN PARK LUKE MULLINS MARY KATE
FRANK BURLEE VANG ELRENA EVANS
MIELLYN FITZWATER KATE McGOVERN
LAUREN MONROE KATHERINE DYKSTRA TRAVIS
SENTELL J. W. YOUNG JOEY FRANKLIN

TWENTYSOMETHING
ESSAYS
BY
TWENTYSOMETHING
WRITERS

EDITED BY

MATT KELLOGG AND JILLIAN QUINT

RANDOM HOUSE TRADE PAPERBACKS ⬤ NEW YORK

Published in the United States by Random House Trade Paperbacks,
an imprint of The Random House Publishing Group,
a division of Random House, Inc., New York.

RANDOM HOUSE TRADE PAPERBACKS and colophon
are trademarks of Random House, Inc.

"Goodbye to All That" by Eula Biss first appeared
in the *North American Review* in 2006.

"My Little Comma" by Elrena Evans first appeared
in *Literary Mama,* under the title "Birthing" in 2005.

Grateful acknowledgment is made to HarperCollins Publishers
for permission to include five lines from "The Secret" from *Betting on the Muse:
Poems & Stories* by Charles Bukowski, copyright © 1996 by Linda Lee
Bukowski. Reprinted by permission of HarperCollins Publishers.

LIBRARY OF CONGRESS CATALOGING-IN-PUBLICATION DATA

Twentysomething essays by twentysomething writers /
edited by Matt Kellogg and Jillian Quint.
p. cm.
ISBN 0-8129-7566-9 (trade pbk.)
1. American essays—21st century. I. Kellogg, Matt. II. Quint, Jillian.
III. Title: Best new voices of 2006.

PS689.T87 2006
814.6'08—dc22 2006045128

Printed in the United States of America

www.atrandom.com

2 4 6 8 9 7 5 3 1

Designed by Stephanie Huntwork

Between the hours of 10:00 A.M. and 11:59 P.M. on November 24, 2005, the inbox of 20by20essays@randomhouse.com was inundated with more than one thousand e-mails. Was it spam? A virus? Were people finally responding to our Match.com profile? No, we still couldn't find a date or a good deal on Viagra. It was simply the deadline for the *Twentysomething Essays by Twentysomething Writers* contest, and as it turned out, nearly everyone—two thirds of the total contestants—had waited until literally the last minute to submit.

According to our colleagues, this meant we were a generation of procrastinators, too busy blogging about our recently diagnosed ADHD or watching the first season of *The OC* on DVD to get our act together and turn something in ahead of time; the contest had run for a full six months, after all. And they had a point. But the more we thought about it, the more we realized that this procrastination wasn't necessarily a generational fault but rather an indication of how today's world works. In an era of text messaging, online shopping, and movies on demand, why would anyone do anything more than a day or two in advance? It's not that we're lazy or bratty or glib; it's just that we're fast. We know how to access all kinds of information, and we have absolute confidence in the tools at our disposal.

In fact, it was precisely because of this technological immediacy that the contest attracted such a large, wide-ranging pool of writers. When we first launched our website, we had two listings on Google;

the next week, fifty; as of this writing, we're at 1,130. Though at first we were concerned that certain groups or types of twentysomethings might dominate the collection—it would be a problem if everyone was from Albuquerque or played the lute or worked at Petco—we were bowled over by the breadth and depth of the submissions we received. We heard from prison inmates, soldiers, production assistants, corporate-ladder climbers, pastry chefs. And not only were the writers themselves diverse, but each also offered a new way of thinking about a given subject. Is ethnicity tantamount to identity or is it a barrier to overcome? Should we be planning careers and families or living moment to moment? How do we negotiate our roles as both someone's child and someone's parent? Do we approach God with skepticism or trust? To what extent can we effect political change? What's funny? What's not? How can we make art that's new, and do we even want to?

Because of this diversity, we had trouble discerning overarching themes in these essays. It seemed almost audacious to make any blanket statements about a generation that so consistently asserts its volatility, but we're nothing if not audacious, so we gave it a shot. We began by doing what any incredibly anal person confronted with an overwhelming amount of information would do: we pigeonholed. Having narrowed the field down to one hundred essays, we subdivided the finalists and slapped on tidy little labels—Ethnic Identity; Cubicle Culture; Born-Again Agnosticism; Indie/Underground/Post-Trip-Hop/Pre-Grunge Revival; Deep, Philosophical, Possibly Drug-Enhanced Ruminations on Life; and, of course, Sex. Lots and lots of sex. Some of the categories, like Gay Issues and Women's Studies, even started to sound like 200-level liberal arts courses.

But ultimately our well-intentioned bigotry was for naught. For example, early on we relegated a piece about a Web-radio obsession to the Technology section. As we moved through the rest of the submissions, though, we saw that it could just as easily have worked under the heading Pop Culture or Career (the author listens to her favorite station to get her through the workday) or Family (she fondly remembers her father's addiction to NPR). And this kept happening. No single

essay, it seemed, fit snugly into a single category. It was as if we were stuck using a Microsoft Outlook approach in a Gmail world. (For those not familiar with the difference, Outlook only allows you to sort each e-mail into a single folder, while the exceedingly brilliant people at Google figured out that you could cross-reference messages by an unlimited number of distinct labels.) Maybe it was just the sleep deprivation talking, but everything seemed to be about, well, everything. We didn't know whether to jump for joy or weep in a corner.

The problem was that such "everything-ness" seemed to spoil any claims of twentysomething solidarity. Our generation has often been accused of political apathy, of lacking the unity of ideology and purpose that the Boomers—our parents—were so famous for. According to popular opinion, we are all supposed to be deeply polarized by the Red/Blue divide. Which side we land on, we are told, should dictate who we vote for, what we wear, how we feel about NASCAR. But, in reality, the spectrum is much wider and more colorful. We are not apathetic; we've simply learned to make more subtle distinctions. Because of the Gmail Effect, we can each adopt a multitude of personas that ebb and flow depending on context. And this, in our humble opinion, is very cool.

A friend of ours once commented that there isn't a twentysomething out there, home-schooled hermits and bow-tied Republicans aside, who doesn't love *The Daily Show with Jon Stewart*. And that was even before the *Crossfire* appearance. So, if we are such a diverse, nuanced generation, why is it that a late-night comedy show on cable TV has become our universal point of reference? Sure, the fart jokes and celebrity interviews don't hurt, but ultimately we watch because Stewart and company have come to reflect our core values: a new brand of humor that recognizes that reality is itself a punch line, a categorically skeptical point of view, and a genuine engagement with the world around us. And these values are what enable us to make informed decisions and keep up hope in legitimately troubled times (e.g., recent elections, natural disasters, the Nick and Jessica debacle, etc.).

The writers in this book recognize the problems, big and not-so-

big, that our generation faces. With hope, intelligence, irreverence, and urgency, they show that we are not to be taken lightly (but not too seriously, either), that we're finally ready to sit at the proverbial Grownups' Table. Like the twentysomethings who have come before us, we've slogged through the absurdities of postadolescence/pre-adulthood and are prepared for anything the world might throw at us—except, God forbid, turning thirty.

CONTENTS

TWENTYSOMETHING
ESSAYS
BY
TWENTYSOMETHING
WRITERS

You know about how I ended up in L.A., how I was drowning in that postcollegiate soup into which middle-class white kids with arty leanings often slip the summer after senior year. I had no particular plans for any particular thing, and suddenly nobody was grading me on the still life of a pear I painted or my paper on the postfeminist ramifications of the film *Alien: Resurrection*. You mean nobody is going to seek me out and give me a job rendering fruit in cheap oils on Tuesdays and Thursdays from twelve-thirty to four? Weird.

It had been six months since I'd stopped taking the little pink pills that had evened out my moods and the old ugly feelings were beginning to rumble again. With the summer getting late and no school to go back to, Martha and I figured we'd leave Ohio and drive around the country awhile, eat Fritos in the car and drink beer in weird bars in Kansas. It was hot and rainy, and by the time we got to Vegas and tried to scrape together blackjack money in the parking lot of the Sahara the adventure was turning grim. I'd lost my voice from yelling over the noise of the passing road and Martha wanted to keep moving west, as she was heartsick about this guitar player in Los Angeles, California.

California.

I grew up smack in the middle of God's Great Ohio, writing stupid poems in Five-Star notebooks, struggling against imagined adversity

and promising to make an artist of myself in New York City as soon as the opportunity arose. Twenty-two years in the Middle West, land of sweaters and heavy silence and three-way chili; California barely existed except as the place the stars lived and loved, the place where skinny people had tans and white teeth and cellular telephones. We stood in the parking lot of the Sahara and looked west over 250 miles of desert and thought, Here we go.

When we arrived in that golden state, after we had left the horror of the freeway behind us, California smelled like flowers. Nothing as domestic as a tulip or a marigold—these are wild and twisting animals in Seussian shapes, red and purple like a gorgeous bruise. Asters and snapdragons and birds-of-paradise push through the fences in the suburbs of L.A., and in the mountains it is wildflowers, lupine and verbena low to the ground, blooming in crazy colors for no one at all. Even the junk flowers—the lush fireweed and the elegant cow parsnip! Stretched-out palm trees in neatly spaced rows look over the neatly stuccoed houses on street after street after street, no big deal, they're just there and that's just how it goes. Strange and magnificent! The middle of September came and classes started up in the Middle West and I stayed in California and got a job.

The first thing you see when you walk into Paramount Studios is a giant cyclorama on the side of a soundstage, a wide blue sky with wild white clouds rolling along the top of it. To the north, above the studio walls, are the Hollywood Hills, and perched atop them is the Hollywood sign, just as white and absurd as you imagine, and beyond that the washed-out SoCal sky reaches blue-brown and constant in every direction, and welcome to L.A. While the leaves turned on the oaks back home, those palm trees didn't bat an eyelash, just kept smiling down on me in my little Ford Escort, zooming off to my new job at Paramount in the morning and zooming back after dark. My job was an internship and it paid $250 a week regardless of hours worked, maybe enough to scrape on back home, but I quickly found out it's a joke out here and don't forget they're doing you a favor because this is how people get a foot in the door.

I worked in a basement, and all day the stars and the big-leaguers trod above my head in what were once Lucille Ball's mahogany offices. On my first day they showed me a roomful of magazines and newspapers, heaps of them, ten copies of every periodical that had, in the past three years, borne mention of Tom Cruise, whose career it was now my job to document in an oversize scrapbook. My tools in this endeavor were a paper cutter and a can of spray adhesive, the fumes of which, by the middle of the day, left me glassy-eyed and floating three inches off the floor of the unventilated basement. And oh, the glamour! Stoned on Super 77, I would pet the dog from *Frasier* when my lunch break and his pee break coincided. The klieg lights came out and they filmed an episode of the UPN's *Girlfriends* on the lawn outside my basement. Did I not exchange words (he: "Windy enough for you?," me: "Yes.") with *Quantum Leap*'s Scott Bakula? This was my first job out of college, and that lot with its fake streets and fake sky was probably the realest thing to come my way.

I took to California like a duck to water. November came and went, and I didn't even unpack my scarf. The Christmas decorations went up and faded in the sun—Santa and his reindeer smiling down on the open convertibles putting down Wilshire in Beverly Hills. I went to the beach after New Year's and called my little brother, snowbound in Ann Arbor, Michigan. "I'm wearing a tank top!" I told him. "Hear that? That's the ocean!" *Wooshhh,* it said, rushing in. *Shhhh,* back out again. Then a moment of quiet. *Wooshhh. Shhhh.* Quiet. *Wooshhh.*

Back at home, we were hurled through the year by climatic changes too swift and cruel to ignore. Summer ticked hot into fall, which cooled into winter, which dragged into spring, and we alternately brought out the sweaters and packed up the umbrellas and dug through the drawer for the swimsuit that had one more year in it. Talking about the weather gets a bad reputation, but when the weather is your temperamental husband and you hardly know one day to the next if he's going to love you right or insult your casserole and try to kill you in an electrical storm—well, that's something you want to mull over with your girlfriends. I had spent the winter of my freshman year

of college in Chicago with the covers of my extra-long twin bed tucked under my chin, staring horrified out the window at the snow that fell and fell and continued to fall. Out of my parents' nest, the winters had been long and mean, far removed from the snowsuited Christmases of my youth, when I was ferried about in a minivan, feet touching snow only when it was time to play in it. This new California January was a marvel.

June first of that year, I woke up and changed the calendar and thought, Summer? What happened to winter, where was the spring? Seasons in California are gentle and mysterious suggestions that usher the willing through the year, but for the willful or the oblivious they hardly exist. Before I knew it, I was twenty-three and my first year in California had passed in a haze of sunshine and strip-mall trips to the all-night taco stand down the street. I was suddenly tan. Tan! In Ohio the sun hides for months at a time and then attacks in a savage burst of heat and humidity, and when I wasn't bundled up against the winter I spent my childhood either knee-deep in SPF 60 or crisped red and blistery like a lizard cooked too long in the sun. Now I looked in the mirror and I was from California.

I had a new blond driver's license that made my residency official, but the terms of my emigration reached deeper. Every morning I woke up, opened the screen door onto my balcony and saw sunshine, and thought, Yes. I am on a vacation life, and my vacation life is a good one. All those feelings of loneliness and upset that I had lugged around since adolescence were melting like butter and zipping up into the ozone, leaving me light and laughing and tan with no unpleasant side effects. With those low thoughts gone, I felt other things slipping away as well, though I only half knew what they were. All I knew was that I wasn't sad anymore—I was in California.

My second year in L.A. passed much like the first: evenly, pleasantly, marked by beach trips and concerts and beautiful days, the stretches of beautiful days broken by spectacular ones. I parted ways with Paramount and started working three jobs: Venice, Beverly Hills, Encino. Los Angeles is 465 square miles of freeways, and depending

on the weather and the time of day, they can be the best or worst thing that has ever happened to you. Live in L.A. long enough, and you will come to navigate them like a sailor catching sea currents: the 101 to the 110 to the 10 to the 405. Hit them right, late at night mostly, with the stars out and a warm breeze through four open windows, hit them at one A.M. with Led Zeppelin or something equally triumphant blasting on the tinny speakers of your little Ford Escort and you will dream of missing your exit and burning into the desert until you run out of gas money or highway, whichever comes first. But the unfortunate daylight hours on the unfortunate weekday? Hang your head, traveler, for the Lord does not hear your implorations. Nothing is crueler than the inexplicable two-thirty jam on the 405, a strip of steaming asphalt set between the unforgiving walls of a canyon from which there is no escape once you have entered it. Stuck in the sun, air conditioner broken, you sit immobile behind a belching yellow school bus, and the only things moving in ten lanes of traffic are the motorcycles whizzing past like drunk mosquitoes.

The lemons and oranges ripened and fell from the fruit trees, and I waltzed into a dreamy job at a girls' high school that offered a respectable salary for a few hours of work on the green and Catholic campus four days a week. In California, high schools are not cinderblock boxes where they seal you up at eight and spit you back out at three blinking at the sunlight. Los Angeles high schools are breezy outdoor places, and when they let you outside between classes you find well-manicured lawns spotted with hydrangea and lilacs. The biggest perk of my job was that it brought many idle hours, hours I used for napping and trying to cook tofu in my sunny kitchen and improving my tan hiking in the hills above my apartment, for thinking about painting my bedroom and pushing my hair down on my forehead to see what I would look like with bangs. I set my alarm for eight just to enjoy the empty mornings, one after another, desultory and mine.

My drive to and from the school came to include that wild road Sunset Boulevard, an exercise in extremes running as it does from the high street numbers and high fences where beat-down Mexican men

hustle star maps to hapless tourists, to the less fashionable guts of Hollywood fifteen miles east. You'll know you're getting there when the gas stations become less and less respectable, and finally, you get to 'exaco, from which the T was pried in a fit of desperation or independent spirit. 'exaco doesn't usually have gas; they're in the used-tire game. In between these two places is the Strip, neon and terrible, looming billboards and nowhere to park for two miles of nude advertisements, some leering in print and some gyrating on giant screens that send weaker motorists careening into one another.

It was on this drive, with its yawning blind curves and occasional mountain views, that I began to feel a *feeling* that third year, coming home every day at six. What a funny feeling, I thought, and turned up the radio and made some phone calls and came home and tried to hush my brain with a few glasses of wine. One morning my alarm went off at eight and I could hardly catch my breath, crushed as I was beneath the weight of the impending morning. The minutes yawned ahead of me, hollow and accusatory, and by nine A.M. I wanted it to be bedtime. I carried a dead thing with me—I couldn't figure out what it was or where it had come from, but I knew that it was dead. Before long I was clutching the steering wheel of my little Ford Escort and weeping into the beautiful wide curves of Sunset Boulevard, trudging into my apartment after work and lying down on the floor to eat a loaf of wheat bread while watching *Buffy the Vampire Slayer,* seasons one through seven, screened in quick and desperate succession from January through April.

I should have stayed happy. Nothing had changed. The sun shone on my apartment, I had money, I had a tan, I had a friend with an apartment on the beach, and there we would sit on warm nights and watch the Ferris wheel turn on the Santa Monica Pier. The school offered me a raise and a promotion, and I lay down on the floor of my living room and wept. All signs pointed to my happiness, but where was it? Sunny day after sunny day I would wake to the smell of hibiscus and throw open the screen door to my balcony and feel that *thing* heavy and black in my gut, ruining endless summer and rotting in the

flower beds. By the time I drove home from work, the Sunset Strip was a grotesquerie, two miles of pornographic traffic to be endured in order to get back home to my television. I was doing nothing.

That's it, I was doing nothing.

I came to this conclusion on a Saturday afternoon in May, lying prone on my couch, staring at the wall, eating peanut butter out of the jar with a spoon (to my credit, it was organic). My dead thing and I sat up and looked at our beautiful apartment. I looked up through the skylight at the beautiful sun and I realized: This *is* the life. California *is* paradise. I could live in California and be content forever, there among the hills and the honeysuckle, but I hadn't earned it. I had shuffled through an exorbitantly priced liberal arts education with slightly less effort than I had devoted to games of Frisbee football, and then followed the path of least resistance into adulthood. I was a jerk, and my life was beautiful and easy, and I was never going to do anything but roll around in the flowers and feel like I had screwed up.

When I moved to California, I stopped writing stupid poems in Five-Star notebooks and started taking walks in the sun. But listen, I like walking in the sun, and there's nothing wrong with that course of events—there was only something wrong with me. All through high school, all through college, some midwestern thing in me was growing and feeding on ice storms and leaf pollen and three-way chili. It made me bite my nails and it made me sad when it rained and it made me stay up nights wondering where it was all heading, and when I went west I shut it down. Hey there, painful thing. Chill out and listen to the surf for a few years. So there we sat: *Wooshhh. Shhhh.* Quiet. *Wooshhh.*

When summer came, I quit my job at the school and packed all my worldly possessions into my little Ford Escort and I zoomed back over the mountains and across the prairie and all the way to New York City, where I had once dreamed of being a very serious and tortured artist. A few months have passed here now, and I am broke and sick and my apartment has mice and no windows in the living room. I'm pasty and haggard and I eat pizza for dinner almost every night, pizza and beer, but that thing has woken up and is moving around in me again, push-

ing me toward something, and it is working, it is growing and aching. Some nights I come home to Brooklyn on the train in time to catch the last moments of sunset throwing wild colors up in the cold sky, and maybe it's because the days are so gray, but every time I see it, it is spectacular, as if there is an economy of beauty here, and no sunset will be wasted.

Now comes the tricky part, the part where ends get tied up and a life lesson is spun. I can say cold weather makes you work harder and crappy apartments aren't good places to hole up and watch 144 episodes of *Buffy the Vampire Slayer.* I can say follow your dreams and work hard in school. But New York is hard and foul-smelling, and the weather is turning terrible in unpredictable ways. There are no flowers in midtown. Tall buildings shut out the sun; I have to wear heels to work. Sometimes I miss California so much my eyes get hot, and I remember how it feels to lie down in February on a hilltop covered, *covered* in golden violets, golden violets and sunshine, and I know that once I get my act together I will be back there, grown up, finally deserving of happiness.

CALIFORNIA THE WALTZ THE MUSTACHE RACE
SEX AND THE SICKBED TRICYCLE PRIME-TIME YOU BACKLASH
THINK OUTSIDE THE BOX BUT STAY INSIDE THE GRID
FINDING THE BEAT YOU SHALL GO OUT WITH JOY AND BE
LED FORTH WITH PEACE THE IDIOT'S GUIDE TO YOUR PALM
SHEER DOMINANCE LIVE NUDE GIRL AN EVENING IN APRIL
CLICHÉ RAPE STORY ROCK MY NETWORK GOODBYE TO ALL THAT
ALL THE RIGHT ANSWERS WHY I HAD TO LEAVE IN-BETWEEN PLACES
A RED SPOON FOR THE NAMELESS MY LITTLE COMMA FIGHT ME
THE SECRET LIVES OF MY PARENTS MY ROARING TWENTIES
IN, FROM THE OUTSIDE THE MYSTERIES OF LIFE . . . REVEALED!
SO YOU SAY YOU WANT A REVOLUTION WORKING AT WENDY'S
JESS LACHER MARY BETH ELLIS BRONSON LEMER JENNIFER GLASER
RACHEL KEMPF JOHN FISCHER SHAHNAZ HABIB EMMA BLACK

B y order of the resident assistant, I made the appointment with the therapist following a fairly major war with my next-door neighbor in the dorm, an altercation involving her assertion that *Growing Pains* reigned supreme over all the eighties sitcoms of the land. I kicked her wall and put my foot through her prized possession, a Whopper banner swiped from the flagpole of a Burger King, because *everybody* knows that *Family Ties* just absolutely *rocked,* at least until the extraordinarily slappable extra child, Andy, showed up.

"I think I need help with stress management," I said to the therapist. I was perched on the edge of a lavender chair crammed hard with foam and embroidery. It was aggressively comforting, this chair.

A manila file folder marked with my name was open on the psychologist's lap. "I see you've been in therapy before," she said.

That would be my freshman year of high school, when I first became strongly convinced that if I did not touch a doorknob with both hands upon entering or exiting a room, the world would implode in dramatic and fully horrible fashion.

"Yes," I said. I had not told anyone that such matters were my chief concern most days, as I was fully aware they were well within the realm of the totally ridiculous.

"Also," said the woman before me with my mental health history

spread on her knees, "you seem to have had certain excessive . . . anxieties . . . concerning use of the Internet?"

That, I hadn't quite been able to hide. When you are fourteen and you make furtive attempts to double back to the pew your family was sitting in so you can scrub away the fingerprints, thus leaving no record of your active Catholicism because you are privately terrified that the Ku Klux Klan is after you, people tend to form the conclusion that There Is a Problem.

Activities such as these sprang from the day I posted a gentle rant to an electronic religious discussion group, in which I'd announced to the whole entire Internet that I was Catholic and that, in my very humble opinion, liturgical dance was the worst thing *ever* and that it made me want to injure people with blunt and heavy objects.

Making this pronouncement, I decided with a terrifying and completely unwarranted urgency less than a week after I'd typed it, was not the brightest thing I had ever done. It was bottomlessly stupid; it was *stupid,* and it was going to get me killed. The Klan! They hate Catholics, they *kill* Catholics, and where better to find Catholics than a public forum? Oh God, maybe they *set up the discussion* for the *sole purpose* of finding some! And there were other people . . . just who, I didn't know, but they were out there and they hated Catholics and they were going to kick my ass.

And the liturgical dancers . . . oh God . . . I'd insulted the liturgical dancers of the earth. They were going to find me, me and my family. Right now they were taking a break from choreographing "Crown Him with Many Crowns" to call out a hit on me, their vaunted and public enemy. Why didn't I just keep my mouth shut? Why hadn't I just endured their "Nearer My God to Thee" kicklines in silence? I had angered them, belittled their cherished way of life, and any second now a gauze-wrapped grenade was going to come sailing through the window. Oh God oh God oh God oh God.

I stayed away from the Internet after that, and not long after came the day when my mother walked into my room with some laundry to

find me breaking open a floppy disk, slicing apart its filmy guts with a pair of desk scissors. She stared at me, a stack of bras in one hand, a pile of Umbro shorts in the other.

"Isn't that," she said, "where the computer saves all the stories and essays you've been writing?"

I glanced down at the torn-away disk label marked with my name—I was going to tear *that* up next, in very tiny bits, and scatter them in a variety of trash bags throughout the house, over a course of many trash collection days, so that no one could piece them together and trace me to it—and looked back up at her, scissors poised.

She twisted her hands in one of my bra straps. "Why are you doing that?"

"I don't know," I said finally, unable to break her heart and let on that I had gone altogether round the bend and was terrified of the frantic electrons that were the Internet, where there was no way to tear up anything you wrote, where God and all His revenge-bent liturgical dancers could find you. Two days later, I was in another version of where I am now—in a therapist's office, in the grips of a chair decorated in Modern American Hotel Lobby, where, for the duration of my high school career, I participated in circular conversations concerning whether or not I was breast-fed, the monotony of which was occasionally sprinkled with moments when the therapist wanted to know, by the way and just out of simple curiosity, if I ever heard voices belonging to famous people or the Devil or God instructing me to, say, shoot the president.

"Well," I said now by way of explanation, "you know."

The therapist closed my file. I settled in and prepared to be casually asked whether I held regular conversations with the Lord of Darkness.

Instead she was eyeing my hands. "You have dry skin," she said.

"I wasn't breast-fed," I said, nodding.

"Dry skin on your hands and nowhere else," she pointed out. "They're chapped almost raw."

"You know what?" I said, rising. "I have a class."

"It's almost as if," she continued, examining her ballpoint pen, "you've been washing them with some fairly strong soap. Pretty often, actually."

Oh dear.

"It's okay if you do," she said.

Ohhhhhhhhhhhh . . .

"Do you have a lot of unwanted thoughts and worries, Mary Beth?"

"I'm having some *right now*." I bent down to retrieve my backpack.

"Are those fears over events you intellectually know aren't likely to happen, but you can't stop worrying anyway? And do you feel you need to check and arrange things a lot to relieve the worry—not just leaving the curling iron on, but more out-of-the-ordinary things, like rereading pages in a book over and over, avoiding certain numbers. . . ."

I sat down again. "Three!" I said. "And six!"

"It sounds like you might have obsessive-compulsive disorder."

"And I'm afraid that if I sit in a chair that a guy's been sitting in, I will become pregnant!"

"Let's make another appointment so I can administer a screening test."

"I'm afraid I'll catch AIDS from library books!"

"Okay, well, maybe we can skip the screening test."

When one has obsessive-compulsive disorder, insufficient amounts of the neurotransmitter serotonin prevent proper communication between one's orbital cortex and basal ganglia, resulting in unwanted obsessive thoughts, even though the patient is fully cognizant of the inappropriate and nonsensical nature. To sum: The brain is on a constant short circuit and therefore shits a brick. You don't die from OCD. You just wish you would.

Patients can tackle the symptoms of it—the liturgical-dancer panic, the frantic mental urgings to run for the bathroom sink—with behavioral therapy, which involves extensive and intense work on retraining one's brain by forcing oneself to face, even encounter, those aspects of life that one most fears. When the therapist suggested this—she en-

couraged me to, for instance, wear my boyfriend's boxer shorts for a day without washing them first—I communicated that I'd really rather not by way of throwing up in her floral trash can.

The other course of action is to ingest staggering amounts of government-regulated, mind-altering substances. I was all for this.

The Luvox, the "serotonin reuptake inhibitor"—they could have called it Warmed-Over String-Bean Vomit, for all I cared, as long as it curbed the overwhelming urge to carry my own toilet paper into public restrooms because God only knew what kind of AIDS-riddled microbes lurked within the tire-size rolls—tamed the OCD to a manageable if irritating mosquito whine. Life as a Luvox-sedated obsessive-compulsive is like arising each morning with a slightly pulled calf muscle: You can run, walk, stretch, and kick perfectly well, but not without an eternally twinging reminder, a tiny pinprick of fear. There is always sewage in the serotonin canal.

The OCD flows through my family like a Purell-purchasing version of the Force: My great-grandmother had it. My grandmother had it. I have it. But I also have the gift of receiving a diagnosis in an era when personal problems are quite the thing, as evidenced when my girlhood hero, Mary Lou Retton, told the world that she has an overactive bladder, easily the most important celebrity endorsement of a bodily dysfunction since Jerry Mathers bravely denounced psoriasis. So far, those of us with OCD have netted only former *Double Dare* host Marc Summers, but as awareness increases, we might be able to score us someone on the level of a Loni Anderson or—dare we dream—a Bob Barker.

E veryday life is a soapy film coating seas of panic and second-guessing. We seek constant reassurance from those without OCD that our fears are groundless, thus unwittingly sweeping friends and family members into the sticky, clawing net.

And I'm one of the lucky ones. Some OCD patients, unresponsive to treatment or just plain unaware that there exists a name and a lot of slanty Latin words for what they're feeling and thinking and doing,

spend hours before the mirror, parting their hair just . . . exactly . . . right. Others feel forced to hoard mail, sit on every single piece of it, hundreds and hundreds of little Ed McMahons smiling out from beneath the kitchen table, in between piles of 1987 *People*s, peering up from behind the television set. There are those compelled to count objects—windowpanes, words, songs on the radio—to a certain number for a certain number of times. Many can't stop tearing out their own hair. Sometimes an OCD patient cannot leave a room without holding a certain word or phrase in his mind. Mothers double over in the fear that they will somehow harm their children; children erase holes in their math homework, frantic that they haven't printed out their numbers in precisely the proper fashion.

Me, I just spend an inordinate amount of time worrying that, virgin status notwithstanding, I will come down either pregnant or HIV-positive. So: a *Hannity & Colmes* session between me and my serotonin . . . holding myself a delicate distance from a gentleman's crotch . . . these are simple things, really.

Try telling that, however, to the gentleman. The experts have informed me that such fears are quite prevalent among OCD patients who have grown up steeped in Catholicism, a religion that kind of frowns upon premarital sex; but if that's really the case, we would have popped up with a Saint Simon of the Antibacterial Soap a long, long time ago.

As I began dating more and more, and the Luvox-pumped serotonin levels went up and up, I wasn't sure if I felt uncomfortable with the nonsex I was having because of the obsessing and compulsing in my head or because of the Blessed Virgin statue on my windowsill. On dates I would toss my hair and lean forward with wide eyes and feign enchantment over butchered acoustical versions of "Gloria"; then I'd return to the dorm, stare up at the stained ceiling, and anxiously await my period. My other friends, when they had pregnancy scares, at least had the preliminary fun of the thing.

Every time I fumbled through a darkened dorm room in search of my underwire bra, I had to sort it out like dirty laundry: Did I feel cas-

cades of unease after I sat up on the couch because I was afraid that HIV had somehow magically leaped into my bloodstream, or because if an anvil came crashing down upon me through the ceiling, it meant big-time hell for me?

By the end of my college career, I had it pretty well figured out—when I felt like a slut as I was dropped off, it was the Catholicism; when I merely felt like shooting up a horse tranquilizer, it was the OCD. On a good night I felt only one or the other.

I've been through four boyfriends and two therapists since I was diagnosed, and the only ones not currently eyeing me from a distance of at least seven states are the therapists.

The first boyfriend, to his everlasting credit, broke up with me because he was an idiot and a child and was feeling, and I quote, "trapped" after I insisted that he remove the pictures of his ex-girlfriend from his walls. Obsessive-compulsive disorder, whatever—just don't come between him and the woman who'd asked for a restraining order.

The second boyfriend, a little worse. When I explained the condition to him, he had no problem with it as long as his wang was satisfyingly chunged, and when I told him I felt uncomfortable or frightened, he tended to become very, very concerned with how incredibly frustrating all this was for him personally. "I just . . . I just need some time to come to terms with this," he said once after I asked him to stop, tears spilling down my face. He then turned his face toward the wall.

I sent that one packing after he shipped me an anniversary present—we celebrated it in late February—with a card reading "Happy Anniversary to a Great Couple!" and a bag of Valentine's Day candy with the 50-percent-off tag still dangling.

The most earnest one lasted all of seven months. He did his best, God bless him—came to a therapy session with me, looked up the Obsessive-Compulsive Foundation on the Internet—but the problem with him wasn't so much the number of women he'd been with before

he began dating me (nine) or the fact that, as a non-Catholic, he'd never experienced the faith-based restrictions I faced (nine!); it was more that he'd never been in a relationship with a heavily medicated lady before, even though, to be honest, the only OCD skin off his nose (*nine*), other than the fact that one of us had to have her underwear on at all times and was afraid to sit on certain spots of the bed, was to periodically endure the offhand question "So you did test negative, right? . . . *right*?" (*Nine!*) And so all of a sudden here was this poor fellow in a relationship with a woman who drew her knees to her chest in paroxysms of panic every now and again (NINE!) after definitely not having sex, so I should not have been too horribly shocked when the word came via e-mail one early morning: "I've come to the conclusion," he wrote, "that OCD is not something I could spend the rest of my life with."

After I read this, I sat on the floor and cried a whole lot, and then I took myself for a wee-small-hours drive, at the end of which, the odometer, I could not help but notice, stood at 33,033 miles.

For all this, however, for all the Luvox and the neurons and the occasional field trips to the fetal position, most people don't know that I have OCD until I tell them about it; one of the main symptoms of OCD is that its patients rarely exhibit any. We *know* that crabs cannot be transmitted via Blockbuster rentals; we are fully aware that no misfortune shall befall us should we become the sixth person in line rather than the fourth or seventh or twenty-eighth; and for the most part, the dishes get washed and the TPS report gets faxed without anyone knowing that our neurons fear otherwise. Much as the fears loom and snarl on the inside, nearly as bad is the fear that somebody else will know they are there.

I could be sitting right smack next to you in a movie theater, in the pincers of an OCD attack, terrified more than anyone has ever been, and the only sound you will hear, the only sight you will see, is Tom Hanks before you delivering a soliloquy to a volleyball, a thing bad enough all on its own.

For we are actors, consummate and professional actors, we members of the OCD Guild. There should be a separate Oscar ceremony each and every year specifically for obsessive-compulsives. "And the award for Best Excuse upon Getting Caught Backing In and Out of a Doorway Seventeen Times goes to . . ." "The nominees for Outstanding Adeptness at Covering Up the Fact That One Is Counting the Number of Syllables in the Sentence One Is Currently Speaking are . . ."

"Think of the most scared you've ever felt," I'll say to people who ask me about it. "It feels like that, only all the time, every single second of every single day." People will cock their heads and conjure up the top of the roller coaster or the day Dad found out about the dent on the Wrangler.

If you're missing a leg, people get that, it's *right there,* they're not going to ask you to help move the couch. Where OCD is concerned, where the absurd meets cover-ups of Watergate dimensions, it's not so self-explanatory. Go ahead, give it a shot: "I'd love to play tennis, Alan, but I can't serve game point because I have a strong aversion to the number three."

It's simpler with women, with friends, with men who repulse me sexually, because once the bottle of wine is half gone and the other party has slipped me a secret of his own, it's not a far leap to slur, "Did I ever tell you that I can't let myself inhale if someone's talking about AIDS, that I'll, like, hold my breath for, like, *ever* because I toooooootally freak out that if I breathe in while someone's even *talking* about it, then I'm afraid that means I'll get it? Iddn't that fucked *up*?" I have no problem broaching the subject under these circumstances, for if the other party freaks and bolts, I can watch him walk away without wondering whether I have just truthed myself right out of a potential groom.

At what point does one inform a budding love interest that one has qualms turning a page in a magazine if the last word of the last paragraph is "death" or "baby" or "positive" or "wrong"? First date? Second? After he's seen you without makeup? Before or after the check? "I'll have the surf and turf, and by the way, in the rare event this

evening that your pubic area should brush mine and I run shrieking for the shower, don't take it personally." I feel an obligation to run some sort of public service disclaimer, a PG-13 warning that She's Got Issues; and I feel I need to lay it all out for each potential suitor before he starts building up feelings of the for-life variety. It would not be sporting of me to allow the Serotonin Express to mow him sideways after he has been so foolish.

Sometimes with OCD there are only fear and the fetal position, no washing or checking or counting, just plain old ordinary terror that comes and goes as it pleases. Here, I'll use an example we can all recognize:

"Hello, I'm anthrax, and I'll be your OCD trigger today. Worried yet? . . . worried yet? . . . worried yet? . . . No? What about that box you opened the other day, with the address labels you ordered from New Jersey—you really aren't sure which post office that came through, are you? How about now? . . . No white powder, but then again there doesn't necessarily have to be any, you know . . . Oh, there you go! That's a lovely panic attack, right in the middle of the *Cheers* rerun, very nice. Good girl! Good girl: Get up, look at the labels, think about tossing them out, wash your hands, can't be too careful! Lookit, I'll allow you to watch the first twenty minutes of *Skating with Celebrities* in relative peace, then I'll come back and check on you, okay? I'll see ya. . . . In the meantime—oh dear, is that a headache coming on? Sore throat? Oh, doesn't matter, you know that by the time the symptoms come on, it's too late anyway, you're dead. Wash your *hands*!"

This happens every now and again, when real-life worries and normal-people stresses ooze out of the basal ganglia in the form of some truly fer-weird mental experience. It sucks when this comes to pass, because the OCD, it does this on purpose, digs deep into your psyche, submarines down through sugar-cookie recipes and the brand of socks that don't crunch up when I run and how Colorado smells in the morning; and then it roots out the diamonds, the good stuff, the things that mean the most, and it clamps on and it contaminates.

Months ago, as my thesis deadline closed in, I began to shift uneasily and look over my shoulder every time I prayed the Rosary, suddenly and for no reason at all fearing an apparition from the Virgin Mary, somehow convinced that such an appearance would signal the end of the world. (The OCD is overfond of fretting about the apocalypse, apparently unaware that its arrival would neatly counteract all of the other calamities it usually shrieks about.)

Here was a powerful religious figure whom I normally enjoyed hanging out with, prayer-wise, and the fear spread to going to Communion and then Mass itself. I swept every Mary statue in the house into a box and hid it behind the Christmas decorations, the gold-painted halos and the tiny white hands clinking together as I fled from room to room, beside myself at my feebleness in the face of such illogic: Like the boyfriend who sent me on my way once he realized that his discomfort with the OCD was greater than his love for me, I was shoving away someone I loved and leaned on because I was afraid.

At such times I wish very hard that I had done less learning and more drinking in college, that I had developed the ability to drain large amounts of liquor without having to toss it right back up at the bar. Nights, wandering the blazing house in fear of the Virgin Mary (I felt quieter with the lights on somehow, protected by the blazing glow of the GE bulbs), I would pause before my father's liquor cabinet, arrested by the rows of see-through Scotch and dark, engulfing Jack, square and sturdy in the bottle. The thick phantom sensations of the two times I have been full-blown drunk would slide into my bloodstream and extremities. Anesthetized, dead: It would be so nice, I'd think, running a palm over the decanter lids, to be numb, and hurling. But the Luvox doesn't work as well with alcohol in the system, makes you sleepy, and so I'd keep pacing, next room, next worry-go-round.

These phases never last long; they level out, once medications are adjusted and exercise is attended to, and I sink back into the blissful state of normality—to bitch, without impunity, about the mere existence of Jessica Simpson! The sublime joy of going to my dead-end job

every morning! Normal is lovely; the grind is a salve. Those of us with OCD live for the days when the counting is unconscious and the flashes of discomfort exist as a mere itch on the anklebone; when the battery-acid fear is far off on the horizon somewhere, and the house may be exited without tossing all the matchbooks in the bathtub first.

That is why, in the aftermath of September 11, I watched with equal parts pity and dark amusement as the nation had a bout of the serotonin grippers. What's this, don't you feel safe in everyday life anymore? Do you fear that the calm Delta fabric print of the seat back in front of you is the last sight you'll ever see? Are you slathering yourself with Germ-X every time you page through the Lands' End catalog? Longing to go about your day worried only that your TiVo commands were set correctly? Pull up a chair and have a Luvox: You've just taken your first step into a freakier world, young Skywalker.

Normal people, people in Nebraska and Delaware and Utah with no prescriptions to fill, were forced to redefine bravery as they beheld cranes lifting entire fire engines from the smoking hole in the concrete that was once the World Trade Center. To me, a person whose most frightening, thick-scariest task was to log on to the Internet so I could close my online account during my liturgical-dancer phase, anyone who ran *at* danger, on *purpose,* was a *god.* Army guys and fire chiefs and police officers—my God, imagine the mean people who must hate *them.* How do they get *up* in the morning? Terrorists . . . death threats . . . smallpox . . . poison in the water supply . . . that was small potatoes, that was amateur hour. I panicked over microorganisms in my juice box way before Tom Brokaw ever did, man, eons and ages before *Newsweek* deemed it fashionable to fling oneself hysterical over baby powder on the bathroom floor.

So, the whole Mary thing.

The Our Lady of Lourdes statue and the Rosaries, they continue to reside with the Tinker Bell Christmas stocking and the *Grandma Got Run Over by a Reindeer* CD. I go to Mass, but I'm typing this quickly, nervous clicks on the keyboard, because the topic gives me

the d.t.'s. We continue in a nodding, proper Protestant relationship, the Virgin and I, and probably will until the next fun topic screams down the brain pike.

And . . . that's it?

That's never it. That's OCD: The nice ribbons and sharp paper edges are gone, frayed out of existence by fear and flinching and sorrow.

But what if . . .

And how about . . .

That is how OCD goes, and that is what the life is like: the endless march, the daytime drama with no final episode, on and on with predictable camera angles and ridiculous plots and new actors taking over the same character as the rest of the townsfolk pretend not to notice. Fear, adjust, fear again: The needle skips, the gramophone gets a kick, and the dance, it goes on . . . never as a waltz, though . . . in that dance, you count by threes.

The curtains are the color of blueberries. It's difficult not to notice them. They sway hypnotically with the warm air rushing into the bus, and because it is hot, all eyes are on the undersize windows. The air cycles in, pushing the curtains back and forth in a game of tug-of-war. It's as if the curtains sense the nearby turmoil, and through their constant shifting, they help the wind communicate with us. *This breeze will be the last gentle thing to hit your face.* Swoosh. *There's nothing gentle about war.* Swoosh.

We are in Kuwait and it's hot—miserably hot. At four o'clock this morning, we moved from a cramped tent in Camp Wolf, just outside Kuwait City, to a cramped bus headed for Camp New York, one of several U.S. military posts scattered throughout the Kuwaiti desert.

Sweat drips from our brows, splashing onto the seats in front of us, our chins, our weapons, our Battle Dress Uniforms. This is my first big sweat during the deployment and certainly not my last.

Jones looks exhausted. His head, like everyone else's, is covered with a shell of Kevlar, and he rests it on the seat in front of him. His weapon points awkwardly toward his boots. At nineteen, he is the youngest member of our company. I can only imagine the things running through his mind: Why Iraq? What's happening back home?

What if I need to kill a man? What if I'm killed? How does my mustache look?

My father has a mustache. For as long as I can remember, he's had one, a row of straight dark hairs piled on top of one another like lumber. When I was a kid, he'd come in from outside—the cold midwestern wind blowing another snowstorm across the Dakotas—and there'd be ice hanging in shiny, clear strands below his nose, coating the bristly hairs. In the basement, as he removed his snow boots and the plastic bread bags that kept his feet dry, my father would slowly warm, sitting on that green vinyl chair placed awkward amid the furnace, deep freeze, tools, and other amenities that cluttered the unfinished basement. My brother and I would watch from the stairs as the ice on his mustache thawed and the slick, dark slash of hair under his nose reappeared. We wondered when our own lumber piles of hair would sprout.

Like many young boys, I wanted to be like my father. I wanted a mustache. However, I often romanticized my mustache, thinning it out and curling it, like Peter Sellers's 'stache in the *Pink Panther* series, or growing it dark and thick, letting it sag like Wyatt Earp's.

Every now and then, as if he wanted to create this huge surprise, my father would shave it off, paying little regard to what people said. My mother thought it made him look younger. But for me, it made him look strange, deformed or deranged. It seemed as if his mustache had walked right off his face, leaving a blurry substitute for the thick hairs that had complemented his rugged appearance. My father's mustache was like a crooked nose or dimpled chin—strangely alluring and somehow oddly appropriate.

I have no idea which direction we are headed. I don't even know if we are still in Kuwait. This is what I do know: We are on a well-paved highway; there is garbage everywhere; and we all look like wet seals, drenched in sweat, with long, confused faces. Not only do the few people we see along the road look unpleasant, unhappy, and sad, but everyone on this tiny bus senses the misery and lets it consume them.

My face is damp from sweat, my eyes are stinging. My head hurts from the helmet, and my muscles ache from traveling. Yet my ass hurts the most. The half-inch cheap cushion between me and the iron seat provides little relief.

The blueberry curtains are proving to be more harmful than helpful. They get in the way of the air, but if we pull them aside, the Kuwait sun comes down on us with a vengeance. So we just sweat.

Kuwait is all sand. The country, with the occasional clump of trees or cluster of gray, windowless homes, looks like nothing more than a giant sandbox. In fact, that's what we've begun calling it—the Sandbox. We first heard the term from some sergeant in Fort Carson before flying over, yet we refused to believe it. He'd say, "When you're over in the Sandbox, you'll understand the importance of cleanliness" or "You better clean your gas mask daily, because once you're in the Sandbox, that thing will fill up in seconds. And if your gas mask is full of sand, it's going to be hard fitting your head in."

This sandbox is nothing like the sandbox I had when I was a kid. My parents created three sandboxes on our farm—one for my brother, one for my sister, and one for me. Each was made out of an old tractor tire and positioned throughout our farmstead. Thinking back, I realize that playing in my childhood sandbox—making those roads and cities, filling up my Tonka dump truck with load after load of sand, or creating houses out of packed wet sand in the shape of a bucket or a cup—was simply preparation for what I was going to do over here.

I turn away from the window and the endless desert. The bus is loud. Not from talking but from driving down the road, windows wide open and the old Marcopolo engine coughing up years of sand as it goes along. We are quiet. Rainman sits next to me, his hands cupped in his lap, his forehead dripping, and his expression blank. He stares at his boots. We sit in the back, on the long seat that stretches across the entire bus. The seat is raised slightly, and Rainman's in the middle, as if at the head of a grand table, staring at his boots, which stick out into the aisle.

"We were just at an airport. Why couldn't we have taken a heli-

copter there?" he says without looking up. His cheeks are flushed, and there are bags drooping under his eyes. Anyone could gather from his face that we've been traveling for three days.

"You forget. This is the army," I say.

"Well, it would have been a hell of a lot quicker than this shit. Where the hell are we?"

I scan the rest of the bus, looking for an answer. Martin is reading a magazine—*Newsweek*—which he brought with him from the States. Beaming on the cover is Jessica Lynch. When I heard the story of her capture, I stored it in the back of my head, along with thoughts about home, friends, and family. Stories like that only make heading to war more painful, and pushing them out of your mind is the best solution.

Roach and King are both asleep, resting on their rucksacks, piled like bags of coal next to them. Roach is softly snoring. Viv is anxious or has to pee, I can't tell which. He keeps shifting around in his seat, alternately looking out the window and watching the rest of us. The curtains don't seem to have the calming effect on him that they do on me. Everyone looks on edge. Even Johnson's whistling, which drifts quietly around the bus, has little calming effect.

The driver seems like the only calm person on the bus. He's a Kuwait native. He wears a long white robe and a deep blue scarf wrapped around his head. The only visible part of his face is his eyes, dark and darting. He fits here in a completely different way than we do. We are camouflaged with the land. He is camouflaged with the people. Our new desert-camouflaged uniforms are the perfect shade of nothingness, which is exactly what the U.S. military is going for. *Get in and make it look like we aren't even there.* The driver's white robe is clean and pure: the color of peace, surrender.

It's something the military pushes upon people. The Kuwait natives surrender to our neediness. We need them—to drive our troops to outlying posts, to find the land mines, to translate the words, to pump away our waste. But do they need us? What benefit do we bring to these people?

I notice Jones look up, almost as if to answer my unspoken ques-

tion. With his forefinger and thumb, he gently smoothes the fine hairs above his lip.

"Have you ever grown a mustache?" Jones asked me one morning.

He was standing by the mirror. We'd been packing, and there was a sense of excitement as we stuffed DCUs, boots, and gear into the olive-drab duffel bags. It's like sifting through the remains of a tornado, separating the good and useful from the useless.

"What do you mean grown? Like petunias?" I replied, looking up at him.

It seemed odd to talk about a mustache as something you grow. It was as if we were two old women comparing gardens, one asking the other if she'd ever had success growing blue-hubbard hybrid winter squash.

"Yeah, grow. How else would you say it?"

I didn't know. I doubted I could grow a mustache or a garden, so I had nothing to say.

"Do you think I'll need these?" I asked, holding up a pair of mittens with fur on the cuffs.

"It's the desert, not the Arctic."

Earlier that morning, we'd been told that we were headed for Kuwait. After being strung along for two months, we were finally headed somewhere. Now it was time to sort out the stuff we needed from the stuff we could leave behind, with our families, friends, and our country.

Jones and I had been roommates ever since they moved us into the barracks. He married before we left, one of several rush weddings to reap the benefits married couples receive, such as extra money for your wife. I'd met his wife once, the day before we left. They were headed to the courthouse following formation. During family time the following day, they sat in the corner of the auditorium, enjoying each other's company and their new titles—husband and wife. In between talking with my parents, I watched them. They talked as if they were

the only people in the room, ignoring everyone else and the upcoming goodbyes.

"I've always wanted to grow one, but I know Maria wouldn't even look at me if I did. So I was thinking of starting one now."

Maria had flown down to Colorado three days earlier. Now, with Maria gone and not knowing the next time he'd see her, Jones was looking at doing a little experimenting.

For me, growing a mustache always seemed like a rite of passage from boyhood to manhood. Having a mustache meant you were a man. You'd finally proved that you were meant for manly ordeals. Most of the guys in our company had smooth upper lips, including me.

I had never grown a mustache. I didn't want Jones to know that. The mustache simply didn't fit in with our generation. Having a mustache was like rolling your jeans, a fad that eventually faded with time.

Yet we were days away from heading overseas, to a war that required boys to become men.

"I'll tell you what, we can both try growing mustaches," I said. "It could be a race. Whoever grows the best mustache wins."

"Oh, a challenge, then? You're on."

Jones reached over the boots, uniforms, canteens, flashlights, shampoo, suspenders, gas masks, and other equipment littering our floor. We shook on it, agreeing to begin the next day. Our belongings began to separate into piles, and among these piles we started a competition, hoping, I think, that a pile of hair under our noses would help disguise the fear on our faces.

Suddenly, the reason we're in Kuwait makes sense, and everything is silent. A calm engulfs the bus. The whistling has stopped. The bus has cured its cough, and the wind—the wind is still, unwavering. It simply ceases to exist.

This is our equivalent to riding into battle, six beat-up Marcopolo buses charging across the desert. It isn't gallant. It isn't elegant. We aren't the cavalry, the infantry, or the artillery forces. We don't have

the tanks, the guns. We're engineers. We have hammers and wire strippers and monkey wrenches. For us, cruising across the desert in beat-up buses is as grand as it gets.

We have turned off the paved highway onto a thin dirt road. The countryside has opened up into a field of nothing, sand for miles upon miles. The six buses form a line, like ducklings, making their way down this sand trail to their home—our new home.

Roach and King are awake now; the dirt road is too bumpy for sleep. Everyone is surveying the land, peeking out from behind the curtains to get a glimpse of what is in store for us.

Abruptly, the bus jerks to the left, forming its own trail through the sand. I look back and notice that it is barely a trail at all. It's a slightly more traveled line of sand than the one we are currently on. There really isn't a road, and the buses, instead of following one another across the desert, begin to spread out, side by side, racing across the sand. Six tiny Marcopolo buses cruising across the Kuwaiti desert. The race has begun.

Martin puts down the magazine and glances over as two buses glide past us on the left. I pull back the curtain, getting a glimpse of another soldier peeking beyond his curtains as another bus passes us on the right. We've been traveling for about three days, shifting from one post to the next, and this is the first real excitement of the trip.

The land doesn't stretch on for too long before we begin to see signs of military life. An old trailer-bed lies wasted and empty in the sand. Other vehicles are left abandoned along the road—an old five-ton truck, tireless and half covered in sand; a broken-down Humvee. I begin to wonder if anything lives in this desert.

Rainman jabs me with his elbow. "Look at Johnson."

Johnson is two seats in front of us, his back to the aisle, looking down toward his waist. He has a Coke bottle and is peeing into it. When he finishes, he turns to the rest of us, a smug grin on his face as if he's accomplished something no one else could. We give him looks of disgust, knowing that we would do the same thing if we had to.

"What? I had to go. Who knows where this damn base is!"

Five minutes later, the bus slows and we stop. I glance out the window as soldiers begin exiting the other five buses. Some just stand around, hands over their eyes, looking into the desert, surveying the land. Others stretch, arms jutting straight into the sky, chest bowed out, welcoming the new environment. About fifty yards away, a line of soldiers begins to form, their backs to the buses, as they urinate into the desert. *This is now our territory. We claim this for the United States of America.*

We eventually climb back onto the buses and continue our trek toward our next home. We don't know where this base is. We're racing toward an unknown place, an invisible target. I imagine the American camps strategically hidden in the Kuwaiti desert, with secret routes and unmarked paths. There will be no maps, no signs—only a handful of obedient bus drivers who know where the bases are, and they aren't telling anyone. By frantically racing toward these unmarked places, the drivers are distracting us, taking our minds off the fact that we are riding into war. Instead, we're filled with excitement at the possibility of winning a race to an unknown (and possibly secret) place.

We come to a sign, the first sign I've seen out here. It points us toward Camp New York—right. The buses file down to one line again, our bus bringing up the rear. I look up at the bus driver with disappointment. But the race isn't finished.

We pass through a narrow part of road between a small patch of brush and an even smaller sand dune before the land opens up again. We spread out, each bus taking its own path, separating into its own lane for the final leg.

After a while we pass a line of Abram tanks. They are lined up, like they would be in a military handbook. They're stopped, silent and beautiful, like geese waiting in a marsh, fuel cans, rucksacks, and gear dangling from their boxy bodies. Soldiers poke their heads out the top. Their faces are dark, covered in sand, dirt, and sweat. I wonder

how long they've been in Kuwait. How long have they been in the sun, the rays licking their faces? How long has the sand been whipping up and spraying their brows? How long will it be before we wear that same bitter, worn face, and what will it take to get there?

I sense we are close. If nothing else, I imagine the rough terrain is the military's last attempt at diverting people from their secret bases. Each time we hit a bump, sending us toward the ceiling, I look over at Rainman, who gives me a look back: *How does a helicopter sound now?*

Nothing can explain our relief at seeing Camp New York. We follow the other buses through a gate and onto a base that looks almost abandoned. Coming to a halt, the driver—our savior, our guardian—looks into the mirror above his head. With his eyes, he says to us, *We're here.*

Three days after Jones and I shook hands, we're on a plane headed for Kuwait. I splash water on my face and lift my head to the tiny restroom mirror. The weak light barely catches the whiskers poking through below my nose. I turn my head, left then right, trying to cast some light on the few hairs on my upper lip. Laughing, I exit the small bathroom, noticing the people lined up down the aisle. How long was I in there examining my new mustache?

Newark looks so large. Glancing at the city below, I realize that this city, foreign to me because I've never been here, will be the last American city I'll set foot in for quite a while. The seat-belt light comes on, and the pilot explains that we're landing soon. We need fuel.

They don't even give us a gate. We exit the plane onto the tarmac of the Newark International Airport. We stand in a circle, stretching, smoking, joking, taking in the last American air for miles.

"So, Lemer, does this count?" Elijah asks.

Elijah and I argue about what countries and states we've visited. When counting, I don't consider countries where I've been in only the airport. For Elijah, the airports count.

"No, of course not," I say. "How can it? It's only the airport."

"So you wouldn't even say that you've been to New Jersey after this?"

"No."

It's almost a game. He argues with me just to argue, and I comply because I have nothing better to do.

"Why not?"

"It's not real."

"Well, neither is your mustache."

That gets everyone laughing. I smile, laughing along, rocking from my toes to my heels, thumbs tucked inside my new BDU pants. I somehow imagine the camouflage spreading from my pants up onto my face, covering the blood rushing to my cheeks. I turn to look at the plane, pretending that the remark doesn't hurt a little. Jones is standing by the plane with Roach. His mustache looks so much better than mine. At nineteen, he can grow a better mustache than I can at twenty-four. Jealous and embarrassed, I begin walking back to board the plane.

Once the plane is loaded, fueled, and ready to go, the flight attendant announces that our next stop will be Milan.

"That's in Italy," she adds with a sense of excitement.

Elijah looks over at me and raises an eyebrow. He knows I've always wanted to go to Italy.

I n sex ed, they tell you all about normal sexual development. The trajectory of your sex life is supposed to be narrow and straight, passing through preordained landmarks—the prepuberty hormone spike that makes you rub eensy-weensy genitalia against bicycle banana seats, the first-time hand-on-thigh fumblings of teenagerdom, the early-adulthood serious relationship that careens from experimentation into mom-and-pop warmth and the necessary question of "Is this what my parents' sex life was like when they first met?" What they don't tell you about are the detours. Your lover might die. You might wake up to find him dead. Gone. And then there is just you and your libido and the question of what sex in the new world will look like.

Neil was twenty-seven and I was twenty-four when he was diagnosed with leukemia. As for most twentysomethings, mortality was a subject eternally deferred for us. But the weekend after the doctor put his hand on Neil's shoulder and bleated out his diagnosis, I met my boyfriend at a motel in his hometown on Long Island to exchange words only whispered at the Jewish family functions we regularly attended: [*pursed mouth*] "cancer," [*moue of distaste*] "chemo," and [*shhsh-ing finger to lips*] "treatment." It was not the first time we'd met at this anonymous motel near the Long Island Rail Road station. We had been convening in a dun-colored room on the third floor

every weekend since the doctors began to suggest that the swollen lymph nodes on Neil's neck and shoulders were not the sign of a local infection but of something far more, um, global, something insidious, circulating, buzzing. Neil had returned to his parents' nest to deal with the bad news, and every weekend I would visit him, the chug-chug of the train carrying me from the city into a territory of anxious conversation and too-tight hugs.

Often, he would get to the hotel before me and sit in an armchair by the window to wait for my arrival. When I entered the room, he would hold me at a distance and look at me for a moment before reaching out to take my hand and place it on his erection-distended zipper. "I am so glad you are here." He would squint through his glasses and touch my hand. "Look at what you do to me. It's been a long time since I've had one of these." I would fondle his pants and wonder why moments of randiness and vulgarity were so beautiful during this time of crisis. Having Neil's denim-cloaked erection in my hand felt like the opposite of the uncertainty of his disease, I guess. For the most part, erections are a sure thing—a gun introduced in the first act that's sure to go off in the third if you handle it right. It is shocking, I know, to speak of erections and sexual interludes while death is looming. Cancer works very hard to make life unsexy. Freud was right. The only thing that can beat the sex drive is the specter of death. Every kiss or touch is undermined by the images a potentially terminal disease tattoos onto the surface of your mind. White blood cells strangulating your loved one. Cathodes distending his neck and chest like a modern-day Frankenstein. Hair loss. Emaciation. It is coming. And, well, for the time being, at least, you are not.

Leukemia carries with it particular visions of disaster. It was hard not to allow my imagination to take elephantine footsteps ahead of the situation when Neil took me into his arms. I would think about how leukemia makes your body produce blanks. White blood cells without the capacity to do what white blood cells do best. Red blood cells like mules, dead-end hybrids, unable to function. Wastes of space, they crowded out all the green terrain in Neil's body. They si-

phoned off his strength and left vast lunar landscapes behind them. Sometimes I touched Neil and his skin felt cold and I imagined the Pluto that was his innards, the world inside his body that was orbiting so far from the sun.

The dehumanizing aspects of the treatment were even worse than the images that plagued me when I pictured what the future might bring. The first thing the doctor mentioned after handing out Neil's diagnosis was sperm. More precisely, she said that Neil might want to leave some sperm samples at a bank called Cryotex Labs as soon as possible, like this minute, like now. "Well," she said, "what we're about to blast you with kills a lot of things inside of your body, your reproductive capacity being one of the first entities to meet its demise." "La-Z-Boy comfort awaits the patrons of Cryotex Labs." That's what the brochure in the waiting area said, at least. The pamphlet also featured a small insert about the laboratory's prominence among professional athletes. "Groin injuries are part of the game for baseball players. They play it safe by leaving something behind at Cryotex Labs. Cryotex Labs, the first in safety." But, we didn't feel safe.

Neil told me that when he was led into one of the hidden masturbation rooms at Cryotex Labs' sperm bank, he felt like he was entering a bat cave. There were rooms it recalled: the secret room under the stairs where your two-headed brother would be kept; the S and M dungeon that a suburban couple maintains behind their fluorescent-lit den. The juxtaposition between the public and private spaces was perverse. The sperm bank's reception room, reeking of antiseptic and nervous men trying to mask what they were waiting to do in a cup backstage, versus the private depositories located off long hallways, the creepy closeness of those rooms where you do your business, seal the deal, wank—whatever you want to call the sperm-depositing process.

Antique copies of *Hustler, Juggs,* and *Swank* littered the cupboards. The walls were tacked with pinups, spanning decades of titillation from subtle Betty Grable–esque poses to seventies cheesecake pix. Sexy photos so densely papered the place that they formed a kind of space-age wallpaper. Some of the posters were dog-eared and a bit

stained, and Neil couldn't help but wonder if his battered immune system might be leaving him open to contracting whatever weird germs the weird men who had inhabited this room had left behind them. It was like the room of an adolescent boy who sleeps under photos of naked women as some kind of fort or bulwark against pimply loneliness. It was like the room of an adolescent boy who tries to touch at intimacy by rubbing his face against the pinups of nudie magazines until they begin to sweat and run with moisture. It was a sad-ugly room.

It was a sad-ugly disease, depleted of glamour, whatever its well-meaning and beribboned denizens might suggest. When I visited Neil in the hospital after his chemotherapy had started, he scuffed his white-socked feet along the floor, searching blindly for his slippers. I pushed my feet under his hospital bed and kicked the slippers his way. I tried to be unobtrusive about getting the shoes, like I would be about letting an eight-year-old kid win at checkers. Neil slid his feet into the slippers and then sat on the side of the bed looking at me. It was the first time our faces had been so close since his admission to the hospital. I looked at him. "Don't look at me like that. I want to kiss you when you look like that," he said as he turned his face away.

We couldn't kiss. We couldn't kiss because mouths are full of billions of microbes and critters and tiny breaks in gum lining. My mouth was no exception, and a kiss from me could communicate something far more than love and warmth to Neil. It could communicate something that would have left him hobbled and legs waving in bed, Kafka's Samsa-bug come to life.

Months later, though, after multiple chemos and a failed bone marrow transplant and family drama and Neil's death, it wasn't these dystopian postcards from the sickbed that I remembered most. It was the fact that during Neil's lengthy and wholly unsexy illness, he had never ceased to be sexy to me. We flirted, we canoodled, we talked about sex, and we had sex when Neil was sick because, well, sex wasn't death. It was the antithesis of death, and damn if it didn't feel good to forget for a while that nothing we could dream up could act as an effective talisman against the iceberg floating along the horizon

into our sights. After Neil's diagnosis, we led an airless life filled with take-out Chinese food and a bed that dwarfed our shared existence, Alice-in-Wonderland-style, growing and filling minds that should have been taken up with twentysomething concerns. Instead of thinking about Neil's illness, though, we thought about how not to leave the bed: how we could spend twelve hours touching and laughing and weeping and singing in a bed like a boat. A bed like a boat that was sinking.

We imagined mocking Neil's illness and its emasculating powers by making a jokey promotional video for Ara-C, the chemo compound Neil received daily during his inpatient treatments. Neil wrote the script.

[A closely shorn] Neil: Everybody tells you about the downside of being diagnosed with cancer.
[Camera pans back to show wide-angle shot of the hospital room with me sitting on the edge of Neil's bed]
[A *sotto voce*] Me: But, we'd like to tell you about some of the, ahem, benefits. Let us show you what chemo can do for your libido.

They were distancing mechanisms, now that I think of it, the playful commercials and the bed-soaked existence. Furtive embraces and black-humored jabs at Neil's illness and treatment were welcome existential breathers from thinking about death. For me, they had an added benefit. They allowed me the illusion that I would always be approaching Neil's prognosis as part of a dynamic duo, a twosome who could feint and jab together at this overwhelming new opponent, cancer.

But then Neil died. My friends treated me with the type of reverence usually reserved for South American shamans. "You have sipped from the River Styx and lived to tell about it." They were comfortable with the occasional teary jag or sentimental reminiscence about Neil's all-around loveliness, but nobody wanted to hear the truth: Neil was great in bed. When your lover dies, it is the body as much as those intangible qualities of the personality that you miss. I wanted to tell them

and everyone that what I missed was sex with Neil, taking naughty baths and using fingers and tongues and toes to explore whatever pockets of the other we could reach. Eulogies praised Neil's imagination, his writing prowess, his generosity and warmth. I praised these qualities, too. But praise be the body, I told them. It is only in such praise that I could give Neil back what leukemia ended up taking from him, trace the contours of what he lost: his material form, with its capacity for messy emissions and spontaneous boners, parted lips, enveloping bear hugs and leg cramps, beautiful all.

I wanted to explain to my friends and family that it was only by praising Neil's body, his prowess as a lover, his unique hands and eyes and chest that I could hope to restore his particularity. Neil was a material boy. A boho Jewish gal's dreamboat, he was a man equally comfortable having sex all day and doling out stories and whitefish around my grandmother's kitchen table. He was of that elusive species hunted by urban ladies of a certain age, the aw-shucks writer boy who turned me on with his horizonless imagination, as much as with his self-lacerating wit and gorgeous prose. I used to call him my Proust, still churning out stories from his sickbed. That was part of it, too. Insisting upon Neil as embodied was an insistence on the realness of the sickbed, on the realness of his illness, the material reality of night shakes and nausea and pain that accompanied his many months of illness and treatment. Illness is supposed to be romantic and meaningful, right? That's what art tells us. The consumptive cousin making eyes at Isabel Archer in Henry James's *The Portrait of a Lady*. Or think of the opera. The divas are little more than a series of sexy terminal cases, women slo-mo-swooning to the ground in the last act like interlocked paper dolls. Talking about the body, the details of what happens to the human body during illness, is the quickest way to defetishize illness and its effects.

Of course, it's not entirely altruistic, my refusal to reduce Neil to the ether, my desire to resurrect him as an entity both embodied and real. After Neil's death, I experienced an extreme form of what long-distance lovers feel, the sense that they want to lick the phone, the

closest thing they can get to a material incarnation of their mate. Like these lovers, separated by thousands of telephone polls and thruway exits, I felt the distance between Neil and me as a vastness that I wanted desperately to shrink. And so I praised Neil's body and all it had been to me. Without his body, there was only this liquid, aqueous longing.

Even more confusing than the physical experience of loss that accompanies the death of a partner, whatever one's age, were the expectations that came along with having lost Neil when I was only twenty-five years old. Where was a twenty-five-year-old widow supposed to go? In what sort of community, dating or other, could such a person fit? As I saw it, I had few options. I could become a retirement-community hottie, raising tents in pleated polyester pants from Boca to the Palms as I lowered the median age of Shady Meadows by forty years or so. My new boyfriend Saul-ie and I could hold each other companionably through the night and spend our days with heads bowed beneath photos of our lost belovеds, Esther and Neil, like they hadn't so much died as had the audacity to go off and marry goys. Another option: I could move to a war-rent nation where young women buried their lovers on a daily basis. I could wear a head scarf and ululate with anguish next to my global widowed sisters. Instead, I was foolish enough to remain in the twentysomething dating scene in the good old urban Northeast.

My first post-Neil man was not, ahem, a rousing success. The fact that I use the term "first post-Neil man" to describe him might explain the inscribed failure of that effort. I would look into this young man's face for signs of Neil-ness. He was sweet and intelligent, but I didn't care. He wasn't Neil, and no amount of caresses would transform him into my lost beloved. For a long time, I felt like I was waiting for Neil to return from travels unknown. Would he stage a homecoming? He might be Odysseus, I thought, but I was a terrible Penelope, impatient and angry, hopeful that my suitors might metamorphose into my absent sweetie over coffee.

Admittedly, I pushed myself to date far too quickly, thinking that if

I had to mourn, it might help to have someone to cry alongside me. But whether I knew it or not, I was transmitting my disappointment and wish for Neil's return to every man unlucky enough to cross my path. So haunted were the men I casually dated by the thought of my idealized former love that they would discover traces of him throughout my apartment, mistaking framed antique postcards for photos of him and used ticket stubs for sacred relics of our shared past. I didn't help matters by conveying my loss to my new paramours as early as possible in the relationship. A man with whom I had gone on three dates and with whom I'd just had a hearty bedroom make-out session confessed some problems he'd been having with his family. Seeing my chance, I blurted out, "Yeah, that sounds rough . . . Um, I had a rough time recently, too . . . About a year ago, my boyfriend, the man I thought I'd spend my life with, died of leukemia."

"Wow . . . that was difficult, I'm sure," he said before awkwardly baring his teeth. "Huh." Silence. He looked longingly at his pillow, whether with the idea that it would make a good instrument to smother me or with the sense of "Why didn't I lapse into unconsciousness when I had the chance?" I couldn't tell. But I could tell that he was not going to call me again. It was often difficult to constrain this Tourette's syndrome of the unconscious when meeting a potential suitor. After having told me about his most recent long-term relationship, one first date said, "Wouldn't it be funny if our exes ever started dating?"

I held my hand over my mouth, trying not to emit the words. "Our most recent exes would date only if your last gal pal was an inveterate necrophiliac."

It was hard not to emblazon my difference from those I was dating onto a placard that I held in front of my chest to advertise my loss and keep my distance. Later, I realized that this urge to confess might get me more than I had bargained for, namely the men who are turned on by female misery, the Supermen sans capes. I am tough and demanding and snarky, a bossy Jewish girl with a bottomless sexual appetite. In other words, I make a really bad damsel in distress. It was often comical to see the newest superhero-in-training puff out his neuras-

thenic chest and encourage me to cry out my loss on him. It never worked, and it only made me long for Neil to untie me from the metaphorical railroad tracks and usher me back into the familiar.

A year plus later, though, I started to see something. In the messy world of twentysomething dating, Neil's death was a strange gift, something infinitely painful but instrumental, useful in that seeing how men respond to the story of his death is a finely honed barometer of compatibility, kindness, for-realness, intelligence, and unconventionality. And finding someone who gets that I need to appreciate my sex life with Neil as much as my sick life with him is awe-inspiring. If you find someone who can handle sex and death, well, I think anyone would agree you've got things covered. Early on in my relationship with my present beau, as is my wont, I told him about Neil. His response was radical. He didn't look away from me or blanch or hold out paternal arms in which to enfold me. He just listened to me and told me that he admired my strength and that he knew from death, and then he kissed me.

When I met my boyfriend's relatives at a family party, I knew I was home. He and his cousins kept a running tally of how many times death was mentioned by their parents: whether their parents were singing the praises of those who had died, were in the process of dying, or—please, God, no—might die if they weren't careful to watch their cholesterol or diabetes. The number came out to twelve, but I was told that twelve was a small number of deaths to be discussed at a family-wide party and that everyone had been on best behavior, trying to impress me by muzzling their morbidity and dark Irish humor.

On our fifth date, my boyfriend smelled my hair and said, "I love what you smell like."

"What do I smell like?"

"A combination of Secret antiperspirant and Home."

I smiled. He didn't realize what I was thinking at that moment. I'm sure we were thinking about different things at that moment. I imagine that he was thinking about the grandfather and aunt who died young and his miniature self afloat in a kiddie pool and the musty

smell of his attic bedroom filled with indie-rock posters curling at the edges and a personality that was too big for that tiny room. I was thinking that it must have sunk down into my DNA, thick like silt, that comfort with endings and bottomless things, with sex and death. My comfort with those things once known as the private things, the behind-closed-door things, the best-swept-under-the-rug, kept-within-the-family things. The stuff my mother and grandmother and all the nurturing matriarchs in my family couldn't help plunging into up to their elbows, the unfortunate reality that comes of caring for and loving the bodies of others. My genetic material, soupy with loss and desire. He could smell it and he felt at home. And so did I.

On Thursday afternoon I can hear them tapping on my window. I go around the side door to let them in. They walk right into the kitchen, both of them carrying orange sodas and candy bars. Christian is done with class by one-thirty on Thursdays, and I imagine Eric is probably skipping French. Christian is eating a Hershey's milk-chocolate candy bar. Eric's is Special Dark.

"We came here earlier—"

"You were still in bed."

"I just walked in and stole your Neutral Milk Hotel CD. I'm not giving it back."

"I thought you had class at eleven-thirty. Are you sick or something?"

I nod. It's two o'clock in the afternoon, and I'm still in my pajamas. I spent the better part of the morning throwing up in a bucket next to my bed. I don't have a headache yet, but I can feel one forming between my temples.

"I'm sorry. We don't have to eat in front of you if you're sick."

I shake my head. There are only two people in the world I would want to talk to in this condition, and both of them are eating Hershey's chocolate in my kitchen. "I'm fine. I just wish I could throw up."

I excuse myself to the bathroom. There is a weird sort of intimacy involved in talking to friends while kneeling in front of a toilet.

"Just make yourself do it," Christian yells from the living room. "You'll feel better afterward."

I gingerly stick my index and middle finger in my mouth. I pull them out before I even reach the back of my tongue. "I can't. It's like touching my own eyeball."

"You're not really touching anything. Just stick your fingers down your throat as far as they'll go until you feel like throwing up. I'll do it for you if you want."

"What, stick your fingers down your throat?"

"No, stick my fingers down *your* throat."

I'm pretty sure this would be crossing some sort of line, but I can tell he's serious, so I consider it anyway. "That's kind of disgusting, isn't it?"

Eric pipes up from the kitchen: "I think it's kind of hot."

Never in my life did I imagine I would have friends offering to forcibly make me vomit for my own well-being. This is how the week begins.

On Tuesday it snows six inches, but by nighttime it's warm enough. We each pile on three layers of clothing and trek up to the quad at midnight for a snowball fight. An hour and a half later, we're walking back to my apartment for hot chocolate, and Eric stops on the sidewalk next to my building.

"Sweet, it's still there," he says to himself.

I look down to where his feet are. ERIC ♥S YOU is spelled out in footprints in the snow.

"Hey, I wrote you a message!" he yells to Christian, who is a few feet behind us.

Christian catches up, looks down at the ground. "I love you, too."

He says it quickly, like he's not used to saying it really, so this must be a fairly recent development between them. I'd suspected it for a

while, but hearing it now makes me realize there is an entire world between the two of them that I am not even tangentially involved with.

Christian has squarish features, lighter hair, more muscle, taller maybe. On a good night he has a sort of Peter Pan syndrome, this impish quality that makes everything we do together—smoking pot, buying cigarettes, asking hypothetical questions like "If you could kill any one of your professors" or "If you could be raped by any pop celebrity"— seem both innocent and conspiratory. It is this quality that makes him the center of our group, the focus of everyone's love and attention, and in spite of this love or because of it, there are nights when he seems profoundly lonely and unhappy. On these nights he develops a blank stare and sits apart from me and Eric, like he's working through something very important that he doesn't want to say out loud.

Eric has a rounder face, darker hair, a deeper voice. He talks louder than Christian, yells more often, and cries much more often. Worships David Bowie. Chain-smokes. Makes enormously inappropriate comments for shock value and humor. Occasionally wears eyeliner and gets away with it. From the way he dresses and wears his hair, you could mistake him for a rock star, but it's his hugs that are the best measure of his personality: openly emotional and awkward, afraid to begin and afraid to let go. He gives the all-time greatest hugs in the history of hugging, like he's full of emotion and unsure what to do with his arms.

There are subtle differences between them, but I'm watching them now, fitted coats over Adidas jackets, scarves, and straight-legged jeans, and they look like bookends. They've been dating almost as long as they've known each other, as long as they've been in college, and they've cultivated a collective taste in music, a collective wardrobe, a collective memory. They're a set, and they know it.

"We're disgusting," Christian says. "We're like an accessory. People don't really know us; they just show us off to their friends. 'I'm such a diverse, open-minded person. Have you seen my cute gay couple?' "

"You're not an accessory."

"Maybe not to you," Christian says. "You're different."

"Like a third wheel?" I ask.

I've never said it like that before. I don't think they even consider it, but the thought has definitely crossed my mind. I want to hear them tell me I'm wrong.

Eric shakes his head. "You're not a third wheel. We're a tricycle."

Kirksville sits in the northernmost corner of Missouri, right on the Iowa border, next to a state park, endless acres of farmland, and a large lake. In the summers it is hot and muggy, and in the winters it is so windy that walking half a block across campus between classes is unpleasant. And yet somehow it's the end of January, sixty degrees, with a mild breeze. This is not a phenomenon likely to repeat itself, and we are determined to take advantage of it.

We end up at the park, a pitiful little display with only a few slides and some monkey bars set over a twenty-by-twenty patch of gravel. On the edges of the gravel stands the skeleton of a swing set, the swings taken down for the winter. Near the road is a gazebo with a few picnic tables and a wading pool that has probably been drained forever. We climb onto the metal contraption that houses the slides. On top of the curly slide, there's a small pointed dome, like the tip of a castle you'd see in a storybook.

"It's like a tree house," I say, climbing in. "I used to come here and read in the fall. I wish I'd had more guy friends when I was a kid. Like a best friend I'd grown up with."

"We'll be your guy friends," Eric says. He examines the top of the slide. There is graffiti charting the shift from childhood innocence to adolescent angst: "I like me"; "David's mom is so dumb she sat on the TV and watched the coutch"; "The pool sucks cocks"; and the final word in playground denigration, "David is a child fucker."

"I wish I was a kid," Christian says, which is ironic, since he basically is one. "You guys want to have a sleepover?"

We spend most nights in Meredith's apartment. It's a studio, just a glorified living room that adjoins a kitchenette on one side and a bathroom on the other. In the middle of the room is Meredith's twin-

size bed, leaving just enough room for a couch facing the thirteen-inch TV/VCR combo, a small round kitchen table with scarcely enough space for Meredith to eat off of, let alone the three of us, and Meredith's desk. There are movie posters, framed pictures, collages, and drawings on the wall. There are stuffed animals pouring out of foot-lockers and gathering on the bed. There are art supplies spilling out from under the couch. There are books stuffed onto the shelves of the desk and movies packed under the TV stand. The furniture is virtually every color imaginable, from the lime-green-and-pink bedspread to the pink-yellow-blue-and-green-striped couch. It is literally the happiest place on earth.

Right now we've got blankets spread out on the floor, and we're dipping cheese pizza into chocolate sauce while listening to Belle and Sebastian. Meredith has been drawing on her bed, but now she's packing an overnight bag to stay at her boyfriend's. She used to hang out with us more, but that was before she was deliriously happy with her relationship.

"I want to stay in this apartment forever!" Eric says. He's stoned, but it's not an overstatement.

Meredith smiles. She's standing at the door with her bag in her hand. "Okay. Stay here as long as you want. Just turn off the light and the TV when you leave."

I used to dream about getting married, about getting kids and a husband and in-laws like a deus ex machina to solve all my loneliness. I've been dating Clint on and off for over a year now, the last three months of it long-distance, even. Marriage is something that I might be thinking about, as a twenty-one-year-old girl, but lately, it hasn't occurred to me.

"Let's buy a flat in Scotland and all live there together. We'll have beautiful experiences all day, and at night we'll write about them."

The new dream: me, Christian, Eric, and Meredith move to Europe after graduation and form an aesthetically governed commune. One room for all the greatest books in the world. One room for the

greatest music ever written. A private screening room with all the best movies. An endless supply of coffee, cigarettes, and typing paper. We will live by the principle of aesthetics: Members are allowed only to create and consume beauty.

We explain this to Meredith, and she laughs and smiles but says nothing. It does sound ridiculous when you say it out loud. I think about Meredith sometimes, about how her life is progressing in this normal, healthy way, and mine—ours—seems to be regressing somehow. Is getting older supposed to mean wanting the things grown-ups have?

Later that night we lie on our backs in the dark and talk about being kids again.

"I was so pissed when I turned thirteen," Eric says. "My dad stopped letting my girl friends sleep over. It was so ridiculous. I don't even think he cared if I was attracted to them or not. I think he just wanted to force me to grow up. 'It has to happen eventually,' he said. I don't know. People act like kids are in such a hurry to grow up, but I really don't think I went through that. I mean, even then I was angry. I was terrified."

Saturday. I am uncomfortably spooning on the couch with my boyfriend. He's come up from Carbondale for the weekend, and we've spent almost all of it watching movies. I am bored out of my mind.

"So, what do you want to do?" he asks me.

"Oh, whatever."

"Come on . . . let's do something fun."

"What exactly did you have in mind?"

"Whatever you want to do."

"Um."

"What's the one thing you want to do more than anything in the world right now?"

I want to curl up in the fetal position and go to sleep. I want to

chain-smoke an entire pack of Camel cigarettes. I want to lock myself in my room and read plays all night. I want to get fucked up with Eric and Christian and have a sleepover.

"Nothing."

There is a long pause in the conversation during which I think about what a mean joke it is that mothers tell their daughters love is the most important thing that will ever happen to them, because I'm here now, and it isn't.

"That's sad. You can't think of anything?"

"No . . . Yes. I'm sorry, I'm being a bitch. I haven't had a cigarette in two days. I think I'm finally getting addicted or something."

"Yeah, I heard that happens."

"That was subtle."

"I'm sorry. I'm not judging you. Why don't you explain to me why you smoke? I don't understand. I want to."

Clint is a grad student studying clinical psychology. This means he is an extremely caring and understanding person. It also means that we are incapable of having a fight; instead, we have awkward conversations about our feelings. It used to be something I really loved about our relationship. Most guys are bullies, they'll say, "I'm angry at you," but Clint is never angry at me. Sometimes he "feels there is a lot of hostility between us," which I'm fairly sure is the case right now.

We didn't used to be like this. We used to rent cheesy B-horror movies from Blockbuster and try to guess whether the leading lady's breasts were real. We used to buy paperback romance novels and take turns reading aloud from them. We used to have a good time just lying in bed, hanging out.

"Fish kiss!" I'd yell, and we'd suck in our cheeks and press our lips together.

"Lazy kiss!" he'd say, and I'd apathetically move my motionless mouth to touch his.

"Ze passion!" I'd announce, and we'd suck face like they do in old Hollywood movies.

But right now I don't want to do any of it. I just want this weekend

to be over so I can hang out with my friends, who are probably out somewhere having a wonderful time without me.

"Are you upset about something?" he asks me. "Do you want to talk about it?"

"I don't want to talk about it."

"Do you want to go to bed?"

"Not really."

I look at him. His hair is greasy—it hasn't been washed in two days, and his ears stick out a little. One side of his chin is longer than the other. His shirt doesn't fit right. When I was in Ireland over the summer, I cheated on him with a boy who was in my workshop group. He was decent-looking: better than Clint but slightly overweight. There were other guys who hit on me, but he was the only one I fooled around with. We kissed three separate times: big, moist kisses when the lights were out in our Dublin hostel. He knew what he was doing.

I decided not to tell Clint when I got back to the States, but the guilt was enough that I broke up with him for three months. When we got back together, he didn't ask any questions. He is the most forgiving, understanding person I have ever met, and I can say without qualification that I will never find anyone on earth who loves me as much as he does.

He looks at me, his eyes searching to figure out the right thing to say, the magic that will fix things between us.

"Do you want to watch another movie?" he asks.

I nod and pop another tape in the VCR.

I have class the same time Eric does, one room away, in Baldwin Hall, Mondays, Wednesdays, and Fridays at eleven-thirty. At eleven-twenty on Wednesday, he's already waiting for me outside Baldwin, lighting his Camel.

"I thought you smoked Marlboros."

He nods, finally getting a flame, puts away the lighter, and exhales. "Buy one, get one Camels at Kum & Go. Want one?"

I shake my head. I've already got two packs in my purse, having stopped at Kum & Go just before class.

"How's British Romanticism?"

He nods furiously. His eyes get about three times as big as they normally are. I have never seen a communications major so excited about reading *Frankenstein.*

"Mary Shelley is so hot. Did you know she and Percy had a three-some with her half sister? My professor was telling us about it in class, and I'm like, 'Shit, that's *hot,*' because it is, I mean, it just is, and these fucking freshmen around me look at me like I'm some kind of pervert." He takes another drag and exhales. "Whatever. I don't even care. Whatever."

"I've been thinking about threesomes lately," I say tentatively. "It's just weird how if two people have sex, it's about love. But if three people have sex, it's some sort of fetish thing. Like three people can't possibly be mutually in love. It just seems sort of arbitrary, making two the magic love number." I look at him. This may be getting a little weird. "I mean, hypothetically speaking."

"No, it's okay. I mean, I've thought about it, too. If it happens, it happens. Whatever. It's not like it's something I'm going to regret."

The bell rings. We finish our cigarettes.

"So . . . sleepover tonight?"

"Yeah," he says, pushing the big glass-paneled door open. "I'm excited."

The first sleepover was in September—we didn't plan it. It was a Saturday night, and we almost fell asleep watching *The Royal Tenen-baums* for the thirtieth time. We were sharing a blanket on the couch, but the couch wasn't very big, so somebody—maybe me—came up with the bright idea of all of us sleeping in my twin-size bed. None of us are particularly large people, but even still, it took some maneuvering.

"Christian, you have your hand on my breast."

"I know. There's nowhere else to put it."

"Can I put my hand on your dick?" Eric asks him. It might have been a joke.

"Please don't."

"I know, I know," he says quickly. "I'm joking, I'm joking. I promise."

"You're not joking, I can feel your hard-on."

"I know, I'm sorry. I'm sorry. I'm so horny. I'm sorry."

"I'm sorry."

"Rachel, I'm sorry."

"I'm sorry, Rachel."

"It's okay."

"I'm going to sleep now anyway. I promise. I'm sorry."

I couldn't sleep. I must have gotten out of bed around six-thirty. My right arm was completely numb, and the rest of my body was slowly slipping off the bed altogether. I went into the living room and slept on the couch. Three people simply cannot fit on a twin-size bed.

So much is being left out here. If this were a different sort of essay, I would tell you about how Christian and I used to make out when I was on a break with Clint. I would tell you about the presents we got each other for Christmas. I would tell you about how I get jealous when they talk about other girls, how I worry that my mother would be ashamed of me if she knew I've been stoned every day for the past two weeks, how I've waited my entire life for friends like these and I'm terrified of graduating next year and losing them forever. But that isn't how I feel right now, and it isn't how I want this to end. Right now we're smoking cigarettes in the rain outside of Baldwin Hall. Right now we're watching *The Land Before Time* in Christian's parents' basement. Right now we're rock-and-roll gods dancing around Meredith's apartment to David Bowie. Right now we're having a snowball fight on the quad at midnight, and we are the three happiest people on earth.

About a year ago I was watching MTV. Between teary close-ups on *The Real World: Philadelphia,* MTV was trying to sell me on the idea that I could text "62443" to my mobile phone and for 99 cents get Petey Pablo's "Freek-A-Leek" ringtone. For another 99 cents I could get matching wallpaper. For yet another 99 cents, I could get a cute animation of Petey grabbing the mic that all my friends would LOVE.

And I thought, Huh, so that's what the kids are doing these days.

And then the fear set in.

It wasn't that I worried I was turning into my parents, who still don't quite know how to check their voice mail. I could order the ringtone just fine if I wanted it. But I didn't want it. I like hip-hop just as much as the next guy, but on my phone?

That's okay, right?

I didn't know.

I thought, Who even watches MTV anymore? Cool kids hate MTV.

But I didn't quite believe it.

Pretty soon niggling doubt turned into full-on crisis.

I recently bought a new pair of shoes. They're red Puma sneakers. The exact make, if you're interested, is called H. Street. After losing my bearings on ringtones, I stopped wearing them. Completely.

I don't wear them because I don't know whether they're cool or not. I don't know whether they're appropriate to wear at a party in downtown Manhattan or if I look like a third-wave poseur from the Jersey suburbs.

This is more than just your average sartorial conundrum. Maybe MTV and sneakers don't mean anything to you, but to me the situation betrays a horrible inevitability: The mainstream—the flow of ideas that I trust on a day-to-day basis as a giant point of reference—is running dry.

If this seems like an absurd thing to worry about, let me assure you: It's a problem for you, too; you just don't know it yet. It's in my professional capacity to tell you.

Ten to fourteen hours a day, I work for a futurist consultancy. My company gets millions of dollars a year from huge multinational corporations to predict how consumers' attitudes and behaviors are shifting and how those shifts can be exploited for money. Specifically, I collect cultural specimens—a television channel for obese people, a palm-shaped man-made luxury island off of the coast of Dubai, a magazine about suicide—that outline five-to-ten-year changes in consumer behavior. My bills get paid because the world is saturated with billion-dollar entities run by legions of people who have entirely lost touch with what other people want. These corporations hire people like me simply because I pay closer attention to life than they do.

I figure out how to better provide people with what they want, God help us. I figure out how to better target people.

Once upon a time, popular culture was a common touchstone for people's communication. Fifteen years ago, if you walked by the watercooler at the office, you could immediately pick up shared banter about last night's prime-time TV. But now the mainstream is splitting into millions of tiny tributaries.

And this is going to be very bad for me.

But not just me. I'm on the older end of Gen Y, or Millennials, or Echo Boomers, or whatever you want to call us. My generation is going to crash and burn spectacularly. We're not going to achieve a

single thing because we're not going to notice there's anything to achieve. We're coming of age in a nasty transitional period.

But I'm jumping the gun a bit.

The mainstream serves a purpose: If you understand the movement from start to finish, you can gauge where you stand in it. It's the way that different people reach simultaneous consensus about when to wear suits with shoulder pads. Or skinny ties. Or red Puma sneakers.

At the top of the stream are people who are so passionate about things that they are willing to suffer personal disadvantage, social and physical repercussions for activities deemed unacceptable or dangerous by society at large. In advertising-speak, they are called Innovators, and they are responsible for generating the raw material for "original" ideas. Both dreadlocks and Dr. Martens are commonplace in today's culture, but once upon a time dreadlocks were worn by a fringe religious sect that believed the Ethiopian emperor Haile Selassie to be God, and Dr. Martens were worn by ultranationalist skinheads who used them to stomp minorities.

If you move a level down the food chain, you find the most despicable people on earth. They are sometimes called Influencers. Influencers are people who think of themselves as cool and work hard to cultivate this identity. Influencers are culture's middlemen; they create nothing, but they quickly adopt fringe ideas once some of the social unacceptability has been absorbed by innovators. Think Madonna and pinup sexuality. Think Trent Reznor and anger. Think Danny Boyle and heroin.

Influencers broadcast ideas to Early Adopters, masses of fearless consumers who in turn begin to convince society at large that an idea is okay. What was originally a statement of self-definition ("I'm like that") becomes a statement of taste ("I like that").

When enough people ascribe to an idea or trend, the people for whom self-definition or being cool is important become antsy. They know they're not like everybody else, so they look for new innovations to define themselves. New innovations mean new Innovators, and the cycle starts all over again.

Take techno, for example. Techno got its start as a computer innovation in the eighties. Synthesizer technology gave us MIDI, which stands for musical instrument digital interface and lets us write a sequence of notes that can be played universally on any MIDI-compliant synthesizer. If this sounds uncomfortably geeky, you can probably guess why. Waxing rhapsodic about MIDI-patch changes, grid quantizing, and pitch-wheel modulation isn't exactly socially acceptable.

In the mid to late eighties and early nineties, computer advances pushed MIDI synthesizers from the realm of computer dork to a larger audience. Suddenly, musicians (some in Detroit, some in Bristol, some elsewhere) figured out that you could program crazy beats into synthesizers (or, more recently, groove boxes) and dance the fuck around. Preferably on a drug called MDMA (methylenedioxymethamphetamine, or Ecstasy), which was also relatively new.

But at the time, most people thought computers were for guys with comb-overs and Coke-bottle glasses. Instead, DJs skimmed this subculture for content and then threw it down at clubs. A few musicians brought extensive synthesizer rigs, but mostly, it was on wax. Guys like Carl Cox, Danny Tenaglia, Paul Van Dyke, and a late-night radio host named Liquid Todd started to blow up, just because of their ability to move the crowd all night. Club kids popped E, sucked pacifiers, wore JNCOs, and waved glow sticks. For a while, life was beautiful.

Then a funny thing happened. Madonna did a techno album. Gavin Rossdale had his late-cycle grunge tracks remixed. And pretty soon guys from Staten Island were showing up at raves and spilling beer on people.

If 2002 rolled around and you were still listening to your Global Underground two-CD mix featuring Sasha and Digweed, chances are people laughed at you behind your back.

I know it still seems like ideas travel from Innovators to the masses in a linear fashion. If anything, people today are much more self-aware of their place in the mainstream, helping the transitions through innovation, influence, and mass run even more smoothly.

I can assure you this is not the case.

The problem is that the transfer of ideas through culture is no longer linear, but we won't notice this change until it's too late to adapt—culture is fragmenting, and we're already entrenched in our fragments.

When I turn on the TV, all I see is hip-hop. It's possible that you turn on the TV and all you see are home-designer makeovers. There's been no shift in the greater cultural context; we've each simply become a market of one person and now believe what we see to *be* the greater cultural context.

And this is just the beginning. Pretty soon everything you see in media everywhere will be exactly what you want to see and nothing more.

This is all the fault of the computer.

Yes, but every generation thinks world-changing upheaval is an inevitable—

The computer.

But history is a naturally cyclical—

The computer.

When cultural anthropologists in *Jetsons*-style flying cars look back on our piddling post-analog society (notice how everything today is defined as an expired or "post" relationship to the past?), they will recognize the computer for doing two distinct things to human society.

The computer has exploded the amount of sheer content we are exposed to every day. If I wanted to, I could learn about the latest Japanese schoolgirl fads while reading instructions on how to build pipe bombs, while chatting with a pharmacist in Saigon, while checking my stock figures, while researching cell-phone radiation, while watching videos of American civilian contractors in Iraq getting their heads sawed off.

And to think my parents had to settle for *Consumer Reports.*

But by the same token, the computer has isolated us. It's done away with social stigma. If, in the old model of culture, people had to find fringe and dangerous ideas to differentiate themselves from the

masses, the new model of culture is one in which there is no cost to differentiation. Thirty years ago, if you were a neo-Nazi, you probably kept it to yourself. Now you can find hundreds of thousands of Web pages supporting your point of view.

The net result is, if you don't like your current worldview, you can just go find a new one, because there will always be someone to validate you. There's no longer a progression of ideas from fringe to mainstream. Essentially, our personal understanding of what the world looks like "out there" is a direct reflection of what we believe is "out there." It's almost like the computer wrapped a warm, self-segregating blanket around each one of us and told us that all the things about us, each and every one of them, are A-OK.

In 1994 I got the Internet. Horrified by the social wasteland that was middle school and savaged by the awkwardness of puberty, I quickly found solace in the America Online of yesteryear. Although Netscape and Mosaic had been released, creating greater possibilities for a World Wide Web with graphics, hardware limitations meant that most of the Internet was still text-based.

In the fictional world of RhyDin, part chat room, part desperate imagination, I found friends with names like LdyTera3 and Ranger-Blue. Disputes were settled with a primitive dice-rolling script. The heaviest damage you could inflict were two 20s on virtual twenty-sided dice, but since there was no official scorekeeping, most everyone improvised the effects. It wasn't a chat room, it was the Red Dragon Inn. On any given night, a collection of mechanized battle-bots might be fraternizing with scantily clad illusionists and mustachioed knights. Characters ordered drinks in every currency imaginable, and in a profound display of geek-inspired time-wasting, someone would actually type descriptions of fetching, pouring, and delivering drinks.

While I quickly outgrew the fantasies of my newfound stomping grounds (to this day, I don't know how so many computer dorks afforded the hundred-dollar phone bills), my involvement in such abstract communities yielded music and culture that never could have

permeated my suburban existence otherwise. I went through a Swedish death-metal phase, particularly favoring a group called Bal-Sagoth, who screamed songs about the gore of medieval battlegrounds. I discovered a zine by a British man who went by the name Sexbat and wrote at length of the day Bauhaus disbanded and the chilling effect it had on Brits everywhere. He also provided meticulous care instructions for the feeding and maintenance of your pet rat.

One day, while combing for links to the complete text of the Necronomicon, I stumbled upon a site called shownomercy.com. At the time, the site seemed to be run by a group of British medical students who liked to post sarcastic profiles of one another. They also liked to extensively catalog forensics pictures of suicides, grotesque accidents, and mutilated bodies. At the ripe age of fourteen, I couldn't quite believe that such a thing even existed. Entranced, I clicked on a link labeled "shotgun head."

Before my very eyes materialized a picture (at ancient modem speeds) of a half-naked man slumped forward over a shotgun with the left third of his face spattered against the back wall of a double-wide. The picture was in black and white, which exaggerated the sheen and texture of the mess. I didn't sleep well that night.

A day or so afterward, still upset, I happened to mention this to an Internet friend I talked to nearly every day. He said, and I paraphrase, "Man, that shit's hilarious. When my girl left me, the only thing that kept me going was looking at pictures of the guy who got his hand in a meat grinder. 'Cause, you know, your life can always get worse."

I thought the Internet looked the same to everyone. With one notable exception, I saw only what I wanted to see.

I guess he did, too.

Is it such a bad thing that everyone can now sate their base desires with the click of a button? Maybe it's not. After all, billions of advertising dollars are wasted every year in an attempt to figure out what people want when, in reality, people are already shouting it with their remotes and their beliefs. The more content available, the more people

will be able to demonstrate their desires. And the more people demonstrate their desires, the more things can become available. Sounds great, right?

Sure, but not for me. Or the rest of my generation, for that matter.

One of the horrible parts of growing up is realizing that your fundamental perception of life's truths is going to become obsolete. The game changes, and so do the players.

The world's up and changed on me.

Imagine for the moment that you live on a street in a quiet little suburb. Pastoral, sure. But you're afraid to go outside your front door. Why? Because none of your neighbors speaks the same language. They don't have the same customs. Imagine your neighbor decorates his house with pictures of accident victims. Or Beanie Babies. He doesn't care what you think, because you don't enter into his worldview. And you, vice versa.

Once upon a time, the Melanesian tribes of Papua New Guinea lived in isolated valleys. Each village had its own customs and language. Nearly a thousand independent societies developed side by side, due in part to their separation. This is not so dissimilar from what's happening right now. The modern equivalent is media isolation.

Without a common language of content, without a common understanding of the linear flow of ideas, we all become entrenched in our markets of one, our media fragments. But for people born after the proliferation of computers, this will not be the case. I pick what I see, read, and buy based on who I think I am. These kids understand that they can change the context of who they are by what they see, read, and buy. They are multilingual—they understand that they can travel between cultural fragments. I speak only the language of my fragment.

I need a mainstream. It makes my life easier. It gives me a big gaudy neon reference point on what people are doing and how I can disassociate myself from the rest of fat, beer-swilling America. Or button-down corporate America. Or whiny liberal America. Or whatever other collection of people gets stereotyped for easy consumption.

Stereotyping people makes it easy for me to differentiate myself, so I can always think I'm special. So I can maintain my place in the food chain. Maybe, eventually, I'll understand the existence of other fragments, but only from the perspective of my own.

In ten years, the underpinnings of media and communication will be drastically different. People my age, unfortunately, are in a bad spot. Our prevailing selling point as a market is that we don't want to deal with any of these changes. In demanding the media that reflects ourselves, we demand to be left in the dark.

In a few years, the new up-and-coming hotshots from expensive Ivy League institutions will figure this out. Marketing 101 will boil Gen Y down to its essence: We don't want the boat rocked, we don't want to know what's on the periphery of our vision. Don't try to shake us, just keep selling us the same full-fat, narcissistic version of reality we've found for ourselves. We don't want anything else. Pretty soon the fresh-faced suits will be programming, communicating, and selling me right into my pigeonhole, and I won't even know it. I'll just think that this is the way culture still exists. And it will be my own fault.

Those fuckers.

This story was written on October 31, 2005, as news of the bomb blasts in Delhi came in. Bombs went off simultaneously in busy marketplaces—Sarojini Nagar, Paharganj, and Govindpuri—as the city was preparing to celebrate the festival of lights, Deepavali.

Sarojini Nagar. Paharganj. A DTC bus in Govindpuri. Where were you today? I'm worried for you, my friend. Please let me know you are okay. Send me waves of energy, trembling with relief and gratitude, vibrating in the ears of dogs and fish and birds, but otherwise unheard, unseen, across the Arabian, across the Mediterranean, across the Atlantic. Think of me today, for the first time in years, as I thought of you today, for the millionth time in my life.

But perhaps you are safe and well, and with your leonine nonchalance, you will brush off my overdue, undue anxiety. Perhaps you have already done your Deepavali shopping and are now lighting the small clay *diyas* with your silver cigarette lighter as little Parikram follows you around, step for step, along the contours of the Kirti Nagar apartment-with-balcony that you bought with so much glowing pride two years after you graduated. Perhaps you are holding him to your chest and inhaling the sweet scent of baby shampoo and neediness and feeling lucky to have been spared. He must be what, two, three? Ki-

shan Kawar was standing in the market with his son, Sumit, in his arms as his wife, Vandana, shopped for a pair of sandals, says *The New York Times*. The blast tore his son from his arms.

Remember eating fresh off the stove *chole bhature* at the snack stand in Sarojini Nagar after hours of bargain hunting? The bright white stand with its blackboard menu advertising hot specials was the only location in labyrinthine Sarojini Nagar that I could find on my own. I wonder if it still remains. One always wonders this of places that will never be returned to: *I wonder if it still remains*. Has it changed much? But tonight my question has a jagged edge. I wonder if it still remains. I still have the white silk shirt I bought from a vendor nearby. "It is very elegant, madam," he assured me, "not zazzy."

"What does 'zazzy' mean?" I asked when he was out of earshot and we were walking past the cluster of roadside Romeos lounging in the market, singing *badi mushkil hai, khoya mera dil hai*[1] in insinuating tones. Peals of laughter till someone took pity on me and explained that what he had said was "jazzy."

Sarojini Nagar dressed me. It was the ultimate destination for the particular brand of Delhi University cheap chic that my friends and I had perfected, slowly shedding the marks of small towns in Kerala, Bihar, Uttar Pradesh, Haryana, and West Bengal, provinces that surely existed only to pay tribute to the sweeping-streeted, bougainvillea-lined capital of Shah Jahan and Mountbatten and Indira. It was our skins we were shedding to wear the uniforms of batik and *chikan* and *kalamkari* and *bandhni* and whatever else was trendy on Mall Road that month. But we didn't mind, not us. Perhaps we already sensed then what I can articulate only now, here in a country where the tax forms refer to me as a "nonresident alien"—to step out of your own skin is a condition of existence in India, to speak haltingly in another tongue and jazz up jazzy with zazziness is a way of fitting in with the

[1] Popular Bollywood song, meaning some crap about how life is difficult since I have lost my heart, etc.

millions who don't fit in, who are bursting from the seams of hastily drawn, easily disputed borders.

The black lace shirt, the kind I had promised my mother I would never wear. The bottle-green suede jacket that I wore everywhere during a Delhi corn-on-the-cob, *chowkidars*-warming-their-hands-over-street-corner-fires winter. The unnaturally bright orange skirt in crushed cotton that painted my white bedsheets saffron during laundry. And yes, the purple tunic I was wearing when we first made love.

The terrace of your cousin's apartment on top of Bengal Sweet House in Ashok Vihar. Your neighbors were having a party. We were hungry, we could smell the tandoori chicken. The music was loud, and the breeze was cool after the heat of the summer day. You reached out and cupped my breasts through the thin material of my purple Sarojini Nagar tunic.

This just occurred to me, but the coup de grâce of our relationship was staged on a terrace as well—the cramped *barsati* in Vasant Kunj three years later. By then we had migrated from subsistence-level student life in North Delhi to below-subsistence-level working life in glamorous South Delhi. In keeping with the bizarre, un-Lutyensian architecture of *barsatis* in South Delhi, the terrace divided the kitchen from the rest of the living space. You were ranting at me from the bedroom in your loud "I won't take this anymore" voice, throwing clothes into a rucksack, and I was in the kitchen, determined to be dry-eyed, slicing tomatoes. Suddenly, you came flying out across the terrace like an angry wind, grabbed the knife, drove it into my arm, and announced, "Bitch, this is what it feels like to hurt."

In between the two poles, thousands of chaste pecks on the cheek in front of friends who would have been shocked and disgusted if they knew, and the countless hungry, demanding, worried tendernesses in private. The few fervent moments in early dawn before your mother came to pick you up for a family picnic to Shimla. The instinctive, cowardly drawing of the blinds. The snugness of your hands in mine as the rickshaw lurched over potholes, a reassuring squeeze for each pothole. The softness of a kiss erasing a tear on a mascara-streaked

cheek. The hasty hugs just before the Kerala Express took off from New Delhi Railway Station under the watchful eyes of the respectable Malayali matrons in my compartment.

(To be honest, I never thought I would write about you. You were the black hole in my memories. Please don't exist, I begged you. After I got over you, I did consider turning you into literary capital, but it was too predictable, too childish, too trite. Yet here I am now, fantasizing about you the way writers do about characters, tweaking details here and there to give your character the roundness that you did not have in real life.)

And always, like the perfect soft-focus backdrop of a sentimental Bollywood movie about forbidden love, Delhi rose behind us. Two rupees bought a wildly careening bus ride on the perfect ovalness of the Ring Road. Watch now how each parcel of Delhi gives way to another—the thousands of narrow *galis* between Dilli Gate and Lahore Gate packed with tiny stores selling saris and leather and spectacles and earwaxing services, the predictable traffic jam at Dhaula Kuan, the out-of-left-field peace and quiet of Raj Ghat and Shanti Van and other memorial gardens that the Congress Party liked building for its dearly departed, the smell of *momos* frying in hot mustard oil at Majnu ka Tila, a glimpse of the regal columns of Connaught Place from the bridge over the filth of the River Yamuna, the secondhand book market at Daryaganj stretching for many miles along the dingy street with book lovers crouching on the ground while dogs and cows ambled in between, the lovers cutting classes and dotting the gardens of Safdarjung's old palace, the flower sellers accosting devotees at Nizamuddin's tomb. We wandered into poetry readings and dance recitals in musty government buildings where maestros performed to audiences of three and four. We went into the air-conditioned film theaters without checking to see what was playing, only wanting to escape the barren, dusty heat storm outside. We went into the British Council library or Max Mueller Bhavan when we wanted to feel intellectual with a European touch, when we wanted to build invisible walls between the thousands of desperate immigrant workers from impover-

ished outskirts and our own existential dilemmas—Indian writing in English or translations from regional languages? Was "indigenous people" actually more politically correct than "tribals"? Order Maggie noodles from *bhaiyaji* at the hostel canteen or grab a McAloo Tikki burger at the McDonald's just outside campus? Decisions decisions decisions.

And we argued about each and every one of them. Perhaps it was a passive-aggressive way of fighting the real fights that never took place between us. The fight about whether St. Stephens was an overrated college must have been actually about why our relationship would always be a secret from friends. The bitter argument about whether *Lagaan* was a shallow song, dance, and cricket movie posing as a postcolonial movie was of course about all the other people in your life I was jealous of—one of whom you are now married to. And the accusations that hurled back and forth about Kashmir—alas, those were indeed about Kashmir.

It took me ten minutes to forgive you for the gash on my left arm that day on the terrace of our Vasant Kunj *barsati*. As long as I live, I will never ever be able to forgive you for telling me coolly, "Well, why don't you go to Pakistan, then?" at the end of a discussion about freedom fighters and terrorists. The fault lines were drawn at that moment, carefully and indelibly. Me Muslim, you Hindu. The same fault lines were soon being drawn all over the country. Terrorists attacked the Parliament building. A train burned in Gujarat. All over the country, the instinctive, cowardly drawing of the blinds. My mother hurriedly tried to shut the door of our house in Kochi upon seeing a saffron-clad monk approach, but she was not quick enough. He looked at her with hurt eyes and asked, "Older sister, is there a prayer I can take from you to Ayyappa Swami?"[2]

[2] Pilgrims in South India on their way to the shrine of Ayyappa, a local Hindu deity, often stop to seek alms from the houses they are passing by, irrespective of the religion. But in an atmosphere of increasing religious fundamentalism, saffron robes and flags have become associated with militant Hindu fundamentalists rather than with monks and pilgrims.

The week after the attack on the Parliament, I went to the British Council library. There was a hastily built shelter near the gate containing four armed policemen, an X-ray machine, and a metal detector. It was my first experience of what is today a regular and inevitable part of my life in New York. Yet in markets like Sarojini Nagar and Chor Bazaar, life continued as usual, bravely, smarting under recent wounds but flashing an extra-brilliant smile like a courtesan in a Mughal court who knows she is about to fall from grace. Only for you, special price, two hundred rupees. Two hundred rupees? I am not buying the whole shop, *Bhaiya*. Madam, see quality of this material, it is export quality. Then you should export it, *Bhaiya,* why are you sitting here, go to London with this *kapda*. Madam, see board over there, you are educated person, you know what it says, this is fixed-price shop. Yes, yes, the board is fixed, I can see that. But I am not paying more than fifty rupees. Fifty rupees, madam? *Achcha, aage bhi dookan hai, namaste. Teek hai,* what about seventy-five? No? *Chalo Phir. Arre,* Madam, where are you going in such a hurry? Is this some way to behave with friends? What about one hundred fifty? It's Deepavali next week. You need new clothes . . .

Parikram must be sleeping on your shoulder now. The *diyas* have been lit, the *arti* is ready, the *kaju barfi*[3] boxes and Ferrero Rocher baskets are waiting to be sent across as gifts to neighbors, clients, and in-laws. You are standing on your balcony now, thoughtfully watching the lights glisten in windows across Kirti Nagar, in hundreds of middle-class homes lit up to welcome the lotus-wielding goddess of wealth. You wonder what Deepavali is going to be like this time around. The government has called on people to stay indoors, and armed police have taken up positions in the main public areas. You are praying to all the gods and goddesses you know that the child whose soft little heart is beating against yours will grow up in a safe world, where masked men don't attack the house of the nation's leaders,

[3] Traditional sweets made of cashew nuts.

where chief ministers don't pretend not to see when policemen burn down the houses of one part of the city, where bombs don't go off in crowded markets on the eve of festivals. You think of the first time Parikram called you Mommy, his arms reaching out for you, and you wonder if the other mothers, the ones who lost their children in Sarojini Nagar today, will forgive you for having him alive now. The winter breeze is cold. The next-door neighbors are having a party. The music is loud. The city does not know if it is celebrating or mourning. Shuddering, you step inside and join your husband in the living room, where he is watching the BBC news report on the bomb blasts in India's capital city.

I will stop writing now and listen to cheesy Bollywood songs about communal harmony. The sound track for tonight is Amar Akbar Anthony and A. R. Rahman singing "Bande Mataram." Tonight I will listen to these and hope that you and Parikram and Atul are safe because tomorrow the backlash will begin. Eye for eye, ear for ear, child for child, festival for festival . . .

Sarojini Nagar. Pahadganj. A DTC bus in Govindpuri. Where were you today?

August

"I don't get paid for two months." That's what I should tell the parents during our first open house. "The school board holds our pay to make as much interest as possible for the system. I won't see a check until October first."

Instead, I speak of my qualifications, classes taken, honors received, expectations for my students. This is my first year out of college, and I have returned home to teach fourth grade in the Birmingham public school system. I met my students a week ago. Now I meet the parents.

"We will concentrate heavily on the writing process," I tell them.

"What about math?"

"Hands-on, reinforced with abstract, ability-level acceleration . . ."

"What about conduct?"

"Individual responsibility for participation . . ."

I'm proud of my answers, confident of my capability to surpass No Child Left Behind.

"You don't seem to know much of anything," says one frowning mother.

The muscle behind my eyebrows isn't yet fitted for the teacher stare. I've been practicing it, standing in front of my bathroom mirror, flexing my forehead. It throbs at this interjection.

"You don't seem to know much of anything," she says again.

"If you have a more specific question, I'm sure I can find an answer."

"Bobby couldn't read problem number three from his homework last night. It was badly copied."

"Yes, our copier is broken. That reminds me, if you have printer paper to donate, that'd be great. The school has asked teachers to buy their own paper." (Here, also, I should tell them I don't get paid for two months.)

"My child was very upset about not being able to answer number three."

"Do you have the paper with you?"

"No."

"We'll go over it tomorrow."

September

I learn my children's strengths and weaknesses, what makes them feel comfortable, what makes them succeed. I stay thirty minutes after school to go over long vowel sounds with one student.

In return I become "Ms. Dude," "Emma," "Hey Teacher Lady." Slowly, my slowest learner begins to read. A child who once began each day screaming now finishes his work, all his work, sitting under my desk. We are ahead of other classes by two units.

Because I'm a first-year teacher, I am given forty-seven mentors. They all have plenty of advice. I rotate my one and only daily thirty-minute break among them.

"They talk to you like a friend. This is unacceptable. Demand respect!" advises one.

"You cannot let a child sit under your desk," asserts another.

"Keep a journal for documentation in case you get sued," warns a third.

My favorite, finally, from the fourth: "You have to put your foot down."

I tell mentor number four, who is three times my size, that I am twenty-two years old and weigh a hundred pounds. My foot doesn't make much noise. He doesn't laugh.

I have learned that no one in the education system has a sense of humor.

I think this until I get my first paycheck.

November

I've become used to the interruptions caused by assemblies for special causes.

Cartoons for March of Dimes takes an hour. Afterward, everyone agrees that a thousand elementary school students sitting in a dark auditorium is not a good idea. Lunch for Leukemia takes two hours: one for lunch, one to counsel parentless children. A project for Heifer International steals some of my sanity, as my student from Sudan leaves the assembly fearing her family will eventually die of starvation.

"Maybe it's the way you pronounced 'heifer,' " says mentor number five.

"I don't care about cows!" I scream.

I take half a day off to learn to love the bovine.

When I return from my half-day break, I'm told my class "doesn't do well with substitutes."

One student has written on his chair: "Never leave again, Ms. Black."

"Next time use paper," I tell him.

I ask, "Why is my desk upside down?"

"Principal wouldn't let Daniel sit under your desk," says an honor student.

"If I flip it over, I'm not technically sitting under it," Daniel says.

"Humm," I say.

We spend half an hour relearning to sit quietly in our seats.

My shyest student speaks out for the first time all year. He raises his hand, not his eyes, and very eloquently tells his desk, "Seriously, next time use paper."

Mentor number six reminds me this is not a laughing matter. She says so in the teacher's lounge while feeding construction paper into a lamination machine. This makes me slightly uneasy. She leans closer. The machine hisses and steams, and her glasses fill with fog.

"Respect," she says.

March

We plan for the standardized test, only the standardized test, for a month, with no break.

All extra, non-test-related classes are bumped to two-thirty P.M. The test's new open-ended grid requires six hours' practice a day. In this open-ended grid, children are to answer mathematics questions in their own words, with their own methods, using solely the system set up by the Alabama Reading and Math Test Committee of No Child Left Behind.

THINK OUTSIDE THE BOX BUT STAY INSIDE THE GRID, I post in big letters over my chalkboard.

My students rock back and forth in their seats furiously.

"I hate math," one mumbles.

"All work and no play," chants my back row.

I invent the Geometry Game to prevent anarchy. Children chant, "Parallel . . . cha-cha-cha . . ."

"You are not taking the SAT seriously," says mentor number seven.

And the children sing: "Rhombus . . . cha-cha-cha . . . Right angle . . . cha-cha-cha . . ."

April

The test results come back, and we kick ass.

We write so much in the new grid that children are pulling out magnifying glasses to read their conclusions. We fill those multiple-choice bubbles so beautifully, I want to frame them.

"This is easy," says my back row.

We begin writing research papers in MLA style. We use math books from the grade above. We are the only class that still has time for science and social studies. My children are succeeding. I have never been so proud.

I'm laid off, during lunchtime, on my birthday.

It's nothing personal. The Board of Education fires all nontenured teachers at the end of each school year to keep from paying benefits over the summer. A very pleasant security guard gives me the certified letter and tells me not to cry. He smiles and quickly walks away with handfuls of layoff letters to deliver.

The next day is graduation—at a church. Under normal circumstances, I would object to my students hearing of Paul and chanting prayers during public school events. However, I'm busy dividing my time between the bathroom and the kitchen, preparing food for fifth-grade graduates and guests while dry-heaving what's left of last night's party. I wait tables on weekends for extra income, so my restaurant coworkers threw my birthday party with the theme "It's okay, you can always wait tables!"

"Remember the words of Lazarus—" squawks the loudspeaker from the auditorium. A pulsing begins beneath my eyebrows as diplomas are dispersed.

"Becky Andrews receives our first diploma," reports the loudspeaker. "Becky is receiving an award for citizenship." Clap. Clap.

"Frederic Alexander is receiving 'Most Improved.' " Clap. Clap.

Someone finds chicken salad to apply to white bread. The smell sends me back to the restroom.

When I return, Mark Reynolds is receiving his honors—first-chair trumpet, honor roll, and Earth Day participation award. "Congratulations, Mark." Clap. Clap. Clap.

Parents will come for food when we reach the end of the alphabet.

I'm getting nervous. I stack the sandwiches higher.

Suddenly, there's knocking on the locked doors from parents too hungry to wait for the end. Someone brings out a melon ball, and the sweet, slimy smell of a growing fruit tray pulls at my stomach. Some-

one else combines sherbet and fruit juice. Crackers adorned with cheese cover a tray.

Finally, it's all over. I've survived my first year of teaching.

I learn later, through the teacher grapevine, that my class received the school's highest SAT scores. As a grade level, we rose ten points.

August

I am not rehired. It's cheaper for the school system to find another first-year teacher to fill my position.

I have changed systems, changed schools. Replaced Heifer with March of Dimes, purchased a new journal for legal reasons, and hoped for tenure.

Still, I have taught twenty children. This year I will teach twenty more. I have brought students from sounds to sentences to stories. I have explained multiplication, shown them where they are on a map, taught the difference between warm and cold fronts. I have listened, and heard stories I cannot for legal reasons share. Seen details that others have missed. Overlooked details to see my students. I am proud of what I have heard, of what I cannot share, of what I have shared.

So, if teaching is such a gratifying experience, why do so many teachers leave?

There comes a time in every young man's life when he must bow his head, shrug his shoulders, and say, "Yeah, I'm in a band."

In New York City, that's comparable to admitting, "Yeah, I get on the subway and sell batteries." It's another thing New Yorkers don't need one more of. But I moved to the city believing it had a hole where my angst-ridden pop songs should be. So here's what I did.

I began where all bands begin: Craigslist. I put an ad out for a drummer the week I arrived. It is now a year and a half later, and I've been through six.

The first was a girl. Novelty is priceless, I thought. But Laura couldn't keep time very well and had bipolar disorder. I didn't know if these two things were related. I also didn't know if it was appropriate to ask her to switch poles to accommodate varying tempos. She also drank like a sailor and swore like a lawyer. She dragged me out one night and bullied me into matching her drink for drink. I have never been any good at standing up to bullies, male or female, and I ended the night in tears. (I have a rare condition in which my body rejects alcohol through weeping.) She was given to fits of rage and paranoia, and neither pleading nor depressants could get her to stop speeding up during each song. Ballads started sweet and ended sweaty. Allegro numbers morphed into what could have been used to end hostage sit-

uations. I put out an ad for another drummer a week before our second gig. Laura found it online, confronted me, and a horrible scene occurred in which she called me a "dick." Miraculously, she showed up at the gig and played the best show of her life.

The second drummer was Rob. My biggest worry was that he loved Phish and wore an inordinately long soul patch. This worry became a minor one when he neglected to show up for our first rehearsal and left me with the studio bill. He then disconnected his phone. I had no idea I struck such fear in the hearts of truant drummers. I felt suddenly empowered and despite the rejection went back to Craigslist with renewed authority.

Jason (Drummer #3) was a different type of binge drinker from Laura—the kind whose drumming actually improved with tequila. He could drink anywhere. I once watched him pick out a bottle of wine at a Chinese buffet. Despite his tendency to ramble on about video games and his propensity for Backstreet Boy–style backing vocals, Jason had the makings of a keeper. He was skilled, adamant about the band's success, and came into every practice with new ideas. Then one day I received the following phone call: "I don't know if I can play anymore. I've gone up two pants sizes since joining the band." I personally hadn't noticed. He went on to explain that the two hours a week we practiced interfered with his nightly 10K run. I was impressed. That had to be a first in the history of rock and roll. Jason played one more show with us, then took off to run a road race in Utica.

Drummer #4 was the most evil human being I'd ever met. He sold himself by claiming he was hooked up at Sony. I naturally took him at his word, a word that I later found out began with a "b" and ended with a "shit." The extent of his hookup was owning a PlayStation. He was not only a liar but thick as a plank. But he was an excellent drummer and we were desperate for a beat, so we allowed him to gouge us at a rate of forty-five dollars per rehearsal and a hundred dollars per show. Had he not been evil, this might have been considered a New York bargain. However, an overview of his exploits might explain how it wasn't.

Mikey would show up hours late to rehearsal and still ask for his wages. He would shout "motherfucker" in crowded elevators. He liked to play a game called Throwing Pennies at Shit. He invariably played drums with a trash can at his side so he could let enormous globules of saliva and tobacco escape his lips without soiling the carpet. (He was not without some civility.) Mikey detested the band uniform—white shirt, black pants, skinny tie. In the middle of a show at Luna Lounge, I looked behind me to find he'd cast off his costume to reveal a Tool T-shirt with cutoff sleeves. His blond shoulder-length tresses, which he usually kept under a hat, were now unfurled in full headbanging glory. A charismatic front man can smooth over most stage accidents with a little light banter. There were no words left to rectify the damage Goldilocks Extreme had done to the group's image. That same night Mikey confided in me that his greatest dream in life was to light his hands on fire during a performance.

The most draining of Mikey's personality flaws was his belief that we got along great. He repeatedly asked me to go drinking with him. For the duration of his tenure, I managed to fend him off without revealing my feelings. But when he found himself kicked out of his apartment, my cool wavered. He asked if he could crash at my place and I foresaw waking up to "Dude, I totally took a shit in your sink. My bad." I told him my apartment was too small for guests. He told me he just needed a spot on the floor. I told him I had a rat problem. He said he could sleep in the bathtub. I pedaled my bike into oncoming traffic to avoid further discourse.

In the end, Mikey wasn't totally useless. He introduced me to the guy who became Drummer #5. Bennett Klingman was a smart kid with great chops and the perfect look: skinny, tall, bespectacled. He told me he used to make his living selling PCP, acid, and Vicodin, but since graduating from college had quit messing around with drugs. That was a shame, because now that he was out of the narcotics trade, he was also out of money. He made me feel as if I was two tax brackets above him, yet I was washing my face with stolen soap. I once

bought him a two-dollar hamburger, and he cried. Needless to say, he couldn't contribute to rehearsal fees.

I carried him for five months. His stay was a distance record for the band. I figured as long as I bought him the occasional sandwich, he was guaranteed to stick with it. More fool me. Bennett stopped returning all phone calls and e-mails on March 14, 2005, three weeks before our first industry showcase. It was our most anticipated show to date ("anticipated" meaning two people had made reservations online), and it was not like Bennett to disappear. By this time, the band had acquired a bass player, a teenager of doglike loyalty, and together we allowed genuine human worry to mix in with our usual anger toward drummers. Was Bennett dead? Was he hurt? Could his drug-peddling past have caught up with him? We had nothing to go on. We found his parents' number in Baltimore, but they hadn't heard from him either.

After three weeks of fretting, we had no choice but to put our concern for Bennett's health on the back burner. We shifted into emergency mode for our showcase and hired another drummer. For fun, we'll call him Six-y. Six-y made a minimum of mistakes at the show, and in return, we gave him three hundred bucks. We never heard from any label scouts; however, I did get a call from my bank. We told Six-y "it's been real" (expensive), and between rummaging through the "Server Wanted" ads in *The Village Voice,* I scavenged through the Craigslist mire for Lucky #7.

I didn't close the missing-persons case on Bennett, however, and continued to hunt for him. Mainly for selfish reasons—I felt I deserved some closure. One day while perusing MySpace, I clicked on his profile. It had recently been changed. Under the "About Me" heading, it read, "Hi, I just got back from Burma. I didn't tell any of my friends I was going and now they're all like, 'Hey where the hell's Bennett?' But sometimes you just gotta go to Burma, you know? Ha. Now I've got two wives and six kids. I'm back and I have a job shoveling poop."

I paused.

Then I composed my thoughts into the following:

DID THAT MOTHERFUCKER GO TO BURMA?

I had thought he was lying in a ditch. Apparently, he was alive enough to be updating his MySpace profile, and well enough to be writing poop jokes. (Jokes that I'm sure were hilarious to other drummers but lost on the nondrumming strata of society.) Goddamn it, had he really gone to Burma? Based on the tremendous setback his disappearance had caused the band, I demanded he at least be hooked up to life support with a punctured lung. Anything less was inexcusable. I wondered if I could sue him for the three-hundred-dollar loss of funds and for the millions I deserved in emotional damages. But then I'd still have to find him.

I learned that retribution is not something readily doled out by the gods atop Mount Band. Bennett's betrayal of trust was clearly par for the course, and I never got an answer or an apology. Fellow New York musicians know this hardship intimately, and whenever they hear about my drummer troubles, they usually respond with a great intake of breath and a comforting "Oh, dude. I know." However, nonmusicians from all over the globe continually ask me why drummers are so problematic. The following is a list of possible explanations, compiled from both outside pundits and my own theories. Please note that this list could easily be applied to Chicago, Atlanta, Houston, or any other major city where musicians dwell; however, since the cruelty of New York in general tends to bring out the extremes in already flawed personalities, the list remains Gotham-centric. These are in no particular order:

1) New York City has very few drummers. Housing a full kit in the city of six-flight walk-ups and L-train limited weekend service does not create a fertile breeding ground.

2) Drummers are mentally handicapped. The range of instruments known as "percussion" attracts boys and girls born with

one fewer or one more chromosome than expected. The ability to communicate on a normal level is replaced by an ability to make crashing and smashing sounds.

3) New York City has very few *exceptional* drummers. This is a corollary of Theory #1. A smaller population of drummers naturally assumes a smaller population of good drummers. This explains why most outstanding percussionists in New York will charge as much as "out the ass" to play even the humblest of venues. (*Note: "Out the ass" is an industry-standard quantity ranging from $100 to $250 per performance.*)

4) The desirability of drummers explains why even mediocre ones will fuck off without warning. The average length of time it takes a New York drummer to find a new band is 2.5 seconds.

5) While drummers can easily make money at what they do, singer/songwriters cannot. Most drummers' actions are hence motivated by a sense of superiority. This despite being host to numerous learning disabilities and having absorbed everything they know from Grand Theft Auto.

I impart these explanations not to discourage but to help other aspiring bandleaders relieve some of the stress of their urban struggle. There is nothing you can do to improve your chances of landing a good drummer, but you can at least get by with your standards confidently lowered. Knowing that whatever drummer you find you will not keep may seem like a curse but in reality is a gift. You will enjoy each performance as if it is your last, and you will *live,* damn it! There is joy in discovering which of your microphones delivers the biggest electrical shock when you engage it with your teeth. It will certainly come in handy when you're running through your oldest song for the ten thousandth time with the eight hundredth drummer and you can't help nodding off.

After a dozen or so have sat on your throne, it will appear to you as if the gods are giving you a hint and maybe it's time to pack it in. You've made your catalog of Spinal Tap remarks and cannot bear to hear another. However, one statistical truth will ultimately prevent you from hanging up your guitar: you are not alone. You represent a long march through history between drummers and bands. There was a reason Spinal Tap had so many drummers. Christopher Guest likely suffered through the same parade of stick jockeys that has dogged the careers of countless others. John Lennon complained about finding a decent beat-keeper even in the earliest days of the Quarrymen and confessed to settling for the guy who owned the tape recorder. And finally, there is no doubt in my mind that the lead lyre-ist in a Lower East Rome band plowed through dozens of freedmen claiming to be reliable goatskin beaters but who never turned up for gigs. He and the panpipe player cursed the Fates in frustration but went on, one hopes against hope, to eventually play the Colosseum.

CALIFORNIA THE WALTZ THE MUSTACHE RACE
SEX AND THE SICKBED TRICYCLE PRIME-TIME YOU BACKLASH
THINK OUTSIDE THE BOX BUT STAY INSIDE THE GRID
FINDING THE BEAT YOU SHALL GO OUT WITH JOY AND BE
LED FORTH WITH PEACE THE IDIOT'S GUIDE TO YOUR PALM
SHEER DOMINANCE LIVE NUDE GIRL AN EVENING IN APRIL
CLICHÉ RAPE STORY ROCK MY NETWORK GOODBYE TO ALL THAT
ALL THE RIGHT ANSWERS WHY I HAD TO LEAVE IN-BETWEEN PLACES
A RED SPOON FOR THE NAMELESS MY LITTLE COMMA FIGHT ME
THE SECRET LIVES OF MY PARENTS MY ROARING TWENTIES
IN, FROM THE OUTSIDE THE MYSTERIES OF LIFE . . . REVEALED!
SO YOU SAY YOU WANT A REVOLUTION WORKING AT WENDY'S
JESS LACHER MARY BETH ELLIS BRONSON LEMER JENNIFER GLASER
RACHEL KEMPF JOHN FISCHER SHAHNAZ HABIB EMMA BLACK
ELI JAMES KYLE MINOR COLLEEN KINDER CHRISTOPHER POLING
KATHLEEN ROONEY RADHIKA ... MARISA McCARTHY

am deeply, deeply afraid. Subtract seventeen years from my twenty-nine. I am twelve years old, standing beneath a starfruit tree, standing on an asphalt path lined with banyan trees, their roots extending from ground to sky to ground again and forming great pockets of wild, empty space in the center of their root-branches. Fifty feet behind me, the science laboratories where my chemistry teacher last week was too careless with sodium and set the ceiling tiles on fire. Fifty feet in front, the band room where the Sonshine Fellowship (get it? Son, not sun! Like Jesus, the Son of God, the Light of the world who takes away our sins!) meets every Wednesday morning at six-thirty to pray and sing the happiest of songs all in major keys, except the songs borrowed from the Jews, which are in minor keys and which speed up as they go along and which, when played on acoustic guitars, are faintly reminiscent of sad country songs. And those happy songs make me happy, truly happy, for brief and ever briefer periods of time, but it's those Jewish songs—*You shall go out with joy and be led forth with peace: the mountains and the hills shall break forth before you. . . .*—that really slay me, because there is something *earned* about that joy; it has come from a place of great pain.

The Jews, of course, are going to hell, but, as we students are constantly reminded, Jesus was a Jew, and the Jews are God's chosen peo-

ple, and in fact we must keep the Jews around—this is the *real* reason why the holocaust was so awful, because it was the work of the devil to destroy God's plan for the end of the world, which goes like this: Christ comes back in the clouds, this time on a white horse and bearing a sword, and bodily raptures all the dead in Him—a veritable zombie army—and the living Christians, too, the true ones (not, for instance, the Catholics, who follow a man, the pope; and not, for instance, the Episcopalians, who have placed a premium on the material needs of people rather than their spiritual needs—the Social Gospel, this is called—and so have slipped into heresy). The Christians, living and dead, taken bodily from the earth, leave a void of darkness. Remember, in the Book of Genesis, God promised to save the cities of Sodom and Gomorrah if Lot could find even one righteous man, but none could be found, so God rained fire upon the cities and they were destroyed. This, too, will be the fate of the earth, now that the righteous are gone. The Antichrist has already begun his seven-year reign. The clock is ticking. But—wait!—in the last hour 144,000 Jews finally accept Jesus as their personal Lord and Savior, many of them convinced and converted by two resurrected Jewish prophets. And then the Jews fight alongside the returning army of Christians at the battle of Armageddon, which takes place right in the heart of contemporary Palestine. God's chosen people, old and new, are finally reunited, and live together in the new heaven and the new earth—in the very bosom of God—forever.

But that's not why I am drawn to the Jews and their songs. It's not that I don't care about the rapture and Armageddon and the end of time. I am extremely anxious about it. For the last eight years—for as long, that is to say, as I have had memory—I have knelt in my bed, beside my window, at dusk, and watched the light show of sunset, looking for the crimson bloodstain in the sky that I've been told is a sign of His coming. I have memorized Scriptures—*If we confess our sins, He is faithful and just to forgive us our sins and cleanse us of all unrighteousness*—and I live in fear of unforgiveness, of eternal hellfire, so I am constantly confessing my sins, an ongoing litany, a conversation,

perhaps one-sided, between me and God, that consists for most part of me trying to recount every sinful action (that part is easy) and every sinful thought (that part is hard). To look upon a woman with lust in your heart, for example, is the same as having slept with her. I am twelve years old. I am hard pressed to find a woman upon whom I will be able to gaze without feeling a twinge of lust in my heart. Puberty has come slow—my classmates, staring at my tiny naked body in the shower after physical education class, have made it quite clear that I am deficient in this area of puberty arrival. But not entirely deficient. Sixth-period history: I am sitting behind Jenny Glass.* Her blond hair down to her shoulders, the shape of her hips, the sound of her voice humming softly, soft enough that Mr. Sanders can't hear, but loud enough that I can hear how fully rendered each of her notes, even at so soft a volume such control . . . and then I'm wondering what it would be like to be married to her, and would we share a bed?, and what would *that* be like?, and I don't really know exactly what all that means—I mean, I know that there are parts, and that they fit, that kind of thing—but what I'm really thinking about is what it would be like to *kiss* Jenny Glass, to touch her hair as we kiss, feel it in the webbings of my fingers . . . and my body responds to these thoughts in its new way, and I lean forward a little in the desk, to obscure whatever it is that is happening, but of course it is at this moment that Mr. Sanders has had his say about the battle of the Spanish Armada and is ready for me to have mine. "Kyle?" he says, and I say, "Fifteen eighty-eight," and he says no, it's not enough to just know the date. You have to trace the sea routes on the four-color pulldown map, which he is right this moment pulling down over the chalkboard. Come on up, is what he says. And, right then, I do something that I've seen other people do but have never myself done. I say no, I'm not coming to the board to trace the sea routes on the four-color pulldown map. He asks why, and I say I'm not particularly interested in sea routes, that in fact I *prefer* dates and that I'm tired of being made to do things that I do not want

* Some names and details have been changed.

to do. Mr. Sanders says if I don't walk directly to the blackboard and trace the sea routes that I will get a zero for the day's participation grade and that I'll be in grave danger of making him very angry. I consult my pants. My pants are saying no. Jenny Glass has turned around to look at me now, incredulous—the first opportunity, in fact, I've found to use that word, incredulous; I've been wanting to use it for a very long time, but now, employing it in my own mind, the word incredulous is nowhere near as sweet as I had thought it might be—and I briefly look at Jenny, trying to gauge her reaction to this turn of events, but I find that I am not able to look her in the eye. A slow, painful moment passes. Then, for the first time in my life, I deploy a coping skill that will soon become a lifelong crutch (and will also give those who wish it a reason not to like me): I feign confidence. I say, "Mr. Sanders," and he says, "Yes?," and I borrow a line from a television comedian: "I'll take the zero."

What has this to do with the Jews, their songs? *You shall go out with joy and be led forth with peace,* sure, but first you will undergo great hardship. This from the prophet Isaiah, a truly mystifying figure, the greatest of the Hebrew prophets, come onto the scene at a pivotal point in Israel's history. Twenty years after Isaiah accepted his prophetic mantle, the Assyrians crushed the Northern Kingdom, and the better part of ten of the twelve tribes were taken into exile. (Twelve years old, and I know these things. They teach us these things at my school.) And not long after that, Jerusalem itself found the fearsome army of Sennacherib at its walls, and despite King Hezekiah's recent embrace of what Isaiah had called a "covenant of death" with a political faction that wanted Israel to be more like the Egyptians who had once held their ancestors as slaves—worship their idols; sleep with their women—Yahweh (YHWH: He whose name cannot be uttered on pain of death) delivered the city, and Sennacherib could only brag like a loser. *I shut Hezekiah up in his cage like a bird,* reads the famous inscription; not *Jerusalem is mine.*

Like all the prophets, Isaiah was both trouble and troubled, his destiny sealed when the seraphim cleansed his lips with a burning coal;

and then, no doubt blistered and in great pain, he said, "Here am I, send me!" And then he wrote great, painful, angry poems of warning: *Your country is waste, your cities burnt with fire; Your land before your eyes strangers devour*—and—*the desert owl and hoot owl shall possess her, the screech owl and raven shall dwell in her*—and—*Take a harp, go about the city, O forgotten harlot; Pluck the strings skillfully, sing many songs, that they may remember you.*

I am twelve years old, standing beneath the starfruit tree, on the asphalt path, both hiding from and waiting for my daily beating. I know it is coming, because this morning the other science teacher, Mr. Guy, showed the filmstrip from Answers in Genesis about the fossil record—the dinosaur tracks with the human footprints embedded in them; the fragments of the Cro-Magnon man shown to be a hoax in a side-by-side comparison with a baboon skull; satellite imagery of the petrified remains of a massive seagoing vessel found lodged in the side of Mount Ararat, in contemporary Turkey, where the Ark of Noah was said to have come to rest—and after class my head is so full of possibilities—a trip, perhaps, to Muslim Turkey, undercover, perhaps smuggling Bibles . . . perhaps even long hours under the sunlamp so I could pass for a Turk, following the example of the author of *Black Like Me* . . . and a daring climb with a Sherpa guide who would be proud when I bestowed upon him the Anglicized name of Henry . . . and a dig through snow and ice and earth to uncover, in person, what the satellites had already suggested: the Ark of Noah, proof beyond doubt, real archaeological evidence of the worldwide flood that created the Grand Canyon, the Seven Continents, the washing away of the Garden of Eden, and, at last, rest for the angel who had been guarding it with his shining sword for all those many centuries . . . and also refutation of all the theories, the lies, that modern science has been serving up to support their religion of secular humanism—the Ice Age, Plate Tectonics, maybe Evolution itself—my head so full of possibilities that I forget to go the long way to my math class, around the front of the gym that faces the administrative buildings, instead of the short way, around the back of the gym, near the locker

rooms where Drew McKinnick and his boys lie in wait for me at this time every day. A careless, careless mistake that could have been so easily avoided, but I don't give one thought to it until I pass the pale green locker-room door and forget to notice if it is cracked open or not, and then—WHACK!—McKinnick makes a weapon of the wooden door. It hits my arm with a velocity I could not begin to measure, and sends my body hard to the concrete, and—I have good reflexes; I'm used to this sort of thing—I manage to twist at the last moment, to twist my body around so I land front-first rather than flat on my back, and hands-first rather than headfirst—*bruise the hands, cut the hands; protect the head.* A teacher—good, Mr. Sanders, a good man—comes running from behind, and McKinnick is standing in front of my body—I see him up there, scratching his head, feigning concern, and feigning it in a manner that makes very clear his utter lack of concern—and Mr. Sanders says—he yells, really—"Why did you have to go and do that?" and McKinnick says, "I had no idea he was standing there," and Sanders says, "I doubt that sincerely," and McKinnick says, "On my honor, sir. I feel as bad about it as he does."

I know better. I know better than to say it. But I say, "No one feels as bad about it as I do." McKinnick can't help himself—it's only a moment; the slightest moment; the slightest of slightest moments—he smiles, flashes those dog teeth. In those teeth I see real pleasure, and it's not the first time, not by dozens. And then the smile is gone, and what's back is feigned regret. Sanders has his number, but who is Sanders? What can Sanders do? Sanders is already on thin ice for wiping boogers on the blackboard—to make us laugh; to make us feel better about ourselves; compassionate boogers—and before that, Sanders was already suspect, because Sanders moonlights as the school night watchman, because they don't pay him enough money, because he doesn't have a wife or children so he gets less than the other teachers, and sometimes he watches reruns of *Star Trek* on a black-and-white television at midnight in the principal's office, his feet up on the desk—he was caught once, and everyone knows—and another time he was caught falling asleep at two o'clock in the morning, and another

time at five. They—*They*—say that Sanders jogs home at six-thirty every evening after coaching the junior varsity soccer team and sleeps until eleven-thirty, takes a quick shower, eats some Frosted Mini-Wheats, then humps it back to campus to nightwatch until dawn. That's Sanders, and what's Sanders next to McKinnick, whose father is the mayor of the village of Golfview, a veterinarian wealthier than God who paid for half the new football bleachers? And what's Sanders next to McKinnick, varsity linebacker in the eighth grade, second string already, a mean 220, putting hits on twelfth-grade running backs that they'll remember into their old age? McKinnick, who can crush a baseball, hit a 350-foot shot to left center. McKinnick, who could crush Sanders more ways than one.

The locker-room door cracks open. Jones, Dodd, Graves—McKinnick's boys. Sanders sees them. He says, "You boys get on to class." They pause for a minute. "Now," Sanders says, and they go, and McKinnick starts on his way, too, but Sanders says, "No, you wait," and I want to tell him . . . I want to tell him that what he is doing is a very bad idea. That it's a very bad idea for me. But I can't tell him. I can't say anything, because no matter what I say, it will make matters worse for me later. So I keep quiet. It's hard to keep quiet.

"So what you're going to do right now, right at this very moment," Sanders is saying, "is apologize to Mr. Minor here."

McKinnick makes a sound in the back of his throat—the gathering of spit and phlegm—and then he turns his head and spits for distance in the direction of the hedges that line the sidewalk outside the gym and locker rooms. The spit lands a few feet from the hedges, and—I can't help myself—I say, "Airball," and then his eyes flash like they can, the way I imagine the eyes of killers must flash in the moment before they become killers—and, be advised, I believed, then and now, McKinnick, given the right circumstances, fully capable of killing a man, or a boy, especially a boy, with his bare hands.

He looks right at me and smiles, and this time I detect nothing but the utmost sincerity in that smile—and I know that the sincerity does not attach to the apology he is about to offer, but instead to the retri-

bution, the beating, that will follow—and he says, "Minor, I'm truly sorry."

Sanders says, "Good, then. It's settled. Now, both of you, off to class."

I let McKinnick get a head start before I start walking. I know when we turn the corner, mean Mrs. Tatham, the grammarian, will be waiting outside her classroom door, watching, looking for an excuse to jump down some poor kid's throat. God bless Mrs. Tatham.

McKinnick takes his head start. He rounds the corner, then I do, and he is ahead of me, passing Mrs. Tatham, but then he slows down. She is still watching, so he doesn't touch me, but when I get within earshot he says—loud enough for me to hear, but soft enough that she can't—"It's not settled"—and though I knew, now I *know.*

I am twelve years old, standing beneath the starfruit tree, possessing this terrible knowledge . . . and yet, and *yet,* above me are starfruit, a great many, and I have been picking them for all the years I have gone to this school, ever since I was four years old, and I know how to pick one that is sweet enough but not overripe, and not overly bitter, either. It is truly amazing to me that I am the only person I know, student or teacher, who picks from this tree.

The fruit are green or yellow or brown, their color a measure of their ripeness. I reach up and pick a yellow one, the five points of its star just starting to turn brown. This is how I like them. Just a little sweet, but still firm, not mushy. I bite into one of the points of the star and some juice runs down my face and down onto my hands and into the cuts and abrasions from where I caught myself on the concrete behind the pale green locker-room door after McKinnick hit me with it. There is citric acid in the juice, and when the acid touches the cuts and abrasions, it stings, and I make a fist involuntarily, and squeeze the starfruit I am holding, and squeeze more juice, more acid, into the wounds. *You shall go out with joy and be led forth with peace* is the song I am hearing in my head. *The mountains and the hills shall break forth before you*—all this from the naysayer, the prophet of doom who also wrote, *Your country is waste, your cities burnt with fire; Your land*

before your eyes strangers devour—and the difference, you see, between Old Testament prophets like Isaiah and New Testament disciples is that the joy in those old Jewish writings always rises from the deepest of darkness, and there is no gloss on the darkness. No purpose for the darkness, except sometimes testing, sometimes judgment, sometimes spite, all this attributed often enough to God. No *all things work together for good to them who love God, to them who are called according to His righteousness.* No. All things do not work together for good. All things are in opposition, and the darkness more often overtakes the light than the light the darkness. The darkness is the darkness is the darkness.

And what would bring God joy? A final separation from sin. The destruction of the wicked. The destruction of the world.

And what would bring me joy? The destruction of Drew McKinnick.

I am twelve years old, standing beneath the starfruit tree, holding in my hand the most beautiful fruit any tree in the world has ever borne, and now softly humming the most beautiful, sad song I have ever heard—*You shall go out with joy and be led forth with peace*—and contemplating the destruction of Drew McKinnick.

There is the baseball bat. Maybe *his* baseball bat. I could carry it with me around the corner, make a show of showing it to Mrs. Tatham, talk a little shop about the relationship between baseball bats and grammar. And wait. And when McKinnick rounded the corner, I could draw back that baseball bat and swing it at his head and explode his skull . . . no, watch it swell like a balloon, and then swing it again, and watch it pop, watch the splatter of gray matter and crimson blood stain the sidewalk, and then, in the moment before they wrestle me to the ground, kick that mouth with my black penny loafers, kick every last dog tooth from that mouth.

There is the baseball bat, but perhaps it is not practical. But then there is the gun. My grandpa has a loaded twelve-gauge shotgun mounted above his bed in his trailer. And a kid in my second-period study hall, Lee Paterson, has a book called *The Anarchist Cookbook.* He says it is easy to make napalm. I told him once I'd like to napalm

Drew McKinnick, and Paterson said it would be nothing, that his skin would melt off, that he had tried this himself on a Barbie doll and it had been only too easy.

"But what about a bomb?" Paterson said.

"A bomb?"

"Two or three. Five or ten. Ten or twenty. Plant them all around. Blow the whole school down." He showed me a drawing he had made, a diagram of the school and where the bombs would be placed. A few of them would go inside the air-conditioning units that lined the walls, because the components inside would become shrapnel and take out more people.

Paterson is small, smaller than me even, and I am the second-smallest person in the whole secondary school. Some of the fourth- and fifth-graders are bigger than us. When he showed me the drawing, it scared me, first because I thought he might be serious, and second because I thought maybe I might be capable of doing it myself if I knew as much about chemistry and military strategy as he did. Looking at those diagrams, I thought I could maybe do it.

I am twelve years old, standing under the starfruit tree, eating a starfruit, thinking about blowing up the school, humming a song written by the Jewish prophet Isaiah, holding all these contradictions in my head and not knowing that they are contradictions, waiting for my beating; and then it arrives.

But not the way I think it will.

Because usually when McKinnick finds me to beat me, he brings Jones and Dodd and Graves with him. They make a circle, a loose circle at first, and they yell obscenities and push me from one of them to another and sometimes push me down and kick me and make me get back up so they can push me some more, but then the circle tightens and McKinnick slaps my ears, hard, with his open palm. First my ears ring, and then I lose most of my hearing and it doesn't come back for a couple of hours, and when it does, it comes back with louder ringing and an awful headache. Then Jones and Dodd and Graves hold me and slap the top of my head and stick their spit-moistened fingers into

my ears and nostrils while McKinnick stands over me and flicks the cartilage at the tiptops of my ears with his fingers until the cartilage turns purple, and he keeps asking if I've had enough, and when I say yes, he says, "No, you haven't," and when I say no, he says, "You need to get some humility, boy," or, "Who do you think you're talking to, boy," or, "Say *I'm a dirty nigger.* Say it. Say it." And then I say it—"I'm a dirty nigger"—or—"I'm a queer, I'm a homo"—or—"I fuck my mother"—or whatever other thing he wants me to say, but even then it doesn't stop. Drew McKinnick knows how to hurt a person a hundred ways and more, and there is nothing in the world funnier, so far as I can tell, to Jones and Dodd and Graves than to hold my arms while McKinnick lifts up my shirt and grabs my nipples between his thumb and forefinger and tries to turn them 180 degrees (this he calls a One-Eighty), or to hold my arms and legs, to hold my whole body up in the air while McKinnick slaps at my testicles like he did my ears, with an open palm.

I'm waiting for that. I'm waiting for all that to happen.

But that's not what happens. What happens is I hear my name—"Minor"—and I hear it behind me, from the direction of the band room, where the Sonshine Fellowship meets to pray and sing. I turn around. It's McKinnick, and he's alone. And the fact of this—his aloneness—is more terrifying to me than anything I have ever seen or heard or known or imagined in my entire life.

I am deeply, deeply afraid.

McKinnick starts running, takes off at a sprint, and I turn, too, and start to run. But I am slow. I get five steps, maybe, and he tackles me from behind.

I fall face-first on the asphalt. I catch myself with my hands, and my right hand goes through the starfruit on its way down and rips fresh wounds into my hands, and those wounds are bathed in a tiny new pool of citric acid.

McKinnick is on top of me. He mounts me from behind, starts slapping my ears. "How's that?" he says, and slaps and slaps and slaps and slaps, gets a rhythm going. He reached into my pants and grabs

hold of my underwear with his hand and jerks the cotton into my anus, and pulls, and pulls. I am already bleeding. I can feel the warmth.

McKinnick says, "How's that? You like that? You feel it burn? Burn, baby, burn!" He pulls my underwear up and down and from side to side.

He says, "You know what? I could ass-rape you right now, and no one would know. And if they found out, it's you would be the faggot, not me. You hear me, faggot? Are you listening?"

What does it feel like? It is the most helpless feeling in the world. No one will come for me. If I try to tell on him—as I have done in the past—no one will believe me. I am at his mercy, and I am not sure he has any.

All I can do is go someplace else, to that band room, to Wednesday mornings, six-thirty A.M., where I am singing—where *we* are singing— the words of the prophet Isaiah: *You shall go out with joy and be led forth with peace: the mountains and the hills shall break forth before you. There will be shouts of joy, and all the trees of the fields will clap their hands, will clap their hands.*

That, and this: I will grow up to become a person who will be able to make things like this not happen to other people. And I will tell this story. *This* story. I will make sure everyone knows.

And here I must interrupt the thoughts of my twelve-year-old self to tell you, reader, that I did *not* grow up to become a person who could keep things like this from happening to other people. And until this moment, this moment I am sharing with you, I did not grow up to tell this story. I tried, a few times, and less and less as years went by, to tell this story. But no friend ever wanted to hear this story. The past, they would say, is the past. Or: *That was a long time ago. Get over it.* Or: *Nobody likes victim stories.* And, most often, they would say nothing at all. They would just be very quiet—I could tell, always, from the look on their face, that I had made them uncomfortable by sharing even the opening words of this confidence. I had revealed myself to be a strange and disturbed individual.

I stopped trying to tell the story. I grew up, instead, to become a preacher. Briefly a preacher. Less than two years a preacher. And while I was a preacher I was befriended by a Palm Beach Gardens city worker, a meter reader named Tony Griffin, and it is important to know that Tony Griffin was black and that he was especially sensitive to racial issues, and that I was not—trained as I was, at this school, to not believe in any kind of legacy of racism in America, that any talk of race was necessarily a crutch, an excuse used by black people unwilling to work hard, to pull themselves up by their bootstraps and all that. Tony and I had a falling-out over this very issue. He was part of a small group of single people in their twenties and thirties who met at my house on Thursday nights to pray and read the Bible and play video games, mostly Madden NFL 99, on my Sony PlayStation. And Tony was sure that the people in the group—all of them white but him—had turned against him because he was black. I was convinced that this charge was completely unfounded, and conceded that possibly the others were growing impatient because they disliked his habit of interrupting the PlayStation games to put kung fu movies in the VCR. So we broke off our friendship, Tony and I, over race and video games and kung fu movies. And then I quit being a preacher, decided to be a writer, lived in my car for a while.

I kept a cell phone, though, and one afternoon two years later, it rang—I was near Orlando—and I saw Tony Griffin on the caller ID, and I answered and was glad to hear his voice until he said, "I'm calling because I have leukemia." And then I was making trips to West Palm Beach every couple of months to visit him in hospice. And then we had another falling-out. I didn't know that leukemia was a disease of the immune system, and I had a cold, and I came to visit, and I coughed as I walked through the door, and Tony threw a cup of red Jell-O at my head and said, "Mother*fuck*er! You come in here with a *cold*!" I left the room as fast as I could and closed the door behind me, and I heard something else hit the door, and then: "I don't ever want to see your ass again until I'm *dead* and you're standing over my

wooden box." I honored his wishes for a year, and then his niece called and said, "Come quick, he's got two days."

I walked into the room. He lay on the bed. His family was gathered there, waiting. He asked them to leave the room. He said, "No one will be straight with me. Am I going to die?"

I said, "I don't know."

He said, "Bring me a mirror."

I did, and he looked at himself for a long time, and then he said, "You ever see those pictures of the Ethiopian babies starving in the ditches?"

He bore a striking resemblance.

He said, "You see me, don't you?"

I nodded. I couldn't talk. What could I do? I crawled into the bed with him. He was naked beneath the hospital gown and he had shit himself and some of the shit got on my pants. I held him for a while, and then he said, "You were right about the kung fu movies."

And I said, "No, I wasn't. I wasn't right about anything."

This was death talk we were talking.

Then he said something extraordinary. He said, "I'm still praying for a miracle. I'm still believing for a miracle."

I did not want to tell him so I didn't tell him what I had learned, what life had taught me, which is there's no such thing as miracles. God probably doesn't answer our prayers.

After we said our goodbyes I left and knew he only had another day, probably, and it was not information I was equipped to handle. I hadn't cried since I was thirteen years old and received the last of my beatings from McKinnick. I had hardened myself so I wouldn't cry anymore, and then I couldn't undo it when I needed to undo it. So there I was, driving in my Chevy Corsica down Interstate 95, a little bit of Tony's shit still on my pants, just a little black stain, the little bit I couldn't get off with the hospital bathroom's hand soap and sink water. I was still trying to burn into memory what it was like to hold him and feel his flesh hanging like rags from the scaffolding of his

bones, and to feel like if I held him too tightly I might break those bones and that it wouldn't take much at all. Not being able to cry made it all so much worse. The tightness in my chest was almost unbearable and I needed to somehow loosen the tightness, and even though the air conditioner was making the car uncomfortably cold, I felt a terrible heat in my chest and neck, and the veins in both temples were throbbing so hard I thought the vessels might burst. I pulled the car off on the side of the interstate, near a Jupiter neighborhood called The Heights where an ex-girlfriend still lived with her parents, their house a hundred feet or so from where I was sitting. I wanted to see her. I got out and scaled the six-foot chain-link fence separating neighborhood from interstate. My pants snagged on the fence and ripped a little, and I walked to her house and rang the doorbell. She wasn't there, but her mother answered the door and asked what was wrong and I told her that Tony was dying, and she said she was very sad and very sorry and wished she had time to talk about it but she had to be off to a birthday party.

Then I scaled that fence again, and ripped my pants some more, and that made me angry, ripping my pants. A state trooper a quarter mile away turned on his blue lights and raced toward me. I was standing beside the Chevy Corsica in ripped, shit-stained pants, my chest tighter, my neck hot, a shooting pain running down my left arm, watching the state trooper's blue lights parading like funhouse ghosts against the front of my shirt.

The trooper opened his door and stepped out, and then he looked at me, and I looked at him, and I saw that he was Drew McKinnick. I could feel the beating of my heart through my body. I could all but hear the ringing in my ears, and those old, familiar words: "You need to get some humility, boy." But then I could see that he *wasn't* Drew McKinnick, that he only bore a striking resemblance. The same cold intensity in his eyes, same square jaw, same dog teeth.

A couple of years earlier, a state trooper had pulled my brother over on a dark road—he was still in high school and wore his hair

long—and yanked him out of the car by the arm and threw him over the trunk and threw him around some, asked him if he knew what happens to people who hit cops.

This officer, when he got a closer look at me, puffed out his chest, straightened to his full height. He asked what I was doing climbing the fence by the interstate. He was almost grinning. What passed between us was not unfamiliar. It was a flash of mutual recognition, the thing that two individuals of certain types immediately know about each other. Minor and McKinnick. I felt small.

I told him I was having a hard time and I had stopped to see a friend. I said I knew I should not have climbed the fence. I said I would be glad to get back in my car and be on my way. I asked if he'd let me. I said I was very sorry. I was ready for him to throw me around, *knew* he would.

He waited a long time. He did not ask for my driver's license, and this troubled me. Whatever was going to happen between us was going to happen off the record. His nostrils flared when he breathed. He breathed hard. Each breath was like a calculated blow to the stomach. He put his hand on his holstered pistol. He looked into my eyes, measuring. I could not return his stare and shifted my focus to a fixed space beyond his shoulder, the white of the sky. "What happened to your pants?" he said, and I did not want to mention the fence. He seemed to find pleasure in my discomfort. He put his other hand on my shoulder and leaned over me so I had to look up again to meet his eyes. I told him I had ripped them on the fence. At that he grinned again, the predatory grin. His fingers dug into my shoulder. He said, "I don't want to see you on the side of this interstate again. That's a warning. I only give one. You understand?" I nodded. He sniffed the air, made a sour face. "Do yourself a favor and take a shower," he said. He gave my shoulder one last squeeze, then a little shove as he let go and walked back toward his patrol car and got in and waited for me to drive away.

I stepped into my car and drove away, and he followed me all the way to the Indiantown Road exit, and then I exited and he kept going

north. I pulled into a service station, and then I began to sob. Present or not, Drew McKinnick had undone what he had undone. I could feel him in the presence of the cop. His joy at intimidation. Somehow I had made it possible. My ears were ringing though they had not been slapped. Somehow I still carried McKinnick around inside me. I cried for a long time, and if I said that I was crying for Tony dying, that would be true, but it would also be a very, very small portion of the truth. Mostly, I was crying for the twelve-year-old boy standing beneath the starfruit tree on the asphalt path and waiting for his beating.

When I had cried all I could cry, I started the car again. I dug through my cassette tapes and found one that Tony had given me as a joke. It was Parliament Funkadelic's *Greatest Hits.* We used to listen to that tape in the car all the time. I liked it more than he did.

I was listening to George Clinton go through the ministrations of "Atomic Dog"—*Why must I feel like that, why must I chase the cat?*—and then I was singing along, falsetto: *Nothin' but the dawg in me.*

The cell phone rang, and I knew it must be my brother—he was in Nashville auditioning for a six-month touring gig playing bass guitar for a well-known country singer—and I didn't even check the caller ID display. I answered and said, "Dr. Funkenstein here!"

The voice on the other end was not my brother. It was Tony's niece. She said, "Kyle?"

I said, "Oh, oh, I'm so sorry, I didn't know."

"It's Tony," she said. "He's dead. He died a few minutes ago. I knew you'd want to know."

I didn't want to know. If this, dear reader, was a story like the kind I like to write, maybe there would have been a miracle. Most likely, Tony would die, but something else miraculous would happen. There would be a turn toward beauty that would reflect the joy-from-sadness in the prophet Isaiah's words, the comfort: *You shall go out with joy and be led forth with peace.*

But I can't do it. Not this time. At the funeral, when the other men who had been Tony's pastors gave their portion of the eulogy, their words were full of comfort and hope. They were able to assure his

family that Tony was in a better place, that he was, in fact, in heaven, with Jesus and the angels, held close to the bosom of God. But when it was my turn, I had no comfort or hope left to give. All I could say was that I loved Tony, and that he loved me, and that he was a stubborn and intractable person, and that I was, too, and that I believed, truly, that Tony had found his greatest joy in watching kung fu movies. That was all I could say. And when I was done, I stepped down from the only pulpit from which I had ever preached a sermon, and I walked past the altar, and down the steps, and down the aisle, and through the back doors of the church, and I have not been back since.

CALIFORNIA THE WALTZ THE MUSTACHE RACE
SEX AND THE SICKBED TRICYCLE PRIME-TIME YOU BACKLASH
THINK OUTSIDE THE BOX BUT STAY INSIDE THE GRID
FINDING THE BEAT YOU SHALL GO OUT WITH JOY AND BE
LED FORTH WITH PEACE THE IDIOT'S GUIDE TO YOUR PALM
SHEER DOMINANCE LIVE NUDE GIRL AN EVENING IN APRIL
CLICHÉ RAPE STORY ROCK MY NETWORK GOODBYE TO ALL THAT
ALL THE RIGHT ANSWERS WHY I HAD TO LEAVE IN-BETWEEN PLACES
A RED SPOON FOR THE NAMELESS MY LITTLE COMMA FIGHT ME
THE SECRET LIVES OF MY PARENTS MY ROARING TWENTIES
IN, FROM THE OUTSIDE THE MYSTERIES OF LIFE . . . REVEALED!
SO YOU SAY YOU WANT A REVOLUTION WORKING AT WENDY'S
JESS LACHER MARY BETH ELLIS BRONSON LEMER JENNIFER GLASER
RACHEL KEMPF JOHN FISCHER SHAHNAZ HABIB EMMA BLACK
ELI JAMES KYLE MINOR COLLEEN KINDER CHRISTOPHER POLING
KATHLEEN ROONEY

I was walking along the shoulder of a quiet road in Michigan when a sign promising PALM READINGS caught my eye. The sign, aglow in neon red, sat in the window of a humble white house. Open for business, it tempted.

People who make a living by predicting the lives of strangers have always spoken to my irreverence. Raised Catholic, I was taught to seek counsel in old men wearing white collars. No matter my sins, they prescribed three ourfathers, two hailmarys, and a glorybe. The jewelry-draped psychic was, I imagined, the deliberate opposite of a priest. A palm reader could wear purple eye shadow, smoke cigarettes, and charge cash. If her clientele were dull on a given afternoon, she could entertain herself with more lurid prophecies: lottery tickets bought on birthdays, dark strangers in Paris, breast lumps. I wanted to meet one of these people and hunker down by the crystal ball. "Take your best shot," I'd say with a wink.

Some other time. It was eight P.M. already, I reminded myself. I still had a mile to walk before reaching my hotel. But before I could even get to the edge of the palm reader's yard, my feet stopped, reconsidering my flimsy excuses.

Why not?

My day's work was complete, and no one was waiting back in the hotel room. I didn't know a soul in Ann Arbor, or all of Michigan, for that matter. I turned back toward the house, not quite decisively, and approached the porch. Soon I was on the porch, my hand reaching for the door.

Knock, knock.

"Who's there?"

"Sorry."

"Sorry who?"

"Sorry-just-wondering-about-the-palm-readings?"

"MOM! LADY HERE FOR YOU! C'mon in."

"Wow, what a . . . *purple* room."

"You can sit. My mom's getting outta the shower."

I sat in the purple room with a quiet boy and thought about all of the things a quiet boy might wish his mom did instead of palm reading: filing medical records, driving buses, painting toenails? Anything, really, that didn't involve opening the front door to wide-eyed strangers.

When his mother came out, towel-drying her hair, she smiled warmly. Her eyes held mine while she uttered a generic welcome. I repeated that I was just there to inquire about the price of a palm reading. She told me to come inside her office.

The office was a freshly painted white room, the perfect size for two strangers sitting face-to-face. She sat down at a desk with tidy piles of books on it. Arranged on the bookshelves behind her were small pastel-colored stones, spaced out liberally, as if each had demanded personal space.

The palm reader was petite and attractive. Her skin was what dated her beyond thirty; shallow wrinkles fanned from the far corners of her eyes, and faded pockmarks covered both cheeks. Her hair was dark blond and hung in wet clumps on her shoulders. She wore faded jeans and a classic gray V-neck shirt. No makeup. No mess of bracelets slid from wrist to elbow, elbow to wrist.

"Twenty-five for palms," she said, and then rattled off a list of higher prices for services involving cards, baths, and crystals.

"Twenty-five . . ." I mulled the price over, then thought about how awkward it would be to turn back now.

A thin white cat slunk into the room, nudging the door partway open. The palm reader cooed at the cat, seeming pleased by the company.

"How old are you?" she asked, making small talk.

"Twenty . . ." Since leaving behind college and all its tidy calendar divisions, I'd had to think harder about my age. "Three." Last year's number kept arriving on my tongue first.

"Young," she judged, widening her eyes slightly. "How did you find me?"

"Oh, I was just walking back to my hotel."

"You're visiting?" She looked doubly curious. "What do you do?"

The answer was too long. I was in Michigan to give a talk to university students about "postcollege adventures" (i.e., any first job not involving a cubicle, photocopying duties, a boss named Stan). I had become some kind of overnight authority on the matter when I published a book called *Delaying the Real World.* The publishing company seemed most keen on my age, not to mention the fact that I was newly back from living abroad and not yet employed by The Man. I volunteered to set aside my job search for a few months to play poster child and promote the book. Michigan was one of the last stops on the publicity tour. For months I'd been spouting the carpe-diem spiel and could now field questions in my sleep. All except one. *The* question that tied up every Q&A:

What do YOU do for a living?

"I'm a writer."

"Books?" The palm reader looked hopeful.

"Yeah . . . one."

From the change in her face, I could tell that this detail impressed her more than it should. She saw some young Danielle Steel, love affairs

with men in tuxedos and stiff Ken-doll hair. Meanwhile, I was still tabulating the contents of my wallet, hoping the grand total cleared twenty-five. The honest answer to the question of what I *did* was simple: nothing yet. The book about delaying the real world had done just that.

"You're a pretty girl," the palm reader commented, keeping a firm gaze on me.

"Thank you," I replied, startled by the flattery. Still, I couldn't help considering how I might appear in the palm reader's office. I was wearing a long embroidered black jacket that belied its sale-rack origin and suggested a hipper brand. Around my neck was a red speckled scarf, and dangling over it were long fake-gold earrings that I always wore for publicity events. The subtle wind-chiming below my earlobes lent me confidence that I had reason to hold a microphone and advise total strangers. Beneath my coat, blue jeans tempered the costume, promising I was somewhat laid-back. See, kids? Take it from me: The cubicle can wait for an adventure or two!

The palm reader leaned her chest against the rim of her tall desk, where her hands were clasped in a fist. If we chatted any longer, she'd gather the equivalent of a Google search on me. I could sense her probing, plotting.

"Okay," I said. "I'll do palms."

She looked unsurprised, nodding once.

The *door* was open. This was a problem. I was about to have my *life* forecasted, and the door was hanging wide open. I thought of the quiet son in the next room, watching television. Would other quiet family members come home? Put the TV on mute? Snicker?

Mortified to show that I cared this much, I got up out of my chair and reached over to close the door. It took one long second. I sat back down, feeling the color in my cheeks, hoping it would pass.

"Give me your palms."

I offered my open hands across the desk.

The palm reader began by using a smooth scalpel to trace the longest creases. The scalpel's metal felt cool and piercing on my skin.

I looked around. The cat must have been underneath my chair; I didn't see it anywhere.

"You'll live a long life," the palm reader began, raising her voice so noticeably that I almost laughed.

Predictable, I thought. Though I didn't disagree. I'd always been able to picture myself as a wrinkly old woman.

The palm reader pulled apart my skin with her thumb, as if she might find something other than sweat.

"You are more of a giver than a taker," she announced. "Some people take more than they give. They *take, take, take.*" She impersonated greed with a snarl and pawing at the air. "But you're the opposite."

I stared at her, not moving. Worse than untrue, this statement was formerly true. Only lately had I felt self-engrossed. It was one of the odd, unintentional trends of my early twenties—like growing fond of the early morning and binge-drinking less. I couldn't say why, but I felt myself molting generosity by the fistful.

"I can sense this about you. An outward current." She sent one arm floating away from her body, her fingers in a fan.

Listening to the palm reader's airbrushed version of me, it was impossible not to wish I bore a closer resemblance.

"You live for God," the palm reader continued, seeming pleased to bear me the good news. "Material things are not your focus, because God is."

Even worse! A holy misreading. I'd been on deliberate hiatus from all things religious for years, calling myself a "recovering Catholic." I hadn't gotten around to finding a substitute for my past faith. Idealism had filled in for a while, then waned, along with my zeal for moving overseas, living out of a backpack, volunteering. Nowadays, self-conviction was my main religion. Bouts of guilt hit only occasionally, like now.

"What I feeeeel is that you're a spiritual being. Deeply spiritual."

The palm reader then paused, inviting commentary on how God and I got along. I stared back with glassy eyes, saying nothing.

She proceeded. When she spoke, she cocked her head to the right

and scrunched her brow as if something were hurting her right above and between the eyes. She made grammatical slips every so often, and it took me a while to figure out that she had a slight Eastern European accent.

"You keep very busy." She was shifting to new territory. "You have gotten very good at filling up your days."

Aha. I smiled slightly. The busy trait was more mine than freckles. There were few minutes of the day you could catch me not moving. Even when pinned at a desk, one of my legs was bouncing below. Sometimes both.

"Lately, this is all you do. Work."

I thought of the hefty stack of papers I'd stuffed into my suitcase to read through during my trip to Michigan. After a full month of working long hours on publicity, I'd convinced my publishing company to sponsor a $2,500 contest. It was open to all twentysomethings who wanted to flee their cubicles for a "gutsy and worthwhile adventure." The company had set up a website and called for entries. Every five minutes, another application blipped in from cyberspace, appealing for money to bike Thailand, to film Belize, to roam Rome. I'd start reading all thirteen hundred of them tomorrow to find a single winner.

"You look for ways to give yourself more work. To stay busy," she continued.

I looked at the palm reader coyly, as if she had just chanced upon my hidden talent. I had a tic. This activity tic—unlike generosity or any other soft patch of my spirit—was something I'd never turn off. I couldn't. Not without large doses of alcohol or a severe cold.

But the palm reader was not charmed.

"And why do you work? Because you don't know what else to do in life."

Her brow was scrunched; her head cocked right. She found this pitiable.

"You don't know what to pull yourself away *for.*"

For?

"You *tire* yourself out this way. Look how tired you are!"

A new reflection overtook my mental mirror. This face was blanched with fatigue, dominated by gray eye rings. *Tired.* I wanted to curl up in the palm reader's lap for a nap.

Stepping into this woman's office, I hadn't worried about self-composure. I presumed that a palm reader could strike a fault line only if there was a fault line to strike. I had no recently deceased relative to channel, no mental demon to exorcize. I was vaguely unhappy, sure, but I figured that was part of young adulthood. The phase during which all expectation yields some disappointment.

But my palm reader wasn't having it.

"I look at your spirit and see no others surrounding it."

Why would I be in Michigan, alone, with her, if all was swell?

"There are friends you've grown apart from. Good friends. Was there an argument?"

We'd hopped from half-truths, to total bull, to nearer-truths, to things my own mother would say about me, verbatim. It was this cadence, more than anything, that was undoing me.

"You've done *something* to push people out. To keep them away from your life."

No one but a palm reader can say these things to you. Family members and close friends might dissect you among themselves, trading the scalpel, but not while you're sitting in the room with naked, red-rimmed ears.

"You've made yourself very alone."

A palm reader on the side of the road in Michigan is distinct for two reasons. One: She'll never see you again. Two: You're the one who knocked on the door, asking for a blind, cold read.

"Why am I hearing the letter M?"

I stared at her blankly and shook my head.

"How about a D. Whose name starts with D?"

No D. I shook my head.

The palm reader was having an unlucky spell. Before trying the letters M and D, she had misfired with the state of Florida, followed by

California. Feeling stubborn, I wasn't about to lend a hand. My cheeks were still cooling back down to a room-temperature pink.

"I sense a problem with your father. What's going on with your father?"

"Nothing, actually." Pops and I got along great.

There's probably some mnemonic device all palm readers use to touch on the big life topics in a sentimental crescendo (**L**inda **G**ave **P**olly **C**rackers **F**or **T**alking: **L**ifespan **G**od **P**ersonality **C**hildhood **F**amily **T**ragedy). I could trace her methodology; she followed my flushes of reaction and abandoned all duds as soon as they fell.

"You lost a man you loved, didn't you?"

Oh no.

"Recently. You lost a man you love recently."

Linda Gave Polly Crackers For Talking LOUDLY. Love. Of course.

I had completely forgotten about Chris. Forgetting had been the intention, actually, after we broke up on January 1. I took our expiration date literally, like a New Year's resolution—to move on, with all of the closure and resolve that had been missing in the previous two years. I was ready to end the weepy drama and get back to work.

"You were with this man for three years . . ." the palm reader tested.

"Yeah. I guess it was like two and a half?"

She nodded as if this precision had been hers all along. The question mark was my doing.

"You broke up with him . . ."

I winced as if the palm reader were holding a sullen mug shot of Christopher H. Heaney across the desk.

"You didn't want to be with him because you wanted to work. You thought this man would hold you back. Just because he didn't have your, your—*drive*, you walked away from him."

It's one thing to tell a woman she works too hard. That she's tired. That she *looks* tired. All these things pinch. But tell a woman she has chosen work over love, and her blood will go cold with self-doubt.

"And this man loved you very deeply."

Of course he did. Of course I did. But how had we flipped straight to the ofcourses when she was just fishing for Florida and bullshitting about my dad. *How,* in all unlikelihood, could she pin me here, walking away from a good man, when it could have been *him, his* workaholism, or *his* infidelity, jealousy, a screaming spat heard for miles around? No. She'd heard the tic again. My curse: to do one more thing, to stay at the computer, to prefer my own company. What the palm reader said was everything I'd always known—loosely, in worry form—about the future. I would end up alone, a hermit with an unused womb and millions of words on floppy disks and hard drives and to-do lists in garbage cans, crossed off . . .

"Listen." The palm reader's affected tone broke off. "I'm not trying to upset you."

What?

I'm not trying to upset you?

This fit least of all. There had been a pretense between us: drama. The space to discount; the space to half believe. Now the palm reader was calling a time-out. Why? Because she *felt sorry for me.*

"I'm just trying to tell you that there's something gone wrong in your spirit that you gotta fix. You're sick with something. And I can't fix it for you."

The palm reader looked fatigued by my case.

I, as a walk-in client, was fatiguing.

"I *can* tell you that you'll get what you're aspiring to get." The palm reader uttered this prophecy as if its doom were self-evident. She pitied me still. "You'll have your success. Just know you'll pay the heaviest price."

Then, with her head still cocked to the side and her brow fully pinched in concern, she concluded, "But I think you know this already."

With that, she let my hands go.

I reached for my wallet—relieved to find both a twenty and a five—and I paid.

The palm reader handed me a white business card with an electric red compass logo. The red logo was tactile, lifting off the card stock, inviting a thumb's stroke.

Readings by Jacey. Helps Love, Marriage, and Business.

I walked back to my hotel along the bland American strip, where the sky had gone ahead and darkened. I flipped through my cellphone index for a semi-appropriate person to call. Of course, there was no such person. What would I say?

Back in my hotel room, I took a hot bath, sitting in the scalding water until I could see a clear line on my skin, mid-drift, above and below the waterline. White skin, pink skin. And then: white skin, scarlet skin. I wondered if other people's skins changed like this, so distinctly, in bathtubs. And how deep the change could go.

In the months that followed, I tried to do many things differently. I tried morning bike rides. Greener groceries. Self-authored prayers. Slower eating. Concerted acts of kindness. Cloud appreciation. A second go with Chris. Tolstoy. CALL MOM written on my hand. Books with pink covers. A third go with Chris. Walks. Church from the very last pew.

In the tradition of resolutions, they all faded. The only lasting change was "what I do." I dropped out of the publicity sprint not long after selecting our champion "delayer of the real world." She had huge brown eyes, enough idealism to infect a small village, and came from Ann Arbor, of all places. With her winnings, she flew off to Ecuador to work with coffee farmers, and I was relieved, on many levels, to pass the baton. Afterward, I went back to the blank page to write again, beginning "along the shoulder of a quiet road in Michigan," where I'd been shaken enough to feel real.

I still have the palm reader's business card in my wallet. I never resolved to keep it; I just keep not throwing it away. Crammed between plastic credit and photo identification, the card reminds me that once, while walking down a nameless road, I looked for an excuse to change.

am so awesome. I am a twenty-five-year-old strapping young lad living with a couple of roommates who just happen to be my parents. Life is good as a ravishing young twentysomething. I am an adult. I scoff at the very notion of permission slips, and I purchase my porn without the assistance of false identification. So what if I still laugh when engaged in an otherwise adult conversation about the "penal code"? So what if I say a few curse words when there is no toy in my cereal box? I am above the jurisdiction of my parents, and there is not a damn thing that you or anyone else can do about it. Basically, I am a fully blossomed badass. Some haters try to say that I still lack general life experience. However, these people were likely abducted by aliens and repeatedly probed with Barry Bonds bobble-head dolls. In any event, the haters and their bobble-heads must agree with the juiced-up experience I possess in evaluating such groups as: elementaries, tweens, and teens. I have actively participated in elementarism, tweenism, and teenism during the darker days of my past. Therefore, it is above mere speculation that as a twenty-five-year-old dominator, I own superiority over all the elementaries, teens, and tweens this world has to offer.

Elementaries

Elementaries are those little shits between the ages of five and ten years old. They are completely and utterly worthless to society. What do they do? you ask. It's simple: They sit around crapping themselves while trying to communicate with you while their fingers are in their mouths. They also are amazed by bouncing things, probably because of their lack of intellect. They are clumsy and produce, per capita, the majority of the world's worst art.

Elementaries are also worthless for the things they cannot, or refuse to, do. For example, when was the last time an elementary drove to the store to pick you up a six-pack? Sheer laziness. Elementaries cannot feed themselves, hold a steady job, or talk in complete sentences. They also wear the most unhip clothing ever. Seriously, nice dinosaur on your T-shirt, you little dork.

I reign supreme over these little fungi for a multitude of reasons. First, unlike elementaries, when I go to the bathroom in my pants, it is only because I drank way too much. Next, I don't talk with my fingers in my mouth; instead, my fingers are scratching my ass, and thus I am still able to communicate clearly with another party. Third, I am amazed by bouncing things only when I attend a strip club; elementaries can't even get in for want of proper identification. Like elementaries, my art may suck, but at least there is some semblance of an idea as to what the f**k I am drawing. I can't hold a steady job, either, but that is only because my boss's wife looks like a hippo and he happened to overhear me discussing her "grande" appearance. The only time I don't talk in complete sentences is when I am using street slang to impress the ladies (i.e., "Baby got dumps, girl)." Furthermore, my clothes may be unhip according to the E! channel, but that is only because I am ahead of the Hollywood trends. Once the urban Speedo, LA Gear high-tops, and earmuffs come back into style, I will be pure butter, baby. Clearly, tit for tat, there is not an elementary in the country who can go toe-to-toe with me.

Tweens

Next stop on the worthless train is the tweens who range from ages ten to thirteen years old. The tweens are so damn annoying, they make me want to jump off a cliff. I like to separate them into three subcategories: tweeny-bopper girls, pudgy tweens, and prepube awkward tweens.

i. Tweeny-bopper Girls

This species of tween is female, and you may recognize them as the ones who never stop laughing at some lame inside joke. They actually look up to teenagers, which in my opinion is like envying the hair on my ass. This species is super-annoying and may be found constantly draining your funds for clothes they will never wear and talking about the prepube hunk on *One Tree Hill.*

First of all, I am not as annoying as the tweeny-boppers because I don't laugh that much. You wouldn't either if the Kool-Aid guy just got a restraining order against you. I don't waste a lot of my parents' money on clothes because shirts that say YOU ONLY THINK I AM FAT BECAUSE I AM NOT STANDING NEXT TO MY GIRLFRIEND are surprisingly cheap. I don't gossip about *One Tree Hill.* I hate that show.

ii. Pudgy Tweens

This species of tween includes the fat kid you just know is going to get wedgied in high school so badly that you just wish he could skip ahead to the point in his chubby life where he works at Blockbuster and belongs to a Burger King Internet chat room. This tween is usually embarrassingly unathletic and self-conscious about his robust physique. I guess I am supposed to be sympathetic to this plump kid's plight, but I am not.

I am in decent shape and do not get picked on for being pudgy anymore. Instead, I get picked on for things I deserve, like being a Peeping Tom at the gym, sniffing my friend's boxers, and running like a girl. Whatever. At least I don't have moobs.

iii. Prepube Awkward Tweens

This species of tween consists of the little dork who always looks like he is wearing an oversize T-shirt simply because he has no chest. Hit the weights, Junior! This kid is also annoying because his voice is always cracking to the point that you just wish his balls would hurry up and drop. He is usually a little wussy, too. For example, he may cry because his body is changing and he doesn't understand why.

Me, I know exactly why my body is changing: Twinkies and Ho Hos. My shirts are not at all oversize. It isn't because I have a chest; I think it has more to do with the fact that I don't understand how to do laundry yet and keep shrinking everything I own. I must admit, though, at times you may find a few oversize shirts lying around my house. But this is only because sometimes my woman leaves her clothes at the crib after a romantic evening. It works out well for me because I can use them as covers for my van.

Basically, these three categories of tweens have one thing in common: They all suck when stacked up to a badass twentysomething like myself. They have two options: shut the hell up or deal with it. As MC Hammer would say, "You can't touch this."

Teens

The most threatening to my sheer dominance of all the groups are the teens. Lucky for me, the teens are dumb as f**k. In terms of their health, teens can't seem to grasp the concept that when everyone agrees something is bad for you, you should probably stay away from it. For example, how many lectures does crime dog McGruff have to give before teens get it through their thick skulls that smoking may actually be bad for you? Still these morons like to piss off the clerk and rob 7-Eleven of their Marlboros as if they were the cure to acne and awkward silences with the opposite sex. Me, I am concerned about my health. Therefore, the only thing I steal from 7-Eleven is the clerk's dignity after I engage him in an unsolicited rap battle ("Your Twinkies are wack, and your face is bucket. You tell me, 'Shut up and buy.' But

I say, 'F**k it' . . . Word?"). He doesn't want none of my hot rhymes, so he just rolls his eyes and calls the cops. But do I steal his cigarettes like the teens? No. Advantage: me.

In terms of driving, these little asshole teens insist on driving fifty miles over the speed limit at all times. Let's weigh the pros and cons of speeding. Cons would include dying a horrifically gruesome death, being featured in the film *Red Asphalt,* and possibly killing a sweet family on their way to church. Pros would include getting to your destination eighteen seconds early or giving a girl the false impression that you are tough. Apparently, it's a tough choice when your head is lodged up your butt. Me, I drive well below the speed limit. In part because I have matured and am more cautious, but primarily because I am focused on the conversation I am having on my cell phone. Advantage: me.

Another thing. Why are these teens so whipped by whomever they are dating at the time? These dumbasses always think they have found their soul mate. How is it that everybody meets their soul mate in high school? Why don't any people in the nursing homes ever blab my ear off about meeting their soul mates while getting their daily enema and cleaning their dentures? Me, I don't believe in soul mates. I figured out in my twenties that if everyone got matched up with someone, it could be bad. I mean, the majority of the world is ugly people. In other words, my soul mate is probably hideous, and I am not okay with that. Advantage: me.

But none of the teens are insecure, right? Wrong. The teens constantly call their significant other at least fifty times a day and cannot handle even the thought of them talking to another breathing person. Me, I don't call my significant other because she must have accidentally given me the wrong phone number. Whatever, I don't even care if she chats online with another person, since it just means more time for me to practice my karate. Advantage: me.

Also, teen priorities are all out of whack. They would rather skateboard and be cool than try and do anything productive. They think skateboarding and acting like a musician makes them better than me. I forgot, the most significant people in the world are skateboarders

and musicians. In fact, I don't think I can make it through two pages of a history textbook without reading about the amazing accomplishments of skateboarders and musicians. Me, I am not coordinated or talented and therefore cannot skate or play music. I manage to be a productive member of society through ridding the world of hunger by conserving food. I only eat when I am stoned. Advantage: me.

Finally, do all teens have to blame their parents for the fact that they suck? Do they really do drugs and drink because their parents don't "get" them? Nobody gets them, because they are morons. Besides, as if having a rough upbringing and not getting along with your parents makes you any different than anyone else. In fact, it would be more of an excuse to cause trouble if you had a strangely normal upbringing in the mold of the Cleaver family. Me, I don't blame my parents for anything except being liars. I mean, I don't get what would make them lie to the neighbors and tell them I am not their son. An exchange student? I don't even have an accent, and I shower. Who's going to believe that I'm from Europe? Advantage: me.

Clearly, I hold the advantage in every significant category over the teen species. It should come as no surprise, since I was totally popular in high school. What? I was. The principal said it was cool of me to take my sister to prom.

In closing, I would like to proclaim the obvious: The best part of being a twentysomething is the sheer dominance I hold over the lower species on this earth, including: elementaries, tweens, and teens. Some may contend that my theories have holes. They may begin to speculate as to whether this means that thirtysomethings and fortysomethings are better than me. My answer. Absolutely not. A lousy thirtysomething is known only for being a horrible TV show in the late 1980s. Fortysomethings? Those old f**ks don't know their asses from their elbows.

SEX AND THE SICKBED TRICYCLE PRIME-TIME YOU BACKLASH
THINK OUTSIDE THE BOX BUT STAY INSIDE THE GRID
FINDING THE BEAT YOU SHALL GO OUT WITH JOY AND BE
LED FORTH WITH PEACE THE IDIOT'S GUIDE TO YOUR PALM
SHEER DOMINANCE LIVE NUDE GIRL AN EVENING IN APRIL
CLICHÉ RAPE STORY ROCK MY NETWORK GOODBYE TO ALL THAT
ALL THE RIGHT ANSWERS WHY I HAD TO LEAVE IN-BETWEEN PLACES
A RED SPOON FOR THE NAMELESS MY LITTLE COMMA FIGHT ME
THE SECRET LIVES OF MY PARENTS MY ROARING TWENTIES
IN, FROM THE OUTSIDE THE MYSTERIES OF LIFE . . . REVEALED!
SO YOU SAY YOU WANT A REVOLUTION WORKING AT WENDY'S
JESS LACHER MARY BETH ELLIS BRONSON LEMER JENNIFER GLASER
RACHEL KEMPF JOHN FISCHER SHAHNAZ HABIB EMMA BLACK
ELI JAMES KYLE MINOR COLLEEN KINDER CHRISTOPHER POLING
KATHLEEN ROONEY RADHIYAH AYOBAMI MARISA McCARTHY
THEODORA STITES EULA BISS BRENDAN DARK LUKE MULLINS

I am twenty-five years old, five foot eight, 110 pounds, with huge dark eyes and long dark hair, and I look totally fucking amazing naked. Like maybe better than I do clothed, although I look good that way, too. I'm not telling you this to be obnoxious, or conceited, or shallow, but rather because it—my ability to look graceful, tasteful, natural while nude—is a salient secret of the success I've enjoyed in a job I've done for the past three and a half years.

My first time was with another girl. I can't remember her name, but she was older than me—although I was just twenty-one, so almost anyone would have been. She was a former gymnast, African-American, with a compact, sinuous, feline comeliness, and it was she, who had lived almost twice my lifetime, who instructed me in exactly how to work it—where to look in the crowd, where to stand on the platform, how to move, how to hold, how to do it without hurting.

I'm not a porn star or a stripper, although some prurient people seem determined to conflate my career with the latter. I'm a professional artist's model, and I'm a really, really good one.

R ight before I took off my borrowed flannel robe for that first bright revealing, I almost said no, almost looked the instructor straight in her appraising eye and sighed nearly inaudibly, "There's been a mistake. I'm afraid I can't take this." But then I swooped the blue-green plaid cotton off my narrow shoulders and let it go. That was that. No turning back.

I 've made thousands of dollars taking off my clothes and letting people draw, paint, sculpt, and occasionally—when I've been really hard up or bored or both—photograph my face and body. I've been described as gazellelike, dancerly, elegant, and lyrically slender. I've been compared to a Byzantine icon, a doomed pre-Raphaelite siren, a Greco-Roman goddess, and a medieval saint. I've been told I look like one of John Singer Sargent's reflective-skinned society ladies come to life, and I've even posed velvet-clad and strapless as his notorious Madame X.

Sometimes I have to pose with another young female model. Often she will have a veritable road map of tattoos, intimate piercings, and stridently unshaved legs and pits. Her head may be shaved. All eyes are not on me.

I am a competitive person—competitive to my uninked, unpierced, and well-shaved core—and these situations find me eyeing the easels to see which of us more people choose to draw.

I almost always win, but it's a foolish competition. It's not like they pay me more.

L argely because of my slender frame, I've been painted in pigtails in the style of Balthus, and because of my vague ethnic ambiguity, I've been sculpted as Nefertiti and drawn as Salome. I've been a Schiele in stockings, a Toulouse-Lautrec in fishnets, and a Modigliani in nothing but a smirk and a hooded gaze. I've been Manet's Olympia, a nymphet, a sylph, and a Matissean odalisque.

Sometimes I have to pose with a man. In these instances, I don't

feel nearly so jealous, which makes me feel bad. I want to be an equal-opportunity competitor and not have my behavior come down to some kind of paradoxical misogyny within me, but I can't. I find the men mildly menacing but largely ridiculous: They're older, grayer, hairier, and more flaccid in every respect than you might expect them to be. No beefcake here. Their shrivelly penises rest fuzzily, baby birds in testicular nests.

None of the women I've posed with have been shaved down there; they have all proudly sported some type of varyingly groomed pubic hair. I'm not shaved there, either. I know you must have been wondering.

I tend to think about death and eternity a lot anyway, but modeling brings my natural morbidity even more to the fore, particularly when I pose for portrait classes, particularly for sculptural busts. Certain professors employ the traditional technique of strewing skulls around the base of the rotating model stand for comparison and contrast—to study the zygomatic arches, the maxillae, the occipital lobes. I feel as though I've stumbled into *The Ambassadors* by Holbein, a composition whose message is heavy-handed but effective.

I've posed as a dead girl, an angel, winged Victory, and Audrey Hepburn. Someone once said that I could be Frida Kahlo sans monkey and unibrow. I've been Lot's wife, half-salt, Daphne, half-tree, Niobe, half-rock. I've been Eve, pure sin; and Mary, the Mother of God, all holy.

The time it takes for me to be any of these people is surprisingly brief. A typical art class lasts only three hours, perfect for the schedule of a graduate student like me. Or, now that I've graduated—become a master of fine arts, as they say—perfect for someone who's always suspected "real jobs" of being bullshit. Three hours here, three hours there, jumping from class to class, school to school, studio to studio, with welcoming little islands throughout, tiny oases of time in which to read and write.

Plus, the pay is outstanding. I won't tell you what it is.

———————

I've been all things to all people of all backgrounds, ages, genders, and levels of ability, and I've loved it. I love to be looked at, and I love to hold very still. My inertia is breathtaking. I could conceivably seek work as one of those mime-y human statues you see in New Orleans and elsewhere, but the pay's nowhere near as good, and I don't want to have to dip myself in body paint or jerk whimsically whenever someone drops a buck in my bucket.

My capacity for stillness sometimes strikes me as ironic, because the on-the-job pickup line I hear most often is "Hey, are you a dancer?"

Nope. I only act like one, nude and frozen.

Along with all the people I've been, there are lots of times I've been no one, no one of any consequence at all, just the nude girl on the model stand. But I honestly don't think I've ever been just me. John Berger says, "To be naked is to be oneself. To be nude is to be seen by others and yet not recognized for oneself. A naked body has to be seen as an object in order to become a nude."

I am a three-dimensional opportunity on which to hone a physical skill. I'm like a prop, a box, a statue, a feature of the landscape.

David finds me no more or less interesting than the stool or fruit he poses me with. He seems as content to paint the bare burnt-out lightbulb rolling atop his coffee table as he is to paint my bare white butt. I first posed for David at the Arlington Center for the Arts, and now I pose for him privately amid doll parts and mannequins in his cramped junk shop of a studio above Central Square, with mounted animal heads on the walls and pins all over the floor. He can't bear to part with any of his paintings, his babies, so they're all there, or at least it looks that way, piled one atop the other, end to end, strewn around— the room's most prominent feature, freckles on a face. Sometimes we talk so much he forgets to paint me, and he just shows me his work, old and new, and we talk about travels, the ones he's made, the ones I intend to make. I am fairly certain he is a genius.

————————

Sometimes people draw me outside of classes and studios, in the warm light of real day, in the proverbial real world. One of my other jobs is in the bookstore of an art museum, and I get approached there a lot. People hit me with the old dancer line as I help them track down obscure books of etchings. A woman watches me as I work at the info station, comes up to say, "I had to tell you, you're beautiful. With that hairdo, that profile, you look like a geisha."

In summer, I sit outside on the benches during my lunch break, and museumgoers, often Japanese tourists, come up and ask to draw me or take my photograph. I say yes, but modeling's made me mercenary, and there's always some part of me that wishes I could charge them, make them pay to even look at me, but of course I don't, can't.

My hair *is* pretty impressive.

I love myself, hate myself: naked contradiction. I possess staggering self-confidence—as you might expect of someone in my line of work—but also appalling self-doubt. I pose and pose, but I think I'm fat, and sometimes I don't eat because I feel I don't deserve it.

I don't think I've ever completed a modeling session without someone—teacher, student, fellow model—remarking unsolicitedly on my willowy thinness. This makes me alternately proud and suspicious: proud that they've noticed, suspicious that they're lying, that I'm actually a lardass.

I know full well that this is colossally messed up.

A self-taught realist painter from Brooklyn, Jeremy is a devotee of Sargent and Lucien Freud. He likes to make paintings that look good, but he doesn't like to lie—he is not forgiving, and paints things as they are. Jeremy says it is much easier to paint ugly people than beautiful ones. Beautiful ones present a higher level of pressure: the challenge of capturing something already aesthetically lovely. Ugly ones you can shape into a beautiful painting through the trans-

formative power of art, or whatever you want to call it. He says he doesn't want to uglify anything pretty. He says that I am extremely difficult to paint.

Cherubic, blond, apple-cheeked Andy—a Ph.D. and former poli-sci adjunct turned karaoke emcee—is one of the few male models who doesn't creep me out. One day we are scheduled together for an open studio at the Museum School, and to ease the workload, we take turns posing. He reads aloud to me while I pose and he rests, "The Secret," by Charles Bukowski: "nobody has the strange and / hidden power [. . .] there are no strong men, there / are no beautiful women."

It is probably good for me to hear this.

Bohemian and devil-may-care as I make it sound, figure modeling is not all glamour and romance, compliments, admiration, and flattering adjectives. It is hard, too, and can be very demanding. Many times, when I was just starting out, I wanted so badly to please the classes, the instructors, that I would throw an especially hard pose and then not move at all until the end of the allotted time. My feet and legs, executing some daring twist, would fall utterly asleep, and I would rise and step off the platform only to collapse embarrassingly on the deadened limbs, a marionette with the strings cut.

Other times the hazard isn't metaphorical pins and needles but, rather, real ones—pushpins, easel clips, nails, glass. I learned quickly to wear shoes at all times when not on the platform, and to this day I come home with the bottoms of my feet burnt-looking from the charcoal that coats a drawing classroom's every surface, like soot on a company town, like ash from a Dickensian factory. If I've been in a sculpture class, my hands and feet are chalky, gray, as if I've just fled Pompeii.

Some of the older models have warned me that taking too many difficult poses will ruin your body, or can if you let it. Above all, you should never try to keep your hands higher than your heart for longer than, say, a five-minute gesture without a brace, or your arms will go numb and it will become hard to breathe.

By now I've learned how not to get hurt, how to shake it out, how to assert myself if I need to, if a pose really kills, but I rarely need to, because I can use pillows, poles, and stools to brace myself, to create gestures that look beautiful and excruciating without actually being the latter. People seem to respond most passionately to the poses that look agonizing, stretched out, and mannerist, to the extent that I have become convinced, like Edmund Burke, that "we have a degree of delight, and that no small one, in the real misfortunes and pains of others."

Maybe people like the more torturous poses because they find them sublime: They find them pretty and scary, and they delight in looking at them but are glad the poses don't contain them. Sympathy and pathos.

My grad-school friends think it's ironic that I can earn more, at this point, for my body than I can for my expensively educated mind. That I can make more cash as a Francis Bacon–esque slab of human meat than I can by using my shiny new poetry degree.

I laugh along, but really, it's tougher than that, and it takes incredible imagination, yogic focus, control, and intuition.

David seems to like that I am an aspiring poet. He likes to talk about how poets and painters are not so far apart, how poets try to do in words what painters try to do with light. I'm not sure what this means, exactly, but I like how it sounds and how it asks me to think about it, to worry it around my head.

David likes to think, and he thinks out loud, and he says that if you have a good book, you can get through anything. I have found this to be the case.

Damon, a drawing instructor and realist painter from Boston University, often has me pose falling: slipping off a chair, stumbling down stairs, like a broken vase, a shattered figurine. He is a gifted artist, one whose work I admire, so I let him subject me to poses I would normally laugh at and refuse. Once after I'd posed for three hours in his studio in Malden, mangled and broken as though having slipped from a tabletop, my shoulder would not stop aching the whole rest of the day.

Damon does not, cannot, pay nearly enough for this type of near-torture, but I told myself I was okay with that. I try to be nice, good, and karmic when I pose for less well-heeled but still talented artists. My kindness, I tell myself, will surely come back to me.

I'm not a masochist, in case you were curious—although I do enjoy using my body in a way most people wouldn't. I don't derive pleasure from the mild pains of modeling, per se, but I consider myself lucky to get paid for doing something so physical, so personal. This exchange strikes me as distinctly satisfying in a system where most workers are more or less alienated from the products of their labor. I consider myself fortunate not to have to sit at a desk doing "work," mucking around on the Internet, haunting the watercooler, filing, dealing with memos, and all the other assorted tropes of the low-level office work I might otherwise be doing.

Jeremy never put me in elaborate poses. In fact, he discouraged them—was singularly unimpressed, disinterested the first time I came to his sublet studio in Somerville and threw some of my best gestures. He was less into generic contortions or gymnastic feats, and more into me, which is to say in capturing me—not only how I looked but also, at the risk of sounding mawkish, the essence of me. And I'm not saying he treated me uniquely; I'm trying to tell you he was unique. He treated the subject as a subject, as opposed to an object.

Posing nude makes you meditate on the Body with a capital B—how we are all, every day, the objects of thousands of gazes, why figurative painting is such an enduring practice—but also about your own particular, lower-case body. You worry if you are going to sneeze, cough, yawn, fart, or itch. Will you twitch? Get a muscle cramp? Will your stomach growl? Is your nose whistling? Are you falling asleep? Do you need to pee? Worse yet, shit? Do you have your period? Is the tampon showing? Did you cram the string far enough inside? Because to leave it dangling would be mortifying, if not to you, then to the class.

For these reasons (and also, occasionally, boredom), I sometimes

like when the artists have music on, noise to cover up any sounds of the body, noise to drown out any thoughts in the brain: self-conscious indie rock, obscure hip-hop, and trippy house music at the art schools; oldies for the Malden sketch group; horrible radio and pop country for Doug the sculptor; Norah Jones, Eva Cassidy, and snoozy blues and jazz for the ladies in Cambridge; Bollywood and world music for David in Central Square; and more often than not, just talking with Jeremy, the easy volley, the back-and-forth of our voices. I loaned him books, and he loaned books to me. (I still have the one about the commune he lived in, the one in Roxbury where he met his wife.)

Modeling inevitably makes me think of all the things I do as a living human being—laugh, cry, bleed—that I one day won't. But the morbidity of art, the inexpressible sadness and promise of being an artist's model, is thrown into sharpest relief when I pose with bones or plaster casts thereof.

When I worked with Amy—a Museum School instructor, herself a former model—on an anatomy class, she asked me to sit with an actual human skeleton belonging to an actual formerly living human being. Understanding the uneasiness that might accompany this arrangement, she said I didn't have to if I didn't want to.

I wanted to. In my head, I named her Ellie, Ellie the Skellie, and I ended up sitting across from her, each of us in a cold metal folding chair, knobby knee to knobby knee, me naked of clothes, her of flesh, and I held her dry, rickety hands and stared into her sockets, thinking of the woman she'd been and the one I'd become. The whole setup was too obvious to be truly scary, so it mostly just felt like what it was: a balanced composition, an effective teaching tool for an anatomical study.

Still, I felt sad when the pose was over. I liked Ellie, and I picture her sometimes, all alone for eternity, aside from these occasional interruptions, in the corner of studio IC-16.

In spite of the perils involved with the unclothed body, in a way I feel more protected naked than clothed. People treat you with a certain respect when they find out you're the model, because you are

doing something that the majority of them would never, ever do. I feel more vulnerable when I accidentally make eye contact with a stranger on the T than I do, for instance, standing nude three feet above a roomful of two dozen Intro to Drawing students.

I've posed in wigs and angel wings, devil horns and petticoats; I've posed wrapped in cheesecloth, vinyl, and magenta tulle; but I'd rather pose in nothing at all. Underwear or bathing suits are the absolute worst; it is hard to wear them without their wearing you. I pose for Drawing in the Galleries on free Wednesday evenings at the MFA in dresses and boots, stockings and heels—because obviously, nipples aren't allowed out in the gallery—and I like this gig, I really do. The atmosphere is romantic, dramatic, and theatrical, and I appreciate that it's free and populated largely by amateurs who may not even have come to the museum with any intention of drawing.

That said, I still prefer modeling nude, for classes or private groups or individuals, because as much as I enjoy bringing art to the people, I like even better to bring myself to serious artists.

Skill levels aside, private modeling is also my favorite because I get to see the insides of people's houses. I expose myself to them, but they simultaneously expose themselves even more to me. It's like being a plumber or a cable guy.

Better yet, it's like being a piano tuner, which is what Jeremy was for a while before he became a contractor. Modeling is sort of a dying art, like piano tuning, outmoded like figurative painting is often considered to be. Personally, I love figurative painting and representational art in general—any kind of art or photography with people in it, anything that hints at characters and stories. I like abstract art just fine, but I prefer works that are about something more than just the paint.

Of course I write, so that's not a shocker.

My comfort level is aided by the fact that I'm never totally exposed. John Berger writes of the nude as a naked body on public display, this display resulting in a disguise that can never be cast aside: "The

nude is condemned to never being naked. Nudity is a form of dress." I'm not sure I'd want to cast off the disguise, even if I could.

Over lunch in the greasy midday dark of Punter's Pub—lunch for me, rather; a beer for Andy, who claims to eat only one meal a day—he asked what my fiancé thinks of my job.

I told him Martin doesn't mind; he finds it hot. He trusts me—and trusts in the gaping difference, the yawning divide, between nudity and intimacy—but he still gets off on the idea of lots of other people's eyes upon me.

Andy laughed at my honesty. I talked about how the majority of my male friends say they wouldn't "let" their women do anything of the kind, which I find preposterous. They also say they wouldn't let them hang out, clothed and in their free time, with the students or teachers who've seen them nude. I don't do this often, but often enough, and Martin doesn't give me shit. He knows I love him.

To be honest, though, there can be erotic tension, however mild, and I like it. I like posing in Jeremy's house, meeting his wife. I like riding the Chinatown bus to New York City with Doug the sculptor, our thighs almost but not quite touching, concertedly giving each other space, on our way to look at art (him) and to spend a blitzkrieg half-weekend with friends (me).

When conversation lapses, I stare at my reflection in the bus glass. I'm dressed up slightly, in a sundress because it's sweltering July, and Doug comments on it.

Someone always comments on it when I'm not wearing much. Someone always feels entitled. Maybe they are. Maybe I'd feel sad if they didn't.

The naked female body is, according to Susan Bordo, "common cultural property."

I got my start in this business at the Corcoran College of Art and Design in Washington, D.C., by responding to an ad in the alternative weekly. I had just been let go from my job in a gallery—for not want-

ing to sleep with my boss, essentially—and I was in desperate need of a way to earn money.

Being looked at and not touched sounded fine with me. "Be a part of art!" the ad beckoned.

In the Middle Ages, there was a popular meditative activity known as *contemplatio mortis,* "a dramatized medieval exercise in imagining one's own death that prepared one for the inevitable end and helped one enjoy the life that remained." (*Opera: The Art of Dying,* by Linda Hutcheon and Michael Hutcheon.) I tend to think of this a lot when I'm posing, how each of these images—especially the sculptures—with proper care and treatment, stands to exist far longer than I do. I'll age, dimpling like a plucked turkey, rumpling like a punching bag. But I will have left a little fossil record of my body through the years, a string of former selves, silly and brave.

As essential as I sometimes feel to the process, it truly is just that: a process. I am one small part of art. Representational painting pulls me in because it suggests a narrative, and I like being a participant in a story that is massive and ongoing.

My own dramatic arc may well have just begun. The learning curve was steep, and now I keep going, leaving a trail of images like bread crumbs in a forest behind me, although I'm not sure where I'm going, or that I'll ever want to find my way back. If I were to turn and retrace my steps, I'm not sure any of the images would show me the Real Me, if I'd get any closer to knowing Who I Am, whatever that means. But if I look over my shoulder, back through the mirrors and the trees, I hear it—Bukowski, via Andy: "don't worry, nobody has the / beautiful lady, not really."

One night in April, when the Chicago weather is still cool enough for us to wear winter coats, my son, Sekou, decides that he needs a snack from Walgreens. It's almost ten o'clock, our curfew, but we have enough time to walk down the block to the store. I hide our crackers under the pillow, and we go downstairs and leave our room key at the front desk. At Walgreens, I buy Sekou some Twinkies. When we get out of the store, he looks around for a place to sit and eat. It's too late and windy for us to walk far.

"Let's sit over there." I point to a small metal fence surrounding the Walgreens parking lot.

Sekou wrinkles his nose. "I don't wanna sit there. The change man sits there."

Down the long stretch of West Lawrence Avenue, where we have lived for the last month, there are several shelters. Sekou is used to seeing people sit on the fence and ask for change as customers come out of the store. Most of the people he sees aren't that old, but the way they slump over the fence, like rag dolls, and the strange bruised color of their eyes makes them seem much older.

At our building, SALVATION ARMY is printed in neat blue letters on a white awning, and it almost looks like someone's house. There are kids in white-and-blue school uniforms, just like Sekou, and babies in

strollers with cute fat feet, and the word LODGE is marked everywhere, on doors, linen, and all paperwork. Sekou passes the change men every morning on the bus as he rides to school, as they sit on the steps to their shelter or lounge on folding chairs in the parking lot. To him, the change men live in shelters. He does not.

I can see the Lodge from the fence, and I know in another fifteen minutes we'll have to go in. I consider sneaking Sekou's Twinkies into our room, even though food is not allowed, but I can see Sekou running up to another little boy in front of a worker the next morning and saying, "Guess what my mama got me last night?"

He doesn't agree with the Lodge rules. On the first night we arrived, carrying our suitcases and schoolbags, we went through orientation. A worker explained the rules: No food was to be brought into the building at all.

When we got to the room, Sekou said, "No food? This is crazy. People live here. We gotta eat."

He had always been a picky eater, and after a few times visiting the cafeteria, we knew the meals were not for us. Once, at breakfast, bacon, sausage, and sausage links were served. Sekou and I are vegetarians. Another time, as I was walking into the kitchen, I saw a lady in blond pigtails coming through the door with an open box of donuts.

"Donuts!" Sekou said, and reached for one.

The blond women smiled at him, gave the box to the cook, and left. Sekou reached for a donut, and one tumbled out of the box. A bite-size chunk was missing from it. I grabbed his hand and pulled him away. One day the children were given Lunchables for breakfast. On the bus, Sekou asked me to open his. I took the carton from him. The expiration date was two weeks before. And so we found ourselves eating out, with friends, or snacking outside on the metal fence in front of Walgreens.

That night Sekou sat on the fence and looked around as if he expected a change man to sneak up on him and take his snack. He looked back toward Walgreens.

"I see a change man," he said. "Except it's a girl."

I didn't know how we had missed her. She was sitting on the curb outside of the store, and she spoke in a voice as smooth as a choirgirl's. "Could anybody help me out with some change, please? Is anybody going downtown? Can I get a ride? I'm going to Harvey."

She was a young woman wearing a scarf and dirty sneakers, and customers saw her as they pulled into the parking lot. They rushed from the cars into the store, then rushed from the store back into their cars. A few of the customers looked at me, too, quickly, without meeting my eyes, as if the woman and I were involved in some scheme. When the woman saw us, she stood up and walked over. She was heavyset, with big breasts, and being a mother, I looked at her and thought she had at least one child. Sekou clutched his Twinkies.

"Calm down," I told him as the woman approached.

"Excuse me, ma'am, are you driving? I'm trying to get to Harvey."

She was about my age, and I wondered why she was calling me ma'am. I looked down at my own dirty sneakers, my schoolbag with the broken strap, and my bleach-splotched jeans. I didn't look any more likely to be driving than she did.

I shook my head. "Sorry. Isn't Harvey a long way?"

She nodded and watched as Sekou stuffed half a Twinkie in his mouth and gagged. I gave him a look and he smiled, chewing fast, cream smeared on his nose. I wanted to ask the woman why she was going to Harvey. Though I had lived in Chicago only a year and didn't know much about the neighborhoods, I had heard several times that Harvey was the murder capital of the state.

She didn't have the dry, cracked skin, swollen hands, or bruised eyes of the junkies I had seen around the block, and she wasn't hustling like the group of teenagers who stood in front of the corner store. I wondered what her game was.

She smiled at Sekou. "He's cute. How old is he?"

"He's five," Sekou hollered, and I smacked his elbow. He didn't like people talking about him as if he weren't there. "You got kids?" he asked her.

"Yup. I got four," she said. Her eyes were as soft as her voice,

and she looked at him with such longing that I knew she was missing her own.

"Where your kids at?" he asked, chewing slower.

She sighed. "They took 'em away. They took my kids away."

We looked at each other, and there was no need for her to explain. In New York, where I was from, "they" were called ACS, Administration for Children's Services, and before that, BCW, Bureau of Child Welfare. In Chicago, they were called DCFS, Department of Children and Family Services. Whatever the acronym, their purpose was not to assist or offer service in any way but, rather, to render, separate, and break apart.

When poor women of color were together, and we said "they" had taken someone's kids away, there was no need for explanation. "They" were the long white arm of the law.

Sekou held the other Twinkie half in his hand and stared at the woman. "Who took your kids? Why?"

She shrugged and looked down at the change in her palm, a few dimes and a couple of pennies. "I don't know why they took my kids. Just took 'em."

Sekou shoved the Twinkie half in his mouth and held out the uneaten Twinkie to the woman. "Here, you could have it," he said.

She shook her head. "Naw, you go ahead and enjoy yourself, baby."

I looked at my watch. It was five minutes until ten o'clock, and I couldn't afford to be late. I needed to stay at the Lodge until I finished my semester at school.

"It's time to go," I told Sekou.

He jumped down off the fence and waved to the woman. She waved back. I started to go toward the Lodge, and then I stopped, dug in my pocket, and gave the woman two dollars. I didn't know her story, but we all had one.

"Hope this helps," I said.

The next day, after school was over, I went back over to Walgreens looking for the woman. I had been thinking about her all day and wondering if she had made it out to Harvey. Sekou was looking for

her, too. He had shoved the other Twinkie in his pocket, and we had gone into the Lodge with it. I discovered it in his coat pocket on our way from school, and he had insisted on offering it to the woman.

"I don't think she's gonna want it," I said.

"Who don't like Twinkies?" he asked.

We sat on the fence while he ate some graham crackers from school. After about half an hour, we left. But I was sure we would see the woman again. I started looking for her from the bus windows on our way to school in the morning. Maybe, when a room was free at the Lodge, I could let her know. Then she could have her kids back and get into some kind of housing program so she didn't have to ask for change in parking lots. Maybe one day, when it was nice outside and not so windy, we could take our kids to the park together. People would look at us, and instead of seeing two beggars, they'd see two mothers with children, and they'd smile. I had big plans for that woman, if only I could see her again.

SEX AND THE SICKBED TRICYCLE PRIME-TIME YOU BACKLASH
THINK OUTSIDE THE BOX BUT STAY INSIDE THE GRID
FINDING THE BEAT YOU SHALL GO OUT WITH JOY AND BE
LED FORTH WITH PEACE THE IDIOT'S GUIDE TO YOUR PALM
SHEER DOMINANCE LIVE NUDE GIRL AN EVENING IN APRIL
CLICHÉ RAPE STORY ROCK MY NETWORK GOODBYE TO ALL THAT
ALL THE RIGHT ANSWERS WHY I HAD TO LEAVE IN-BETWEEN PLACES
A RED SPOON FOR THE NAMELESS MY LITTLE COMMA FIGHT ME
THE SECRET LIVES OF MY PARENTS MY ROARING TWENTIES
IN, FROM THE OUTSIDE THE MYSTERIES OF LIFE . . . REVEALED!
SO YOU SAY YOU WANT A REVOLUTION WORKING AT WENDY'S
JESS LACHER MARY BETH ELLIS BRONSON LEMER JENNIFER GLASER
RACHEL KEMPF JOHN FISCHER SHAHNAZ HABIB EMMA BLACK
ELI JAMES KYLE MINOR COLLEEN KINDER CHRISTOPHER POLING
KATHLEEN ROONEY RADHIYAH AYOBAMI MARISA McCARTHY
THEODORA STITES EULA BISS BRENDAN DARK LUKE MULLINS

Y ou are a freshman in college. Cute, maybe pretty, but not beautiful. College is exciting. The people, the parties, the boys. Nobody expects anything of you. You can be anyone. You can be the wild girl you mocked in high school but secretly envied. You can be the life of the party.

You go to a party with a girlfriend one night in February. It's usually a big group of girls who go out, but tonight it's just the two of you. You are having a great time. You are drinking. You know that you cannot take very much alcohol, so you make sure to take it slow. You are meeting new people. You have been given the duty of serving beer at the party. You feel honored. You wonder how many beers you have had. You think you've only had two, but it feels like six. You realize your friend has left without you. The party is ending. You go outside to catch a cab.

A dark, handsome stranger offers you a ride. "Where do you live?" he asks you. You tell him the name of your dorm. "Come on," he says, "I'll take you." He puts his arm around you, and you begin to walk toward the car. You think of all the other rides you have taken. Those turned out fine. Nice people. You can trust anyone from school, you say to yourself with confidence. It's only a ride. Think of the money you are saving. And maybe you'll make a new friend.

The ride is blurry, a haze of drunken conversation. The ride seems longer than it should be. When the car stops, you realize you are not at your dormitory. You are at a house on a dark street that you do not recognize. You question the driver. "I just need to pick something up," he tells you, "it'll only take a minute." Outwardly, you remain calm, but your mind slips into panic and confusion.

You regain consciousness, never realizing you were unconscious. You are naked. You are never naked. You feel weight pressing down on your small body. You hear unfamiliar breathing. It takes you minutes to realize what is happening. Words refuse to come from your mouth. Your fists do not swing furiously, as you always imagined they would. You do not find yourself kicking and struggling, as you want to. Your body is limp beneath you. Hands roughly run themselves over every inch of your frame. You are paralyzed. Rough chest hairs grind against your breasts. You are whimpering. A wet tongue probes in and out of your mouth, but it does not feel like being kissed. Your arms are pinned underneath your body as you feel yourself thrust against a wall. You find your voice. It must be hard to understand you through the tears. But you repeat "no" over and over again. You are not above begging. You alternate your "no"s with "please"s and "stop"s. Exhausted, you resign yourself to the act.

When it is done, the stranger on top of you rolls over and begins to snore loudly. You are shaking and cold. You feel a strong urge to curl up next to him, to protect yourself with the weight that just violated you, to find warmth and affection where there was none.

Instead, you get up and begin to wander around the strange apartment, naked and damp with sweat. You find a phone. You cannot figure out how to dial. Your brain and body are slow. You collapse in the kitchen crying, at a loss about what to do next. You wait to be rescued, but you are alone. No one comes. You try to compose yourself and, in anger, decide you must take things of value from the apartment, because something of value was taken from you. You grab a bottle of wine that you will later notice from the price tag is worth only $6.99, and a casino chip from Bally's Las Vegas. You go back to the room

where the stranger sleeps and begin to look for your clothes. They lie crumpled up on the floor, ripped off in a haste that you do not recall or want to remember. You find everything except your underwear and socks. You dress quickly and quietly. You decide that it is too cold outside to not wear any socks with your boots, so you begin to rifle through some drawers in the room. You find socks and, in the drawer that holds them, a bank statement. You read the name on the statement. Thirteen times. You promise yourself that you will never forget the name.

You run out into the street, hugging your body in the cold, the bottle of wine in the pocket of your peacoat. You realize you do not recognize the neighborhood. You have no idea where you are. You begin to run down the block. You stop at the end and read the street signs. You promise yourself you will remember the names. It should be easy. One of the streets has the same name as the street you lived on for the first seventeen years of your life. The other is the name of the heroine in a novel you once read. You run for several more blocks. Just unfamiliar sleeping houses. You decide to walk no farther. You see no pay phones, no cabs. A few cars drive by. You try to flag them down. No one stops. You are frustrated but understand how you appear. It is after five in the morning, and you must look like hell. After what seems like hours, you decide to pull the fire alarm on a telephone pole. Your other option seems to be to lie down in the snow and die. And you would prefer to die with a bra on.

You wait. After a while, a car stops, and as you begin to yell to the driver to please call a taxi, two fire engines and a police car pull up to the telephone pole. You begin to panic, recalling that you are nineteen years old, intoxicated, and carrying a bottle of wine in your pocket. Several firemen and a policeman get out of their vehicles. The policeman approaches you. You make the decision to play it cool. You act nonchalant and calm. He asks you if you pulled the fire alarm. You tell him no. You do not believe you did. You are just looking for a pay phone to call a cab, you say, you needed to get out of a bad situation.

You are speaking clearly and slowly, repeating yourself. The men look stumped. The cop turns to you and tells you that you pulled the alarm because you were lost and scared and escaping a bad situation. You stick to your story but mention that it is possible you could have inadvertently hit the alarm in your pursuit of a phone. You ask the police officer to please call you a cab, avoiding the eyes of the firemen staring at you from their trucks. The police officer tells you he will take you back to your dorm.

You ride in the back of the police car in total silence as the strange cop takes you toward familiar streets and buildings. You thank him for the ride and run upstairs. You hug the floor in thanks. You knock on the door of a friend, then decide no one should see you like this. It seems useless to wake anyone else up. You go to your hall bathroom and take a scalding shower. You scrub your skin raw. You sit on cool tile as the water beats down on your head, and you bawl. You remember a character on a television show did this after she sold her body for sex. Though you feel silly and clichéd, you are determined to get clean. You are too weak to stand up and cannot bring yourself to stop crying.

When you are finished, you go to the mirror and examine your face. You expect to look different. You try to wipe away dirt from your face that isn't there. You hate the girl in the mirror at the same time that you pity her. Maybe tomorrow you will feel differently. You crawl into your top bunk before anyone in your dorm wakes up.

You wake up in the morning sick. You spend hours hunched over the toilet, throwing up your insides. You watch people's feet coming in and out of the bathroom. You wonder what they are thinking about you. You go back to your room. Your roommates are gone, and your friends have left you a note outside your door: "Went shopping, figured you needed your rest, will call later to see if you want to meet for dinner."

You sit at your desk for twenty minutes, staring at the window, waiting for something to happen. You realize you will not feel better anytime soon. You pick up the phone and call your best friend at an-

other college. For once she is there. When you hear her voice, no words come. You just sob. Some of the story gets out. She speaks softly and instructs you to go find a friend who is home. When he comes upstairs, you hand him the receiver, and she tells him what she knows. He, too, is calm. He and the friend urge you to call some phone number. You agree. You are done making decisions for yourself. The friend you went out with the night before comes over. She wants to tell you about the crazy night she had after she left you. Your silence speaks volumes to her, and she looks to your other friend. He explains. She cries hysterically as he calls the number on the magnet on your micro-fridge. You try not to listen as he says "date" and "rape." When you hear him say "victim," you pretend he's talking about someone else.

You walk slowly with them to the bus that will take you to the infirmary. You all sit in the sparse, fluorescent-lit room for hours, waiting. You answer questions that you wish people would not ask, and you try not to cry or care as you do. Everyone is nice to you, but they all keep their distance. They look at you as if you are broken, even though you are desperately trying to appear undamaged. Your male friend leaves, at the request of the nurses and the volunteer they have sent for to "guide you through this difficult time." The volunteer and the friend who deserted you just the night before accompany you to the hospital, where you answer the same questions and wait some more. At the hospital, everyone is even nicer. They want to take care of you because you are sick and hurt. They poke and prod at your wrecked body and speak to you in whispers. They take a kit, or they give you a kit. It is a rape kit. When they explain they will keep the kit at the police station for six months, you wonder why.

They are very concerned with your mental state. They give you names of people to see, to call, things to look out for, things not to do. They shoot your friend dirty looks as she cracks jokes to you. You cannot help but laugh at her responses to the inanely posed questions. "What do you do when your roommate becomes anorexic?" the

women eagerly ask you both, as if that is extremely relevant. You glance at each other before she blurts out, "Eat her food." They are not amused as you giggle in the solemn room.

They seem to believe you will have the energy to do things that you cannot imagine doing. You crave sleep. You want everyone to finish this busywork without you. You did as they said, made the right choices, and now you want to be left alone, for your body to heal.

You fall asleep, you in the hospital bed and your friend in a metal chair next to you. You wake up to her eating off the tray of food in front of you. A nurse gives you five thousand pills to take and a shot of water. They are going to send you home. And by "home" they mean your school's infirmary. One final psychiatric evaluation, though. You sit on the floor of a small interrogation-like room. You listen to the sounds of the hospital. You wonder where the real sick people are. You imagine people bleeding to death outside the hospital as ten nurses continually ask you how you are doing.

As you walk through the automatic doors into the fresh air, you think you are free. However, overcome with nausea, you throw up several times on the sidewalk. You insist you are okay, and you get into the campus police car with your two companions, who have become your keepers and your collective voice. The police officer has to stop the car three times on the ride home so you can vomit. You vomit for the next twelve hours straight, while your friend sleeps quietly in the infirmary bed next to yours. For a few minutes, you hate her.

In the morning one of the nurses finds you on the bathroom floor still sick. She insists that you return to the hospital. You are willing to do anything. You just want sleep. You are carted away to an ambulance, strapped to a stretcher, and carried by burly paramedics. You hear the nurse explaining your situation to the men, and you want to stop her, because it's none of their business. The rest of the day blurs. When it's over, you sleep. Four of your friends come to visit. They bring a card, some of your clothes and toiletries, and, by mistake, your roommate's enormous shoes. You sit in the TV room with them for

twenty minutes in silence. You cannot bring yourself to tell them. Your other friend does it the next day.

When you get to go back to your dorm room, you tell everyone that you had food poisoning. When they ask you where you got it, you feel bad blaming the perfectly good restaurant you had eaten at earlier that Friday. Your friends huddle around you and stroke your hair. It hurts whenever someone hugs you. The next week you find out you have a broken rib. It's painful and prevents you from doing much of anything. It's a constant and irritating reminder that you are not normal. Your friends tease you about it lightheartedly and call you "Ribs." You laugh, but you don't really think it's funny.

You decide you need to be normal again and start to hang out with people on weekends, drinking with your friends. But every time you have a sip of alcohol, you are sick for the next forty-eight hours. You still drink with them, trying to make everything the same again. When you go out, your friends watch you and surround you. You cling to them and attempt to enjoy yourself. Your male friends yell at any boy who talks to you and assign one another to "look after" you. You act annoyed, but secretly, you are relieved and grateful.

You think every boy you see on campus fitting his description is *him.* You have long forgotten the name on the bank statement. You politely turn down the offer from a football player to have the team beat him up. You wonder what your answer would be if you knew who he was. The police tell you they have too little to go on. They are irked by the gaps in your memory and put off by the lack of material evidence. You write them off and try to accept that you will never find the person who stole you in his imported car.

Your life goes on. Everything seems okay. Your parents never find out. Your differences are now just your secrets. You eat and put on forty-five pounds to keep other boys away. You are lucky to have friends who were there for you, who love you. You think of the things you will do someday about what happened. You cry only sometimes.

You pat yourself on the back for being strong, but you hate that you had to rescue yourself.

You decide you cannot hang out only with people you knew before forever. You lose some of the weight that's been keeping people away. It takes you a year to kiss a boy, and another six months to kiss one after that. You gradually become more comfortable with strangers, in unfamiliar situations, with unknown boys. You sometimes are able to flirt. Sometimes even well. You waver between the fear that no boys find you attractive and the fear that they do. You kiss some more boys, trying to erase the memory of the one who kissed you. You hope someday someone will love you as more than a friend, as more than someone to protect, despite it all. You joke to your close friends about being "sexually damaged." You look forward to the positive sexual experience to cancel out the other. You meet nice boys and wait for one to fall in love with you. One of them walks you home two Saturday nights in a row. You are drunk and appalled when he stops at the bottom of your stairs to say good night. He doesn't try to kiss you or press your body up against a wall. You are not sure what to think. You are confused. You wonder if he finds you annoying or unattractive. The second time he watches you open your door and walk alone into your house, you are almost crying. You go into the kitchen and ask your friends why. "Maybe," they tell you, "he knows you're worth more than that." Maybe, you think. And maybe someday you will know that, too.

I am trying desperately to be a celebrity in the network of my own digital world.

I want to have more Friendster views than anyone else. I need a blog that other people read daily. My iTunes list is shared. I live for smiles on MySpace, winks on Match.com, and pokes on Facebook. Dodgeball messages clog my cell phone every night. Why, you wonder, should I be obsessed with making fifth-hand connections with virtual people? Because I'm voyeuristic, and you are, too. We love personal information; Internet communities are a popularity contest, and it is no longer chic to be mysterious.

I've had more than two hundred Friendster views in the past week. Beat that.

Every morning before I brush my teeth, I check my phone for text messages and sign in to my AOL instant messenger. I need everyone I know to know I'm awake. Thus begins another day of micro-incremental social climbing. Do I have any new e-mails, messages or views, bulletins, invitations, or friend requests? Do I have recent comments on my blog or mentions on my friends' blogs? My celebrity status is uncomfortably quantifiable.

I flip open my phone and check for last night's Dodgeball mes-

sages. Dodgeball is definitely the most personal and invasive network I belong to. It links my online community to my cell phone, so when I send a text message to nyc@Dodgeball.com, the program pings out a message with my location to all the people in my Dodgeball network. Acceptance into another person's Dodgeball network is a very personal way to say you want to hang out. I flip through the messages to see where and when my friends went last night, tracking their progress through various bars and noting the crossed paths. I check the MapQuest map that displays their locations and their proximity to one another. I note how close Christopher and Tom were last night, only a block away, but see that they never met up.

I log on to my Friendster, Facebook, MySpace, and Nerve accounts to make sure the mail bars are rising with new friend requests, messages, and testimonials. Most of the people I know in one community exist in others, and we are constantly firing invites back and forth to new networks. Not a day goes by when I don't send out or accept a new friend request. It's a beautiful example of mutually assured popularity.

I live for testimonials and solicit them incessantly. Testimonials are the ultimate social currency, public declarations of the intimacy level of friendship. The degree of cheekiness expressed is directly related to personal comfort, like signing a yearbook. I click through the profiles of my friends to the profiles of their friends of friends and friends of friends of friends, always aware of the little bar at the top of each profile indicating my multiple connections. A girl I know from college is friends with my friend from college's best friend from Minnesota. They met at camp in the seventh grade. The boyfriend of my friend from work is friends with one of my friends from high school.

I note the connections and remind myself to IM them later.

On Facebook, I skip from profile to profile by clicking on the faces of posted pictures. I find a picture of my sister and her boyfriend, click on his face, and jump right to his page.

Pictures are extremely necessary for enticing new friends and fans—the more pictures, the better. I change my pictures at least once a week.

There are hidden social codes in every image. Shadows and promi-

nent eyes: not confident about their looks. Far away and seated in beautiful scenery: want you to know they're adventurous. Half in the picture: good-looking but want you to know they're artistic, too. Every profile is a carefully planned media campaign. I click on the Friendster "who's viewed me" bar to see who has stumbled upon my profile over the last day, week, or month, and if people I don't know have checked me out, I immediately check them back. I get an adrenaline rush when I find out that a friend of a friend I was always interested in is evidently interested in me, too, and wants to make a connection.

Just imagine if we could be this good in person. Online, everyone has bulletproof social armor.

Finding the perfect online community is not as easy as it looks, especially when they are all in such constant population flux. Some are too small. Dodgeball is so tiny, it's almost too personal. It takes constant attention. Not only does my online profile need to be tended to and updated regularly, but the text messages demand a prompt response. In order to stay in the loop, I even occasionally have to meet up with the members of my Dodgeball network in person.

Some networks are too large. MySpace is so big that I can't seem to find a place to start my own mini-network and branch out. I have ten profiles but not nearly enough friends. It's just so difficult to find people on MySpace who aren't in a band, because the site allows people to link MP3s to their profiles. This immediately caught on with indie bands who realized they could debut new tracks to hardcore fans and groupies at absolutely no cost. But now it has just become a huge marketing machine, not a way to actually find people and connect. You know what I'm talking about. Band profiles linking only to other bands' pages. The site has even started a record label; buying a CD from the MySpace label gets you an extra picture posting on the site. Groupies rejoice.

I spend the majority of my time searching the Internet for new communities and ways to connect. Are there enough people on

Plazes.com yet? Is it worth it to make a profile on Consummating? Am I hip enough for Nerve? It doesn't bother me that Friendster and Consummating started as dating sites; now they are just networking spaces. Can I be a part of Geocaching.com without having a GPS? Are the people on Fark.com my kind of people, and should I spend my time and energy making a profile?

Fark.com members apparently opened their homes to other Fark.com members who were stranded after Hurricane Katrina. This makes their community seem beautiful and touching. Definitely worth starting a profile. Plazes.com is based on posting your GPS address on Google maps and finding people not just through interests but through exact location. Though it's still in beta state, it definitely has potential. I, of course, have a profile and log in every day. But I don't know anyone else on it yet, so I'm not sure I'm ready to tell my friends.

Why, you ask, do I have to be a part of just so many online communities? Isn't one enough? Isn't it hard to keep track of them?

But I have no choice. I need to belong to all of them because each one enables me to connect to people with different levels of social intimacy. The closer I am to someone in the offline world, the more easily accessible they are online. Don't know you but think I might want you to be part of my network? I'll contact you through Match.com or Nerve. Just met? I'll look you up on MySpace. Known each other for a while but haven't been in touch recently? Friendster message. Friends with my friends, talked at a few parties, and want to get to know you better? Dodgeball or Friendster. Good friends and want to connect more often? Dodgeball. Really good friends? Instant message. I have to admit, I now think of most people by their screen names, even when I see them in person.

Through IM, I talk to my friends in Japan and Jamaica as often as I do the friends I see every weekend. Likewise, I have friends on my buddy list who live in my neighborhood, but we only talk on IM. We would never dream of hanging out in person. We have enough con-

nection online for our degree of closeness and don't need to enhance our relationship by spending time together offline. As Friendster puts it, some people are just second- or third-degree friends.

I also use instant messenger as a tool for keeping track of my exes. I know when they sign on, and I read their away messages. I can keep track of what's happening in their lives without their ever knowing I still care. Good or bad day, sick or asleep, I see what they're doing. I know at all times if and when they're on the Internet. Sometimes they get smart, though, and click the little eye in the instant-messenger bar that makes them "invisible." A much less aggressive move than simply not responding to a message.

After I have checked the status of my communities, I move along to the blogs. Blog content is so niche; if you like a blog, then the people reading it must be just like you. Or you know the blogger. Blogs are the most notorious, easiest, and best way to gain celebrity status and online fans. They are free and simple to start, and growing an audience is as easy as sending out a link to all of your other networks, instantly connecting to form an instant audience.

It is no surprise, then, that the most common blogs are about celebrities. There are over thirteen thousand about Britney Spears alone. Celebrity worship is so rampant that even the writers of these blogs have become celebrities themselves. Celebrities by association.

For instance, Trent, the author and editor of pinkisthenewblog .com, was a kid interested in celebrity magazines. He started a blog and had his friends send him links and pics of their celebrity sightings. When Trent mentioned he was sick, my officemates and I drafted a group e-mail expressing our concern and hopes for a healthy recovery. Eventually, as his website grew, random fans—and publicists—began supplying pics in the hopes of being featured on his blog. Trent started showing up in the pictures with the celebrities. Recently, Nicole mentioned him in her new book. Britney said that she knows her new baby will make Trent happy. Lindsay took press pictures with him.

Trent doesn't write back anymore.

Every homepage wants to feel like a community. More and more, they are trying to extend into the offline world. Sites such as Flavorpill, Dodgeball, and GeoCaching.com encourage and facilitate real interactions between their respective members. Flavorpill throws monthly parties for the subscribers in their network, which have become so prominent that when the Guggenheim cosponsored a party, they reported record ticket sales. The line to get in was two avenue blocks long, and hundreds of dancing hipsters were crammed into the main hall, bobbing heads poking over the walls of every ascending level.

I honestly don't know why anyone wants to socialize in person anymore. It's so difficult to concentrate on talking to just one person at a time. Eye contact isn't all it's cracked up to be, and facial expressions are so hard to control.

I was sick of being in awkward social situations I couldn't log out of, so I joined SecondLife. Every member is given an avatar—a 3D body with a choice of clothing, hairstyle, body type, and gender. Members of SecondLife have SecondLife jobs, families, and friends. The population is more than two hundred thousand, and there are over $120,000 U.S. exchanged daily between members. It's amazing how much real money people are willing to pay for virtual objects. After all, one does need to have a good-looking avatar, and stylish SecondLife attire can get expensive.

The people in SecondLife stand around and talk to one another in small, intimate gatherings. They spend the day gossiping, shopping, fighting, making fun of the flying people, and giving one another tattoos. Oh yeah, in SecondLife, you can fly.

Learning how to fly and fly well is key. Making conversation and gaining friends is tough when you suddenly shoot up in the air twenty feet and kick someone in the head. The veterans are definitely at an advantage because they can stay put long enough to establish relationships. I have been placed initially on a lush tropical island to learn how to maneuver. Once I get better at virtually sitting, walking, jumping, and picking up things and moving them, I'll be moved to the main city.

But I've been called a newborn enough times to know I'm not ready yet. There are no flaws in SecondLife. You don't have to eat, and no one gets sick. All of the members choose their body type, so no one is unattractive.

I can't wait to log back in.

Hanging out in the real world one weekend, I went to a Flavorpill party. I'm well aware that knowing and connecting with online celebrities in the real world validates one's celebrity status in the virtual universe. I was sucking down a cigarette with the head of Flavorpill, decidedly a celebrity in many online worlds, when our cell phones rang at the same time. We both flipped them open to see who was contacting us. He turned to me. "Dennis? He's really got to go someplace new."

I looked down at my screen and noticed that Dennis had sent out a Dodgeball message that he was at a bar on the Lower East Side—the fourth such message that week. I turned to the Flavorpill guy. "I didn't know you were in Dennis's network."

Dennis started Dodgeball.

He nodded. We laughed. I quickly exclaimed, "You aren't in my network, why aren't you in my network?" I couldn't believe it. Here we were in person, both in Dennis's network, but not in each other's. That almost never happens.

Without looking at me, he responded, "Rock it."

"Rock what?"

"Rock my network."

For me, New York ended as soon as it began. The day I moved in to my first apartment, I discovered that the reason the kitchen had looked so big was that there was no refrigerator. I also discovered that water didn't flow out of any of the taps. Sal, the plumber who scolded me for letting him in before I asked if he was the plumber, stood in the doorway to my bedroom after he fixed the sinks. I was staring at a wall, holding a paintbrush and a can of paint. He asked, "Did they teach you to paint like that in college?"

So Sal painted my room while I listened to the story of his life and the story of my neighborhood. It had been Finnish when Sal moved there from Sicily as a young boy, and then it was Italian and then Jewish, and now it was Puerto Rican. After he finished painting my room, Sal drove around looking for used refrigerators, found one, fixed it, put it on my front stoop, rang the bell, and drove away. By the time I got downstairs, the refrigerator had already been stolen.

But that is not the way it really happened. That is how I learned to tell the story of my life in New York. I learned to make my experience of being young and new to the city sound effortless and zany. It was not.

I didn't mention that I couldn't go down to get the refrigerator Sal found because it was impossible for me to carry it up four flights of

stairs alone. It was taken only after I left it on the stoop for an entire day while I tried to think of someone I could ask for help. I didn't mention the animal-piss stink of my room or the extreme aching sense of helplessness that overcame me when I realized that I would have to buy a refrigerator. I didn't mention that I couldn't hear out of my right ear because it became clogged from crying. I didn't mention all the time I wasted in bed, staring at the ceiling, debilitated with dread. Or the time I wasted trying to find out if landlords were required to provide refrigerators in units over a certain size. Or the moment when I confronted the landlord and he laughed at me, saying, "Look, either you take the place as it is, or you find somewhere else to live." I didn't mention hurting my hand when I punched the door frame in frustration. Or my sickening realization that Sal was helping me because I was white. He made me aware of this fact with a barrage of racial slurs that I failed to respond to with anything but silence. Silence because I needed his help and I suddenly understood the contract.

"You gotta get a better lock on that door," Sal advised. I pointed out that I didn't own anything except a bed. "Yeah, well, these Puerto Ricans will steal that bed right out from under you," he said. Silence.

I ran into Sal once more before I left the city. He was getting into a car in Brooklyn's Chinatown with his daughter, who was not white at all. Sal, like everyone else in New York, was not exactly who the story might lead you to believe he was.

I hardly even knew the story back then—I had only a vague sense that the heroine was young and that the moral had something to do with being in the right place at the right time. I was ready for anything. I moved to the city during a record heat wave and calmly braced myself for an entire summer of filling the bathtub with ice cubes to cool my body at night. But it was never again that hot in New York. And I learned every detail of the story just as fast as I discovered its falsehood.

I remember a moment from my first days in the city when I was lost in Brooklyn somewhere around Avenue J. Sweat was trickling over my

breastbone, and the sun was burning my scalp. I couldn't identify the exact nature of any of the businesses I was walking past, but they seemed to deal in car parts. Dozens of taillights in all different sizes and shades of red hung, sparkling, from chain-link fences. Suddenly, I felt a desperate need to call my mother. I tried three pay phones and lost five quarters before I found one that worked. When I got her on the line, all I could do was lean against the searing metal phone booth and sob.

Not that I wasn't dazzled by the city. Every nerve in my body was electrified by New York. I was on an endless sidewalk surrounded by bare bulbs and whistles and sudden flocks of pigeons and huge fading stretches of concrete. I believe that I will never feel like that again—so raw and so moved.

I was always lost in New York, even after I stopped walking east when I intended to walk west. There were just ways in which I fundamentally did not know where I was. I grew up north of the city, in the Hudson River Valley. But the water that flowed through upstate New York might as well have been a different substance than the water that flowed into the New York Harbor. Where I came from, the river smelled distinctly of crayfish and grew a leafy skin in the summer. In the winter, the ice groaned and cracked under the weight of all the surrounding silence. I would not have had any trouble believing, when I arrived in New York, that the water in the harbor had been brought on barges from the polar ice cap. Everything about the city seemed at least that absurd.

I was naive enough then to imagine that living a few blocks from the harbor would be pleasant. And I was innocent enough not to know that I should not walk down the street carrying two melons in my arms at about the level of my chest, even if melons were two for a dollar. From the roof of my building in Brooklyn, I could see giant barges silhouetted against the hazy pink horizon at dusk. I tried to walk down to the water and promptly dead-ended at a huge building labeled TER-MINAL WAREHOUSE. On my way back, a bus driver at a red light yelled

to me that I shouldn't be walking around down there. I got on the bus just to humor him and rode past train yards bordered with barbed wire. Then I took a train to Coney Island.

The station at Coney Island was half charred from a fire decades ago and packed with huge inflatable pink seals for sale. An abandoned wooden box read, THE WORLD'S TINIEST HORSE! Caramel apples were seventy-five cents, and the din of the fair games was intolerable. One freak-show announcer screamed, "If you love your family, you will take them to see the two-headed baby!" It was gross and crazy and base—it was everything I would ever love about the city. The beach was packed with naked flesh and smelled like beer and mango. And the Wonder Wheel inspired real wonder as I rose up over Brooklyn in a swinging metal cage.

Did I know it would all cost something sooner or later? All the bewilderment and disorientation? I'm not sure. But I remember the moment when I realized exactly what it had already cost me. A friend and I thought it would be fun to go ice-skating in Prospect Park, but, like most things in New York that are supposed to be fun, it was miserable. The rented skates were as dull as spoons, the ice was slush, and it was so crowded that all we could do was keep ourselves standing and try to avoid being burned by cigarettes while we were pushed and shoved in a slow circle. We had both been very good ice-skaters as children.

I arrived in New York at twenty-one, with a poor sense of direction and a worse sense of time. I set my watch first five minutes fast, then ten, then fifteen. I was going to stay only six months. I stayed three years, and I never stopped thinking about leaving. But when I left, I left my entire life behind. I have to explain to you why I no longer live in New York, but first I have to explain to myself why I stayed so long. Because what I want to say about living there is that it is not, as the mythology goes, more real than anyplace else. In some ways, it is less.

I noticed during my time in New York that many of the people I met there had a habit of describing how miserable they were, then arguing that they couldn't leave the city because it was so wonderful.

When someone who spends the better part of every day in a cubicle and only occasionally makes it out to sit in a loud, dull bar tells me that she is living in the city for "the pace, the excitement, the culture, the— you know—stimulation," I have trouble fully believing her.

The myth of New York seems to be sustained by the fact that so many people who live there are from somewhere else. They come to the city and immediately dedicate themselves to making it the city of their imagination. The—you know—glittering city of endless opportunity that oozes riches and delights for the young and talented. I also came from somewhere else. Somewhere not far away but so clearly foreign that people often asked what country I was from. I always felt like an expatriate in the city, and I came knowing just a few of the stories that everyone has been told.

By now I consider almost everything that is often said about New York to be false. To begin with, the city is not that big or that worldly. An astonishing number of people who live there rarely leave their borough, let alone the country. And if you are part of the elite, as Joan Didion found, New York is like a small town. A tiny population of New York is rich or famous, and much of the rest of the city is in service to that population. For most people, even the elite, it is a city of drudgery. You sweat in the hot subway station, then you shiver in the crowded train, then you walk for ten blocks without an umbrella through a pounding summer thunderstorm . . . and you do this with desperation, because you have no other obvious choice. You do it every day. There are a series of statements on the supporting beams of one of the tunnels under Forty-second Street that read, OVERSLEPT, / SO TIRED. / IF LATE, / GET FIRED. / WHY BOTHER? / WHY THE PAIN? / JUST GO HOME / DO IT AGAIN.

Those words always affected me, although I never worked long enough at any one job to fully understand that particular brand of drudgery. I read them as words of caution. My work in New York was, like the work of everyone else I knew, whatever I could find. I watered plants in the offices of *TV Guide* at one point, I cleaned a bookstore twice a week for a while, I was a waitress for a few days, I did inspec-

tions of community gardens under the Parks Department for quite some time, I proofread just long enough to learn proofreaders' marks, I did transcriptions now and then, I opened mail, I taught writing for a couple of years, I temped, and I was briefly an editorial assistant at a major publishing house. My job as an editorial assistant was by far the most menial work I ever did in the city. I remember it mostly as a series of pointless trips in elevators. And I remember the way my friend described a similar job: "I professionally destroy paper clips."

But I still believed in the mystical power of the city to transform me into a writer—a real writer. I wasn't sure exactly how this alchemy would happen, which is one reason I kept changing jobs, but I was convinced that just living in the city could make my writing more legitimate. By the time I left New York, I had learned that the distinction between a writer and a real writer is superficial. And I understood the advice that more established writers had been giving me all along. "Move somewhere else—anywhere else," one journalist had recommended soon after I moved to New York. "Pick any other city."

There is a popular legend of New York as the gritty city of hard knocks and rough neighborhoods and real danger and police chases and wild nights. I suppose that watching a bum with no legs being dragged out of his stinking pile of blankets by four policemen is gritty, but it lacks any of the romance implied by the word. Standing for an entire day in a clinic crowded with sick babies and pregnant women because you don't have health insurance and you've been ill for several months also lacks romance. So does spending hours on the telephone waiting for the chance to explain that you were billed twice for the month of June. One of my most vivid memories from that first year in New York is the smell of the oil soap I always used to clean my floors. While I was on hold with the telephone company or the gas company or the credit-card company, I would sit on the floor examining the splinters in the wood and inhaling the scent of oil soap for hours.

Not even the dangers of New York are what the story dictates. I

was harassed by children nearly as often as I was harassed by men in the city. I remember smiling at an eight-year-old boy on the train who stared at me stonily before he half closed his eyes and slowly ran his tongue across his upper lip as he fingered his crotch. While I was working for the Parks Department, I spent most of my time in neighborhoods imagined as "rough," where one or two people might ask me if I was lost. Often I *was* lost, and I got directions that were usually wrong from people who were always nice. The worst thing I was ever threatened with in New York was a lighter. And it was terrifying. But the man standing in the middle of the sidewalk in front of me flicking his lighter didn't hurt me. He stared at me and said softly, "How ya doing, princess?" I told him that I had been working all day and that I was very tired, and he said he knew how I felt and walked away.

I often woke before dawn and could not fall back to sleep. I lay there listening to the car alarms cycle through all their different sounds while my heart raced for no reason. It is hard for me to separate my experience of living in New York from the sensation of reaching the limits of my own independence. I was excruciatingly lonely, and everything was unfamiliar and difficult. But in a way, I was living my dream. Long after I discarded every illusion I ever had about New York, I still treasured the empty fantasy of complete autonomy.

If I had entertained more illusions, I might have been able to stay in New York longer. I might have even considered myself happier. But I was not tickled by the daily opportunity to change trains in Rockefeller Center, I did not feel lucky to be surrounded by merchandise I couldn't afford, and I had absolutely no interest in the nightlife, whatever that is.

I didn't participate in the New York of the collective imagination, which may be one reason why I don't believe in it. My interactions with people I didn't know were always brief and often painful. One afternoon I crashed my bike into a man just as he stepped off the curb in Chinatown. Our heads slammed together, and I fell onto the sidewalk. For an instant I lay there, looking up at an advertisement for Asian escorts on the side of a building, smelling the reek of the fish market and

listening to the humming motor of a tiny scuba diver swimming in a washtub next to me. The man I had hit was holding his forehead and seemed to be getting more and more agitated as people with orange bags of bok choy crowded around me to make sure I was all right while they left him standing alone. Scared and still seeing a few swimming lights from the impact, I got onto my bike quickly and rode away. I stopped after a few blocks and cried hysterically in dismay. No one looked at me. In ways I find hard to explain, most of the interactions I had in New York were like this one. Which may be why I always felt more comfortable simply observing other people's lives.

I watched everything carefully and never quite lost the conviction that I was missing something. So, what's so good about all this? I kept thinking. I suspected that there was a secret I hadn't been told. I was sure that I had only one chance to do the right things and meet the right people and that I would surely fail. Everything was irrevocable and nothing was within reach. The peculiar paralysis I felt when I first came to the city was mostly from the sense that every decision I made would last the rest of my life. I know now that I was right and I was wrong. Success and failure were the terms in which young people who had just moved to the city spoke. It was not a place to live as much as it was a test or a game. I despise both. "Why don't you leave?" I asked people endlessly, even though I could not yet explain why I didn't leave. "Because I don't want to admit that I failed," one friend said. "Because I have to prove to myself that I can do this." By the time I left New York, I knew that success and failure are silly terms in which to speak of living a life.

I read Joan Didion's 1967 essay "Goodbye to All That" before I ever saw the trenches of New York. All I remember of that first reading is that I didn't like the title. I knew nothing at all back then. I did not know that I would return to the essay again and again, and that I would eventually feel compelled to rewrite it.

But I distinctly remember walking down Fourth Avenue in Brooklyn for the first time, past the car wash and the huge windowless ware-

houses and the brick buildings bristling with TV antennas and the bill-board that read SE HACEN. I looked around and thought, with wonder, I'm going to love all this someday. And I did.

Still, I feel jarred by I ♥ NY bumper stickers and repulsed by I ♥ NY T-shirts. Especially now that the slogan has become so fetishized, like the flag. I don't want the New York I loved to be confused with the New York the T-shirts love. That isn't the same city. I didn't love *The New Yorker*'s New York or the New York of *The New York Times*. I didn't love Joan Didion's New York, or anyone else's fantasy of the place. I loved my own experience of the city, which was rarely what I expected it to be. And I loved the people I knew there, who were un-like every character in every TV show or movie set in New York that I had ever seen. I was most comfortable with people for whom New York was not a mirage, and I most trusted people who hated it there.

New York took everything I had. I moved four times, and each time I owned less. I left New York without even a bed. I no longer had potted plants, or framed pieces of art, or a snapshot of my father. I re-member the moment when I threw that snapshot out. I was sifting through my things before another hurried move with a borrowed car, and I looked at the photo, thinking, I don't really need this, he still looks almost the same. That was just before I noticed that my father had become old.

In New York, even one snapshot became too much of a burden to carry from one place to another. The mementos of my childhood began to weigh like lead. And so did my adolescent preoccupation with the real. Like many young people who go to college immediately after high school, I had learned to talk about the real world as if it were in an entirely different universe from the one I lived in. With the blind enthusiasm and embarrassing ignorance of a colonial explorer, I left college determined to discover the real world. I didn't just want to live there—I wanted to be made real myself. This might be the saddest part of my story, because New York did not make me feel more legiti-mate or real. Actually, it made me feel like I barely existed. As I wan-dered through the surprisingly solid streets of that mostly fictitious

city, people often bumped into me surprisingly hard, as if I were invisible. Now I agree with my grandmother, who recently said, "The real question is, what is authenticity, anyways?"

For most of my time in New York, I lived in Brooklyn and worked in Harlem. I considered this a clever evasion of The City. Where I lived was just a place to live, not The Place. And where I worked was just a place to work, not The Place. I rode my bike to work early in the morning, when even the streets of midtown were still empty. I rattled over the Brooklyn Bridge, looking down through the wooden slats at the water below. I swerved through Chinatown. And then I rode up Mulberry Street, through Little Italy, where the street carnival had been the night before. The strings of lights were still hanging but not illuminated. The cobblestones were covered with trash. The sausage vendor was asleep at the wooden counter with his head resting on his folded arms.

The New York I knew was always the city of the morning after the carnival. I rode all the way uptown on First Avenue, from Little Italy to Harlem. I walked from 110th to 140th, from Frederick Douglass to Martin Luther King Jr. Boulevard. I passed murals painted on the boards that covered the broken windows of the old brownstones—the Virgin Mary on one window, Saint Lazarus with his crutches and his dog on the other. I read the messages chalked onto the sidewalk by De La Vega every morning, "You are more desirable as a servant of the machine than as a free thinker." I saw the glorious graffiti on the basketball courts. I stepped over dog shit. I watched the Eastern European woman who worked in the pizza shop grow thin and develop a sore on her face while the boys from the school came in and yelled at her to hurry up with that slice, bitch. I glared at the boys, and they didn't meet my eyes. Almost no one did. I listened to the guys in the bodega betting on the Mets and laughing. I smiled at babies in strollers. I watched kids on bikes ride through traffic and pop up onto their back wheels. Sometimes I ate in the hospital café, because it was the only place I knew I could get spinach for lunch. I watched women in hot, hot dresses, and I watched the men watching them. I listened

to Rosie the police officer singing Aretha Franklin in the bathroom of the school where I worked. I knew, intimately, the empty lots where grandmas from Alabama grew okra and collard greens. I found a cat that had drowned in a rain barrel and was gathering mold. At the bodega on First Avenue, I saw the old man who was always trying to remember my name. "Ida!" he would jump up and yell. "Ursula, Ursula, Ursula!"

This was the New York I loved, with the imperfect, ambiguous, hesitant love that I have come to recognize as my own. It was the city that existed on the margins of the story. It was the New York of Harlem and Ingleside and Washington Heights. The New York of the outer boroughs. The New York of Brooklyn and Queens and Staten Island and the Bronx.

But see, the name of every place in New York serves as a code word or a racial cue. The code shifts slightly depending on who you are talking to, so that at times the word "Harlem" will mean "dangerous" and "tough" and at other times will mean "vibrant" and "real." It is always a setting for our same old stories. What an injustice to a place. A place that is, incidentally, real.

Now my friends often say, "When you come back to New York," assuming, of course, that I will come back. And maybe I will, despite it all. Joan Didion did. But for now I prefer to think that I will go somewhere that is not so overimagined.

I lived in the city just long enough to see Coney Island begin to be destroyed. The spring I left New York was the same spring when I discovered that the old vine-covered roller coaster had finally been torn down. So had the ancient candy shop with the homemade caramel apples. And the burnt train station was being renovated.

It has been said that New York is a city for only the very rich and the very poor. Joan Didion suggested that it is a city for only the very young. In my worst moments, especially when standing on Madison Avenue, I have suspected that it is a city for only the very desperate or the very deluded.

I have often been mystified by Joan Didion's ability to tolerate certain myths while she so fiercely and effectively destroys the foundations of many others. But I know now that it is very difficult to dismantle one story without replacing it with another. The romance of narrative is so hard to resist. Like Joan Didion, I made a yellow curtain for my first bedroom in the city because I had a romantic notion of light and color. My curtain also became grimy in the rain.

It is not that the heroine is no longer as optimistic as she once was. It is that the heroine is not convinced she is the heroine or that the story is true. The heroine knows that New York is just a city—just a place to live. And like any other place, it demands that you make your own story.

I came to New York very young, and I left still young but not the same. The Wonder Wheel is still there, true, but everything else is gone.

Here's what I'm going to do. I'm going to pick a random, repre-
sentative sample of three people in their twenties, assemble
them together, and observe them while they converse. I will
then compile all the data I record and rearrange the information into
a succinct, lucid, and objective essay that will effectively define my
generation with accuracy and finality. I will then sell the rights to this
definition to *Webster's Dictionary,* Universal Studios, or the federal
government of the United States of America, depending on who offers
me the highest bid.

I've done a lot of legwork since that last paragraph. Here are the
people I've found to participate in the discussion. Their names have
been changed. Maggie is twenty-five years old and resides in Berkley,
California, where she failed to get into the college of her choosing but
frequently pretends to be a student by congregating with them on
sidewalks and in parks, passing out various pamphlets and flyers that
are all equally informative on the topics of government, correct moral
behavior in regards to flora and fauna of the Planet Earth, and punk
bands. In order to maintain the facade of being an actual student, she
sometimes stays up nights reading a textbook on abnormal psychology
(aka exceptional behavior, aka sick minds, sick people), but in darker
moments, she realizes that this calculated effort to deceive herself only

confirms her own neurosis. She's also extremely scared that she might have hypochondriasis. Her parents, who reside in New England some-whereabouts, believe she is on scholarship, respect her desire that they not visit her, and send her $2,500 a month for her living expenses. She feels guilty about this but doesn't know what to do. She once used some of the extra money to buy herself and some student friends some high-grade marijuana, but after smoking, she ran out into the streets shouting for someone to call a cop because her heart was going to ex-plode. Maggie won't admit to her friends that she has money, even though she doesn't have a job, and she won't admit to herself that she very much enjoys the benefits of having money. Maggie is white, and every human ancestor in her lineage was also white, but she insists that she has Cherokee blood. Her mother drives a Jeep Cherokee, but that's as close a connection to Native Americans as Maggie has. She hates her mother because she's a materialist and once cheated on Mag-gie's father. She loves her father but is embarrassed that he's an avid duck hunter, plus he fought in the Vietnam War without protest.

Gordon is twenty-nine years old and lives in a wealthy suburb of Cleveland, Ohio, about six miles away from his parents' home. Gordon majored in business at Ohio State but flunked out his sophomore year; he stayed in town for an extra three years so he wouldn't miss out on any keggers with his friends, or brothers, as he called them, even though his own fraternal status wasn't officially recognized. He once tried to kiss one of these brothers after a particularly heavy night of drinking; this led to things, and both of them pretended not to remember the incident the next morning. Gordon's father, Gordon Sr., is the CEO of a multimil-lion-dollar corporation (which I have signed a legal agreement not to name) that produces household products ranging from high-tech mi-crowaves to innocently packaged and euphemistically labeled Stress Massagers for the Common Housewife. Gordon's mother is a big fan of this product, incidentally. Now that his father is selling his corporation to China for a cool $1 billion, Gordon will never have to work a day in his life and hence spends all his time and money trying to figure out what to do with himself. He drinks, gains weight, watches sports and

pornography, buys fast cars and all the newest hair-loss products, and sometimes calls his mother late at night and weeps torrentially, so long as she assures him his father is not in the room. He respects and loves his father, but the only advice old Dad ever gives him is "Son, you just need to find yourself a good woman to take care of you."

Zachary is twenty years old and lives in Savannah, Georgia. Zachary's father was granted asylum in the United States because his political beliefs put his life in danger in Singapore. His mother is the illegitimate daughter of a white traveling businessman from Texas and a Creole waitress in New Orleans. Zachary's parents aren't married, either. His father is in prison for political beliefs he developed after arriving in the U.S., and his stepfather is a homosexual who married Zachary's mother because he believed he needed a beard (this was his own terminology, not mine, mind you) back home in Georgia. Zachary thinks of his mother as this man's virgin whore. Zachary hates homosexuals, heterosexuals, black people, Asians, whites, men and women, small children and dogs, even though there are people (and dogs) who belong to each of these illusory categories who have offered and will continue to offer Zachary pure, unadulterated compassion and love. Zachary also hates the proverbial Old South and hates that he was born there, and he has perfected the art of talking like people in the movies in order to hide the fact that he ever had an accent. Zachary is infatuated with his concept of the bigger-picture U.S.A. The U.S.A. recognized his right to be self-made, historyless, skilled, and judged by his skills alone. The U.S.A. gave him a computer and let him use it however he saw fit.

Enough of these people and on to me. I am the pure observer, and I sprang from my own forehead in order to be born. Although I am twenty-six years old, I have no past, present, or future. I am the Objective Moderator, and henceforth my title shall be abbreviated simply as "Om."

OM: First of all, I'd like to thank all of you for coming today. I hope all of you feel a real sense of pride in being chosen for this discussion that will be used to define an entire generation of our peers.

MAGGIE: I thought this was supposed to be a random sample. How are we supposed to be proud of being randomly selected?

OM: Good point, Maggie, I'd forgotten you stay up all night reading that psychology book and thus know what a real random sample is. I hadn't counted on that. But then again, you didn't exactly get into that fancy college with any of your smart comments, did you?

MAGGIE: What's that supposed to mean?

OM: It means I was using a superficial gesture to make a point of my gratitude for everyone coming out, and the words themselves are meaningless, so it'd be great if you could just shut up and play along.

GORDON: I don't see what the big deal is with college anyways.

OM: Dynamite drop-in, Gordo. The conversation's sort of moved on from there, but we'd love to hear your thoughts. Please, continue.

GORDON: Well, it's just kind of something you do for your parents, and—

MAGGIE: Precisely. You do it for your parents and you do it for The Man. College is an archaic, patriarchal, self-validating institution that doesn't amount to anything more than citizenship training for drones and idiots. Hey, you went to college, didn't you, Om?

OM: You're displacing, Maggie. I'm the objective moderator. My role is to selflessly facilitate a discussion about your own beautiful lives.

GORDON: No, I think she's right. I saw you once; you went to one of those small schools in Ohio. I went to a party there and saw you walk by and completely miss out. Someone told me you played piano so you could get chicks and thought you were above parties.

OM: You have a wonderful memory, Gordon, but again, I'm not the point here. I don't exist. The fact that you were more preoccupied with some guy walking across the street and not the chicks who were right in front of you *is* up for discussion, though, and I think we'll be coming to that shortly.

ZACHARY: What'd you learn?

OM: Pleasure to have you join the dialogue, Zachary. Welcome. To whom are you addressing your question?

ZACHARY: To you, fucker. What'd you learn in college?

OM: Again, I think it's time to move the discussion back to you three. I'm not the—

MAGGIE: Yeah, Om, what'd you learn?

GORDON: Yeah.

OM: All right, if it will help us to move forward. I learned how to write an essay in college.

ZACHARY: Bull-fucking-shit. And you say you've brought us here to say something about *our* generation.

OM: Yep. Absolutely. Now you're getting somewhere.

ZACHARY: Saying something important to or about our generation in an essay is like, I don't know, a dog trying to make puppies by screwing a cat or something.

OM: Terrific, Zachary. You spend an awful amount of time playing around on that computer of yours. It's evident that your verbal skills won't be impelling *you* to write an essay anytime soon, but I like what you're saying. You've got heart. What mode of communication would you suggest?

ZACHARY: The Internet, man. No one ever reads anything anymore unless they have to click on a word to get into some site.

GORDON: Oh, God. I hate all you technobabies. You were all born with plugs up your—

OM: Now might be a good time for you discuss that incident with your fraternity brother, Gordon.

GORDON: What? Oh, come on, I didn't mean *that* kind of plugs—like, spark plugs or, I mean, outlets, you know, three-prongs. They're *plugged in.* Get it? It's a figure of speech. I'm just saying I don't like the way all these kids think the Internet is everything, you know? It's good for porn and e-mail and stuff, but that's it.

OM: Maggie, why are you blushing? Why do you and Gordon keep looking at each other like there's something going on between the two of you that Zachary and I don't know about?

ZACHARY: I don't friggin' care, man.

OM: No one asked you. Maggie, Gordo—how about it? You're in a

safe place here. No one's ever going to read any of this. I promise. Maggie, I want you to tell me what your feelings are right now. How are Gordo's comments making you *feel*?

MAGGIE: Okay. I feel a little awkward about bringing this up, and Gordon, I know you wouldn't want me to—

GORDON: Don't say it. Don't you dare say it, Maggie.

OM AND ZACHARY: You two know each other?

MAGGIE: I met Gordon in a chat room.

ZACHARY: The Internet is everything.

OM AND GORDON: Shut up.

MAGGIE: Here's the deal. I'm a dominatrix, and I'm not ashamed to admit it. Our sexual-preference profiles were a hundred percent match. Gordon and I chatted for a while about strap-ons and how he really wanted to try one. Gordon kept asking me if it really felt like a real man's, and how small were my breasts, and things like that; and then he typed that he would fly out from Ohio to Berkley in his private jet that instant if there was any chance I had a burly chest or facial hair. And it just felt wrong all of a sudden. Kinky sex is great with me, but I want the other person to want *me* to do really nasty things to them, not some fantasy person who isn't even in the room. That's what threesomes are for.

ZACHARY: That's pretty sentimental for a dom.

OM: I guess I don't know you so well as I thought I did, Maggie.

MAGGIE: The need for control is a huge part of being OCPD, Om, if you take a little time to study the *DSM-IV.*

OM: Missed that.

MAGGIE: I'm really sorry, Gordon. It's just that I want you to be okay with yourself, and I just know that you aren't. At first I thought I was just stereotyping you, with all that money and the pressure to live up to the conqueror persona and the aloof father-figure thing and the overindulgent mother and all that, but it really turned out to be—

GORDON: Is this about that llama thing I told you about from my freshman year? Because I thought I made it pretty damn clear that the llama was *female,* and I wasn't the only one involved in that, either.

ZACHARY: I knew he was queer the second I saw him.

OM: That's a hell of a chip you've got on your shoulder there, Zachary. Maybe you should try a little love and acceptance.

ZACHARY: Maybe I should shoot a hippie in the head, Om. My step-dad's a queer, so I can say whatever I want.

GORDON: Listen here, you cotton-pickin', shoe-shining, Commie boat rat motherf—

MAGGIE: Stop! Everybody just stop! Don't you guys see what's happening here? These are all defense mechanisms. Gordon, you're sublimating. You perceive that your homosexuality is unacceptable by society, which is particularly understandable considering the fact that you were raised in a conservative, decidedly non-twenty-first-century, heavily Protestant cross section of middle America, and because you're unwilling to face this pressure and come out of the closet, you channel your sexual energy into illicit acts of homosexuality you perceive as accepted by society, such as raping a llama with twenty other men, or, excusing the llama, just having an old-fashioned circle jerk with the same twenty men.

GORDON: The llama was a girl. Circle jerks are all about the competition.

MAGGIE: Don't be so sullen, Gordon! Don't you know I'm not judging you? Maybe in an animal-rights context but not a sexual one. I *understand,* Gordon. Just like I understand, Zachary, that your desire to belittle Gordon for his orientation is a perfect example of the way you displace the rage you feel arising from your own minority status as a—um—not-white person.

ZACHARY: You snort Ritalin through a straw and have orgies with people wrapped in cellophane, hypocrite. Why's that?

MAGGIE: I suffer from A) attention deficit hyperactivity disorder and B) a perfectly natural desire to be loved, a desire that just happens to manifest itself in certain acts that our society deems marginal.

OM: Getting back to the question of our generation, I'd just like to point out that ADHD, Maggie, is a disease that was invented by a profit-mongering pharmaceutical company that got approval for

their drug from a puppet government that lives in the pockets of corporations; the so-called cure was then mass-marketed to a younger population already so bombarded by the maniacal advancement of useless technology and staggering proliferation of advertisement that it was unable to see the *real* truth that ADHD is the sickness of our collective cultural mentality and not any one individual youngster and hence—

GORDON: What's wrong with corporations?

ZACHARY: Absolutely nothing, Gordon. Just keep wiping your ass with Franklins and don't worry yourself over it. You're queer-queer and Om's hippie-queer is all. What I was saying before Objective Moderator interrupted me, Maggie, is that you think you know me, but you don't know me the way I know I know you, you know. No way.

OM: Doesn't your computer have an electronic thesaurus or something?

ZACHARY: You don't know me at all. You know chapter twenty-four or whatever of some psychology book that's got some section on the ratio of brain capacity to lip size in the lower-class Mississippi Negro—

MAGGIE: That's *so* not true! I *completely* sympathize with you, Zachary, and I'm totally on your side! Racial self-loathing is nothing new to this Native American girl! And I don't just read psych, either. There's James Baldwin, Toni Morrison, Gabriel García Márquez, Zora Neale Hurston, Ralph Ellison, Langston Hughes, um, Chris Ro—

ZACHARY: What the hell do a bunch of dead white males and their fucking books have to do with me? How many forests did you have to level to read all that crap, tree-hugger? Books are a technology of the past; essays are bullshit. Live in the now, my friends. The Internet is everything.

OM, MAGGIE, AND GORDON: Stop saying that!

ZACHARY: I hate all of you.

OM: Even me?

ZACHARY: Especially you, Om. I'm on to you. Gordon's not the only

one who's seen you around before today. I saw you in Savannah, wandering around staring up at the Spanish moss and the lamplight, looking pathetic and lonely. You worked at a little café where surly, middle-aged men like my stepfather would waste the afternoons wallowing in decadence and humidity. You were friends with art-student kids who got out of college and found themselves flat on their asses because they and their rich, stupid parents were stupid enough to think that a college was the right place to teach them—what do they call it?—graphic design and how to get a job with a stupid degree like that.

OM: You used "stupid" three times in that last sentence, Zachary. For your own sake, please buy a thesaurus. And for the record, I don't recall any of my friends or their parents being rich or stupid.

GORDON: What's wrong with being rich and stupid?

ZACHARY: Objective Moderator, my ass. You're pathetic.

MAGGIE: Yeah, Om. Who the hell are you to treat us like this? I saw you working at the cash register in some ultra-trendy, expensive clothing store in San Francisco, ringing up some high-maintenance celebrity and looking like you wanted to stab yourself in the face.

OM: If you were a customer in that place, chances are more likely I wanted to kill you, not myself. Sorry, just a lot of negative energy there, you know?

GORDON, MAGGIE, AND ZACHARY: What are we to you?

OM: You're elves. You're helping me realize my vision so that one day all the children of the world can live in happiness.

MAGGIE AND ZACHARY: You mean we're just fiction.

GORDON: What's fiction?

OM: Don't worry about it, Gordo. And the answer is no. None of you are fiction. You're constructs. You're conceptual building blocks in a dry, cerebral polemic I'm going to call an essay. Some people use a false "I" they've assembled out of ignorance, shoddy memories, and sentiment; *I* use Maggie, Gordon, and Zachary.

MAGGIE: We *are* your ignorance, shoddy memory, and sentiment.

OM: Bravo.

MAGGIE: And do you realize the implications of your actions? The consequences?

OM: Um.

MAGGIE: The consequence of all this babbling is that the only thing you've proved to anyone here is that you're a misogynist, a homophobe, an ageist-slash-racist-slash-technophobe, and you have no respect whatsoever for the beauty of Eastern religions. And you've made a big mistake in giving us specific ages. Plenty of twenty-nine-year-olds are tech nerds like Zachary. And plenty of twenty-year-olds are good old boys. Plus, you're totally frenetic and unfocused; I don't think you'd know a body paragraph if you tripped over one.

GORDON: I don't know what any of that means, but I agree with Maggie. I feel like you named me Gordon only because you think Gordo is a cute frat-boy nickname that makes me sound stupid. And it's a total cop-out stereotype to think all frat boys are gay.

OM: I'm just trying to help you. You see, the reason you're all so conceptually pigeonholed is because we live in a culture where it's extremely advantageous for the powers that be and general modus operandi for you to look at me, yourselves, and everyone else as *ideas*. Narrow ideas. That's what keeps this country running the way it does, like the proverbial laser hippo headed for the cliff. That's what's pouring the barrels of shit salad into the airplane engine. Labels, my friends, all labels and words and false distinctions meant to divide us into the clothes we wear, food we eat, stores we shop in, parties we vote for, programs we watch (and does anyone ever think about how creepy and ominous it sounds to sit silently on your ass for hours at a time watching *programs,* my God, does anyone know what that word means?), the sports we—

ZACHARY: Oh, no, you don't.

OM: Don't what?

ZACHARY: You're trying to wrap things up. You want to tidy everything up and put a big green ribbon on it and say that you made it. You want to have the last word on us. No one's going to do that to me.

No one defines me but me. I'm self-determined. I can say what I want, do what I want, buy what—

OM: *Exactly.* That's my point. You're self-obsessed with a self you've derived almost entirely from capitalist marketing propaganda, and if you live the rest of your life thinking with the same logic, then one day you're going to get so wrapped up in this digitalized wet dream of yours that you're not even going to think twice about it when you receive an encrypted e-mail from WALfbiCIAkgb-MART kindly asking you to use your corrupted genius to build them a special chip connected to a special button that they can press willy-nilly and every human being on earth will bend over simultaneously and say, "Do with us what you will! Give us Life! Give us Death! Give us Plastic!"

ZACHARY: You're a little bit out there on all this conspiracy-theory stuff, Om.

OM: Listen. There will be no mutiny here. I'm going to have the last word on you whether you like it or not, Zachary. I'm the one coming up with all the big questions here. I'm the one—

SHADOW IN THE DOORWAY: All of your questions are roosters. All of your answers are pigs.

MAGGIE, GORDON, ZACHARY, AND OM: Who the hell are you?

SHADOW IN THE DOORWAY: I am a shadow standing in the doorway as though I were a person. My person is lost.

MAGGIE, GORDON, AND ZACHARY: Are you another one of Om's constructs?

SHADOW IN THE DOORWAY: Om is mine. Mine is Om is I'm.

MAGGIE, GORDON, ZACHARY, AND OM: What?

GORDON: You make even less sense than Om.

SHADOW IN THE DOORWAY: Razors fall from my lips and land on raindrops. There is a throat that swallows everything. This throat has three openings and no bottom. Fire swims inside.

OM: I don't know who or what you think you are, Mr. or Ms. Shadow in the Doorway thingy, but I'll have you know there's not a chance in hell that all the questions and answers I've come up with here

are just a load of poultry and pork. Two of us here don't even eat meat. And another thing you should know before you pop your head in the doorway and start preaching at a bunch of strangers—

SHADOW IN THE DOORWAY: In all the vast green world—neither here nor there—there are no strangers.

OM: Whatever, man. Keep preaching. It's a hell of a lot easier to be some floating, nebulous, gender-neutral, paradox-spewing shadow blob than it is to be a real person on a real planet. In particular, we're talking about Planet America here, and the plight of our generation upon this planet. When you showed up, I was just about to say that the acceleration of technology and the mass proliferation of amoral advertisement have created the illusion of a conse-quenceless world, and the fact that our generation has always lived in this world and known no other has profound and dangerous im-plications for our collective future psyche. This needs to be ad-dressed. This just happens to be a discussion room. This is a safe place where we encourage diversity, healthy skepticism, and the free exchange of ideas, even if they conflict. And *questions* are a big part of the whole process of discovery we're trying to encourage.

SHADOW IN THE DOORWAY: All of your questions are roosters. All of your answers are pigs.

OM: Dammit! This is a really complicated world we live in, one that no one could even begin to understand even if they could ask a million questions in a second and answer two million. So I'll be the first to admit that what we come up with here today may not be much, but at least it's *something.* At least we're contributing to understand-ing, and we're making some progress. And then you show up and try to bring everything we've done to a screeching halt.

SHADOW IN THE DOORWAY: When you have truly stopped, you will know your true beginning.

OM: Enough of this jibber-jabber! Why are you here? What are you?

SHADOW IN THE DOORWAY: Yes.

OM: Go to hell! Do *you* know all the right questions, all the right an-

swers? Or perhaps your questions are kumquats. Your answers are marsupials.

SHADOW IN THE DOORWAY: Today. Now. There is only one question, and there is only one answer.

OM: Great! I don't believe you, but welcome to the dialogue. Please, tell us. We'd love to know your question and answer. Today. Now. Define this grand generation, oh, wise one.

MAGGIE, GORDON, AND ZACHARY: Yeah, tell us! We're sick of Om's words!

SHADOW IN THE DOORWAY: Okay. I will tell you. But I have to warn you that it may seem to you that nothing will be finished. You may want more and you may not. But I will be gone.

ZACHARY: Fine, already. We can deal with it. Just fucking tell us the damn question and then tell us the damn answer and we can be done with it.

OM: Where did it go?

THE SHADOW THAT WAS IN THE DOORWAY, SPEAKING NOW FROM ELSEWHERE: Q. Tell me. What is this dream?

A. This dream begins with *Tell me.*

This dream ends with *What is this dream.*

This dream begins again with

This dream begins again with.

OM: That's a big, fat load of bullshit. Now. To the point. Where. Was. *III III III III III III III IIIIIIIIIIIIIIIIIIIIIIIIIIIIIIII????????????*

THINK OUTSIDE THE BOX BUT STAY INSIDE THE GRID
FINDING THE BEAT YOU SHALL GO OUT WITH JOY AND BE
LED FORTH WITH PEACE THE IDIOT'S GUIDE TO YOUR PALM
SHEER DOMINANCE LIVE NUDE GIRL AN EVENING IN APRIL
CLICHÉ RAPE STORY ROCK MY NETWORK GOODBYE TO ALL THAT
ALL THE RIGHT ANSWERS WHY I HAD TO LEAVE IN BETWEEN PLACES
A RED SPOON FOR THE NAMELESS MY LITTLE COMMA FIGHT ME
THE SECRET LIVES OF MY PARENTS MY ROARING TWENTIES
IN, FROM THE OUTSIDE THE MYSTERIES OF LIFE . . . REVEALED!
SO YOU SAY YOU WANT A REVOLUTION WORKING AT WENDY'S
JESS LACHER MARY BETH ELLIS BRONSON LEMER JENNIFER GLASER
RACHEL KEMPF JOHN FISCHER SHAHNAZ HABIB EMMA BLACK
ELI JAMES KYLE MINOR COLLEEN KINDER CHRISTOPHER POLING
KATHLEEN ROONEY RADHIYAH AYOBAMI MARISA McCARTHY
THEODORA STITES EULA BISS BRENDAN PARK LUKE MULLINS
MARY KATE FRANK PURLEE MAUD ELDENA EVANS

The pain developed so quietly that I couldn't tell you exactly when it began. But by early evening, it had my full attention: a sharp, relentless sting in my breastbone. It got worse when I sucked in a breath or pressured it with my thumb. Over the next couple of hours, a throbbing ache gathered in the round of my left shoulder and blasted down to my fingertips. Soon my whole arm felt swollen, as if someone had tied a cord around my bicep and was gradually tightening it, cutting off the circulation. Hours passed as I sat and wondered whether I should get help.

The power was out in my house, as it had been for nearly a week. So by candlelight, I searched through my belongings for a book called *Where There Is No Doctor,* which I had brought for just such an occasion.

It was an odd time in Consuelo, the small town in the Dominican Republic where I had been living for the past year and a half. The failure of one of the country's largest banks had tipped the entire nation into economic free fall: Inflation picked up, electricity blacked out, water dripped from the faucets if it came at all. On more than one occasion, the desperate conditions sparked protests in the streets, which quickly dissolved to rock throwing and tire burning. And since na-

tional elections were just around the corner, the situation was expected to worsen.

Where There Is No Doctor is a health-care handbook designed for people who lack access to reliable medical resources. It's filled with advice on how to diagnose and treat a host of ailments—cold sores, nosebleeds, river blindness, etc.—all by yourself. I flipped through the pages until I located the section titled "heart trouble." I knew that most chest pain was caused by nothing more than a bruised or pulled muscle, often resulting from exercise. However, the book said that chest pain accompanied by pain in your left arm could be a sign of something more serious.

This certainly wasn't my first unexplained health problem. Over the past several weeks, I had become a regular at the local medical clinic. I would show up early in the morning to turn in samples of urine or have tubes of blood drained from my arm. After seeing the results, the doctors would send me to the pharmacy for liquid antacids or pills. Still, the nausea and diarrhea persisted, and over time I grew convinced that something terrible was about to happen to me.

Now this, I thought. I had to get help.

I hurried out the door and made my way along the dirt-cobbled streets, past rows of one-story tin-roofed houses, illuminated by the moon and the sky full of stars. It was well past midnight by the time I reached the convent. The gate was locked, so I scaled the ten-foot-high chain-link fence and marched up to the house. I knew Sister Gibb would be in bed, and the last thing I wanted to do was disturb her, but this was serious. So I walked around to the back of the building and called her name reluctantly.

She answered right away.

I explained the pain I was experiencing and told her what I had read in the book.

"Do you think this is something that you need to have checked out right away?" she said.

"Yes, I do," I told her.

In less than five minutes, Sister Gibb and I were on our way to the medical clinic. As the car bounced over wheelbarrow-sized potholes, she asked if I thought it was time for me to go home.

Sister Gibb was a stern gray-haired nun who had spent over half a century working to end poverty in Consuelo. She had seen scores of other young volunteers come and go before me. Thing is, I had been thinking a lot about going home at that time. I had come to believe that nothing I'd done there had amounted to anything meaningful. Soon I began to reexamine my reasoning for coming to Consuelo in the first place.

Still, I was determined to stay for the remaining two months of the school year, as I had promised.

"Absolutely not," I replied.

The clinic was dark when we arrived, lit only by the flickering light of a kerosene lamp. I woke the two medical attendants and explained my symptoms. I then placed my arm palm-up on a table as they took my blood pressure and injected me with a shot, which helped reduce the swelling.

I was fine, they said. But to be sure, they recommended I go see a specialist in the morning.

I always had a tough time explaining what I was doing in Consuelo. It would have been much easier if I actually were in the Peace Corps, or I really were a scout for the Atlanta Braves. That, people could understand. But the idea of an American volunteering to coach baseball at a public elementary school just didn't make sense.

Consuelo is a southeastern Dominican town of roughly sixty thousand people. It's the kind of place where women gossip while hanging laundry to dry in the sun as old men drink rum and play dominoes. In a country known for producing sugar and baseball players, Consuelo is a gold mine: Sammy Sosa, Julio Franco, Rico Carty, Alfredo Griffin, and a lineup of other current and former professional baseball players have roots there. It's been said that per capita, more pro baseball players come out of Consuelo than any other place in the world. For the

hyperkinetic children who run barefoot past Consuelo's sugar-cane factory, baseball is a way out of their hardscrabble existence. In a place where the unemployment rate exceeds 90 percent, baseball provides hope.

As in most Dominican towns, elementary school–aged children in Consuelo who show athletic potential are pressured to drop out of school and sign on with a private baseball scout, sometimes before their twelfth birthday. Scouts have entire teams of young prospects to whom they provide training, equipment, clothing, food, and often money. In return, the prospects hand over a hefty cut of their salary, sometimes as high as 30 percent, if they sign a pro contract. But the overwhelming majority of these young players never end up going pro, and when they finally give up on baseball, they don't even have an elementary school education to fall back on.

I worked for an organization with a different agenda. Beisbol y Libros (Baseball and Books) operates in the Consuelo public school system and uses baseball to keep kids in the classroom. In order to play for Beisbol y Libros, students must be enrolled in school and remain in good standing with their teachers. In this organization, you have to be a student to be a baseball player.

For a year and a half, I was the director of the program, in charge of the three hundred players, fifteen coaches, two ball fields, and the grounds crew.

The morning after the pain began, I traveled to San Pedro de Macoris, a big city located about six miles south of Consuelo, to the office of a cardiologist whom Sister Gibb had recommended. The doctor gave me the full inspection: He shaved my chest, hooked me up to clear plastic suction cups, switched on a noisy, rattling machine, and asked me a checklist of questions. When it was all over, I sat across from the doctor and waited for his computer to spit out the results of the tests, hoping he'd be able to identify what was wrong with me. Soon we got to talking.

"Oh, you're a baseball coach?" The doctor's eyes widened.

He leaned back in his chair and looked up at the ceiling before re-counting the saga of his own tragedy-shortened baseball career. He had been a good player, he said, an outfielder with a great arm, a real shot-gun. For a while he was the best player on his team. But then one day he just couldn't hit anymore, and after a while he stopped playing alto-gether. As he finished speaking, he looked like he was about to tear up.

The doctor was a big, thick man, and I could believe that he had once been an athlete. Still, it struck me as odd that in a country so en-meshed in poverty, a well-respected cardiologist would consider him-self a failure because he wasn't a washed-up ex–minor leaguer.

The doctor studied the long strip of paper that came out of the computer. There was nothing seriously wrong with my heart, he said. But to be extra careful, he attached a bulky recording device to my chest and told me to come back the next day so he could listen to the recordings of my heartbeat. I asked him if he really thought that was necessary, since his previous tests hadn't turned up anything.

"Yes, it is necessary," he replied sternly. "Because if you die, the American embassy is going to come after me." As if I hadn't under-stood him clearly, he ran his index finger across his neck, giving the universal signal for "chop the head off."

When I first came to Consuelo, long before the chest pain occurred, I couldn't seem to find a way to keep the baseball fields in good condition. I know it doesn't seem like a big deal, but my boss from the U.S. would visit every couple of months, and if the fields looked shaggy, I looked like a slacker. So about six months into my tenure, I made field maintenance my top priority.

At that time the only field worker we had—at least that I was aware of—was a middle-aged man named Kuko (pronounced Koo-koh). Kuko was a mysterious figure; he would appear on the field from time to time with a lawn mower or a rake and took long breaks in the shade with the school's maintenance workers, who were also blowing off work. Kuko had an intimidating presence, tall and beer-bellied, with a

frightening set of front teeth. Despite his terrible physique, he insisted on wearing sleeveless muscle shirts to work.

Kuko claimed to have some grounds experience in the Montreal Expos organization, which made him curiously snooty about the work he would and would not do. For example, he would mow the infield grass but would not chop the grass off the infield dirt. He would ensure the pitcher's mound was in good shape but would not chop the grass near the fence. For reasons that are still unclear, Kuko looked at chopping grass the way most people look at cleaning toilets. As a result, the infield dirt sprouted fluffy patches of grass, making it look painfully neglected.

And so it went for some time, until one day Kuko told me that I should ask the other guy to chop the grass.

"Other guy? What other guy?" I asked.

As it turned out, Beisbol y Libros actually had two groundskeepers on the payroll, and while Kuko was content to do his job poorly, the second groundskeeper didn't bother to show up at all. Once I learned the name of the second worker, I immediately tracked him down.

Eduardo Richardson was the town's star basketball player. He was well over six feet tall, with a muscled frame and a multicolored ZZ Top–style beard. The image of a fiery skull being impaled by a two-handed battle-ax was tattooed on his shoulder. Although a fabulous basketball player, Eduardo was a crappy groundskeeper. But it didn't take an employee of the month to chop grass off a dirt field, I thought. And after he promised he would begin showing up for work, I grew optimistic that he had rededicated himself to his profession.

Sure enough, Eduardo came to work the next day and even brought another worker with him. Eduardo's friend, who was a dwarf, worked steadily throughout the day, slowly chopping the grass off the infield. The next day Eduardo again showed up for work, this time with a different helper. The second friend was incredibly tall, easily over seven feet. He must be the center on the basketball team, I thought.

I was amazed. In two days of work, Eduardo had dragged two different people to work that had a height differential of about four feet. But Eduardo didn't come to work at all the next day, nor the following day. Two weeks later, we started looking for a new groundskeeper. That's how I first met Bellisario.

When I returned to the doctor's office, a day after the pain began, I un-Velcroed the device from my chest and clunked it onto the desk. The doctor popped it open, removed the tape, and slipped it into his computer. Soon I recognized the waves on the screen as the rhythms of my heart. As the lines cut across the monitor, I tried to guess what they meant, which lines were good and which lines were bad. I grew scared and nervous, just like I had a couple of months previous when I waited outside a Santo Domingo hospital for the results of my HIV test. That turned out to be nothing, and everything would be fine this time as well, I assured myself.

When the tape was finished, the doctor used a small model heart to explain what he thought was wrong with me. I had some minor blockage in one of several places in my heart, he couldn't say exactly where, that was causing irregularities in my heartbeat. It was no big deal, he said, nothing to worry about. But when I got back to the U.S., I should have it checked out. And that was it. He gave me a prescription for a special kind of aspirin and sent me on my way.

On the bus ride back to Consuelo, I thought about the diagnosis. My heart? Could that have been what was making me sick this whole time? The doctor said it wasn't a big deal, but it had to be connected to my other health issues. The best thing to do, I thought, was to get back to the U.S. so I could get checked out by a real doctor. That was the only way I was ever going to feel better.

Sister Gibb was at the convent when I returned. I explained what the doctor had said and told her that I thought I should go home. She agreed that it was best.

For the next two days, I hardly left the convent. There were people I needed to say goodbye to, but I couldn't face them. I felt ashamed

that I was leaving before the school year had ended. Instead, I stayed inside and wrote letters, maybe fifty of them, to families who had fed me, friends who had helped me learn Spanish, and coaches I had worked with. I even worked up the courage to write to Bellisario. It was a small problem with my heart, I explained, that was forcing me to return to the U.S. to see the doctor. I assured everyone that it was not serious, but I probably wouldn't be able to come back. Less than forty-eight hours later, I was gone.

Sister Gibb had recommended Bellisario for the job opening created by Eduardo's departure, so we hired him. He certainly needed the money. Every morning Bellisario would appear outside Sister Gibb's window with his homemade tools, asking if there was any yard work that needed to be done. Sometimes Sister Gibb had work, sometimes she didn't. On the days when there was no work, Bellisario and his family went hungry.

Bellisario arrived to work each day in a sun-faded navy blue polo shirt that looked huge on his unnaturally thin frame. His hair was short with gray trim, and his skin was the pitch-black hue of his Haitian ancestors. Bellisario's lifetime of hunger and hard labor in the sun showed in his behavior. He moved slowly, he forgot things, and he often seemed dizzy. As he worked, groups of small children would sometimes gather around him, pointing and calling him names, trying to provoke an angry response. More often than not, the children got what they wanted and ran away cackling.

But Bellisario was a diligent worker. Never late. Never missed a day. Every time I passed by the fields, he was out there, bent over at the waist, slashing away at grass and weeds. Plus, Bellisario was grateful to have the work. He seemed to believe that the position had been delivered to him directly from God and that I was some sort of intermediary. Once he opened his arms to the sky and told God to strike him down with lightning if he ever slacked off. The fields never looked better.

Soon, however, Bellisario began asking me for things, begging.

First it was an advance on his salary, then money for food, then there was a family emergency, then clothes . . . He started showing up at my house early in the morning, calling my name until I woke up, then asking to borrow money.

At first I didn't mind. It felt good to help the guy out. So I'd give him whatever I had on me, or arrange to get him an advance on his salary. No big deal. But gradually, my patience eroded. It was always something with him. A family member was sick, the food was all gone, the man who had loaned him money last year was threatening to beat him up if he didn't get paid immediately. It started to get to me. It shouldn't have, I know. But I began to resent Bellisario for being so needy. I mean, what the hell is he doing with his salary, anyway? Why can't he make it to the end of the month like everybody else? God, it pissed me off.

Then everything changed. It happened during a practice for the rookie team. The rookies ranged in age from five to nine and were the youngest group in the organization. As the little ballplayers zipped across the field, I had to remain alert to ensure that the outfielders didn't slam into one another or an errant bat didn't decapitate an on-deck hitter. It was hectic.

In the middle of it all, Bellisario put down his tools and approached me. I could see his exhausted figure walking toward me, trying to get my attention, but I pretended I didn't see him. It was a move I'd been using for the past couple of weeks, as my resentment for him had increased. Can't he see I'm busy?

He spoke in his usual subservient manner, staring at the ground and unsteady from the midday sun. He asked if he could have an advance on his salary. I could have taken care of it right then and there; all I had to do was walk over to the school and tell the principal to cut Bellisario a check. But I was so pissed off at him. Why couldn't he manage his money responsibly, like the other coaches? I wasn't going to be his ATM any longer. So I told him to go to the principal's office and ask for the money himself. There was pain on his face when he

heard my answer; we both knew that Bellisario never got an advance unless I was there to approve it. But that was his problem.

As he walked toward the school, Bellisario turned and asked me, "How much does blood cost?"

I had no idea, I told him.

Practice went on for another half hour before Bellisario appeared again, saying that the principal had refused to give him the money because I wasn't there. I told him I would get him the money, but he would have to wait until after practice. As he moved off the field, he asked me again about the price of blood.

How the hell should I know? I thought.

For the next two hours, Bellisario sat in the scorching sun, watching a group of toddlers chase a baseball around the field. When it was over, I walked Bellisario up to the principal's office. Along the way, he again asked about the price of blood. I said I didn't know, but the usual five-hundred-peso advance should cover whatever he needed. We entered the school's main office, and, with my approval, the principal wrote a check to Bellisario right away. As we walked out of the office, I asked Bellisario why he wanted to know the price of blood, simply to satisfy my own curiosity.

It turned out his sister was, at that very moment, in the final stages of a grueling battle with AIDS. The doctor had told him she needed blood as soon as possible, but Bellisario had spent all his money. Having no other options, he had come to me for help. And I had told him to go fuck himself.

About three months after I returned to the U.S., I got an angry phone call from my boss. He had just gotten back from a trip to Consuelo and was steamed that I hadn't bothered to remove any of my belongings from my house before I left. Shirts were still on their hangers, food was in the fridge, and books were opened to dog-eared pages.

"You might as well have left the TV on," he barked.

Nobody understood why I had left Consuelo so abruptly. I just had

to get out of there. I didn't like the person I had become. After college, I had gone into international volunteer work because I wanted to help the world's most vulnerable people, people just like Bellisario. But after almost four years of work in Africa and the Caribbean, it felt like any other crappy job. Over time, giving money to Bellisario became just another pain-in-the-ass task that I had to do at work, like mopping the floor or taking out the trash. But Bellisario was a human being, and I had somehow lost sight of that.

I had gone to Consuelo to help people, and I wasn't helping anymore. Once I realized that, the only thing I could do was leave.

My health problems worked themselves out when I got back to the U.S. A doctor examined me and said I had some minor irregularities in my heartbeat, but it was nothing I should be concerned about. The pain in my chest and arm also relented, and I have come to believe that it was only a muscle injury.

It took me longer to understand what accounted for the nausea and sleeplessness, to understand that there was more to it than just bad drinking water or being homesick.

It's a typical Saturday morning.

I wake on the old beige couch with the pattern of brown flowers in my parents' wood-paneled den. I wake with a longing, a dull ache. I've been dreaming again about that guy who hacked his own arm off. The hiker. He had recently told Tom Brokaw about being trapped in a remote canyon, his right arm pinned under an eight hundred-pound boulder, and about the way he broke his own bones, cut his flesh, arteries, and muscle, ripped through tendon and nerve to escape. I had watched the interview, transfixed, finding myself turned on by the hiker's shaggy brown curls and by the brutality of his struggle. Ever since, I'd been having visions of him laying me down on copper-colored earth.

I slip my right hand under my blanket, under cotton underwear once dark blue, now barely blue, bleached in the wash. My fingers move in a familiar way, pressing warm skin. The hiker and I are in a canyon, in the sunlight. I tingle. It's amazing what this guy can do with his good hand.

Then, in the next room, movement. The flick of a light switch. My mother steps to the kitchen sink, ten feet from where I lie. She turns the faucet and begins washing dishes and humming. Lemony soap bubbles float toward me. One drifts to the end table near my feet, dis-

appearing as it touches a framed photo of my sister and me holding hands at Disney World.

I shut my eyes. I try to shut my ears. I will my mind to return to the hiker. But what is that tune my mother is humming? Linda Ronstadt? Carly Simon? Sheena Easton. The one about the morning train. The one that is now the sound track to my hot canyon action. "My ba-by takes the morning train. He works from nine to five and then!"

Hiker, I tell myself. Hiker. Hiker. The way he looked when he showed Tom Brokaw how to rappel. Tom Brokaw rappelling. No, no. Hiker. Under my down comforter, I begin to sweat. The prickly, balled-up couch cushions sting my bare skin. I shift. I inhale sharply. I'm ready. The hiker leans down and whispers in my ear: *The pain of cutting my arm off with a dull pocketknife was the exact opposite of the exquisite joy of being inside you.*

And then, disaster.

My father enters the kitchen and with him the queer chemical odor of the nicotine gum he chews ferociously. A retired cop, he is returning home from his security job. As he unloads his gun, a bullet escapes the clip and drops onto the table. *Bounce. Bounce. Bounce.* The bullet hits the floor and rolls, rolls like an eight-hundred-pound boulder over my desire.

The hiker gets up and walks off, disgusted. I withdraw my hand.

When I first moved back in with my parents at the age of twenty-six, I did not call it "moving back in." I called it "staying with for a little while."

At the time I was fresh from a six-month trip to Mexico. I'd gone there to get my head together after quitting my job as a reporter at a small newspaper in New Jersey. It was my first job out of graduate school and one I did not have the stomach for. To do it well, I had to do things that felt obscene: watch the fire consume the home; record the politician's vitriolic comment; ring the doorbell of the woman waiting to hear if her husband had made it out of Tower One of the World Trade Center. For the two years I worked at the paper, I felt

anxious on good days and body-and-soul-tormented most of the time.

I returned from my travels ready to take another stab at making my way in the world. I had a new problem, though. Debt. The money I owed was to my parents, who—unwilling to see me plunge into the kind of credit-card debt they had always painstakingly avoided—paid my bills while I was away. The bills were substantial. For the first time in my life, I had spent money I did not have, each purchase driven by a childish certainty that I deserved a reward after soldiering on for so long in a job I loathed.

A credit-card statement showing purchases from my last full month in Mexico, December 2003, is fairly representative: $161.59 on a rental car used for a four-day road trip; $87.41 to change the return date on my plane ticket home (again); $40.40 on dinner with a friend; $108.27 on a plane ticket from the Oaxacan coast to Mexico City; $24.25 on books; $20.62 to get my hair blown out for a New Year's Eve party; and $9.81 on chocolates, for a total of $452.35.

I'd also spent thousands on tuition to a Spanish-language school and lodging. Not to mention the staggering monthly cost of maintaining my health insurance. All told, I owed my parents about $10,000, a sum I could not even begin to fathom. Would $10,000 fit in an eight-by-ten envelope? In the trunk of a taxicab?

Because I couldn't comprehend my debt, it didn't panic me. Months of finding my way alone in a foreign country had taught me that I could handle things. It was winter and I was tanned, flush with the afterglow of travel. Looped around my neck was a skinny gold scarf that I'd bought in an Oaxacan market from a woman who had convinced me it was a talisman.

There was no room for me, really, at my parents' modest one-story home in northern New Jersey. My younger sister had long ago taken over the bedroom we'd shared as girls. But my parents offered to let me stay on their couch until I could afford to pay my debt and move. I was grateful. I imagined myself a willing serf, living on land that did not belong to me, working to earn my freedom.

Above the couch was a picture window with a view of the Manhattan skyline. During the day, I watched the light fall on the buildings and thought, as I had since I was a little girl, that it was a signal to me. In the late afternoons, the sun flashed intricate patterns on skyscrapers, a special coded message. *Not yet, not yet,* it said. *Soon.*

I told only close friends about my return to the nest, reasoning that my stay would be so brief, no one else would ever need to know about it. "I'll find a job, pay what I owe, and move to the city," I declared, as though all of this would require little more effort than placing a catalog order. Then I made a critical mistake. I said, "I'll be out of here by July." I did not know that, in speaking those words, I had just broken the first rule of reentry, a rule straight out of our own president's playbook: Never set a pullout date.

Back in my small hometown, I felt like a child who had somehow stolen a glimpse of the future. Every bra-snapping boy I'd gone to grammar school with had become a cop. They patrolled the same few blocks over and over in sleek black-and-white police cruisers, circling like sharks. I saw their puffy faces in my rearview mirror as I drove to the post office to send out batches of résumés.

The girls I knew, too, were grown up, so grown up that they had to clip their cell phones to their waists whenever they left their homes, in case a baby ran a fever or a husband needed to know where his navy pants were. Meanwhile, I used my cell phone to place calls to my parents that sounded remarkably like ones I'd made as a nervous eighteen-year-old: "I shouldn't be too late. Yep, I'll be careful with the car. No, no drinking."

The news was full of people in the same predicament. Apparently, moving back in with your parents was a bona fide trend, a new rite of passage; almost eighteen million eighteen-to-thirty-four-year-olds were living at home. Every journalist, cultural commentator, and sociologist had invented a different weird name for this unfortunate lot: adultescents, boomerangers, kidults, thresholders, twixters.

"Most people moving home today will find that the stigma of liv-

ing at home has all but disappeared," assured Elina Furman in her book *Boomerang Nation.* Her expertise came from the rather dubious achievement of having lived at home herself until the age of thirty. "Boomerangers are proud, loud, and not afraid to show the world that they mean business."

I was neither proud nor loud. I was, in truth, mortified. The way I saw it, returning home was worse than if, like my younger sister, I had never left at all. And I wasn't in my early twenties, right out of college, when such backslides were acceptable, even expected. I believed there were noble reasons to move back home (caring for a sick parent) and there were practical reasons (saving to buy property), but paying off chocolates and blow-dries charged on a Mexican holiday didn't fall under either of those categories.

Though a friend of mine (I'll call him Chris) lived at home for what I saw as a sound reason (putting money aside for a condo), he felt ashamed, too. He'd recently initiated sex in his car rather than bringing a date back to his parents' basement.

"So I had lunch at the Outback Steakhouse," he told me on the phone one day.

"Mmm," I said, watching television. The commercial that I hated was on. It was for a bank and showed a young woman—small and blond and pixie-faced and probably freckled—in a city, on her own for the first time. In a nauseating montage, she collected her first paycheck, bought a bulldog, sat on her bed and puzzled over her checkbook, threw down her debit card at brunch with girlfriends, panicked at the ATM, then, finally, confirmed her bank balance on her cell phone outside a movie theater and—Phew! The pet store check cleared!—rushed into the arms of the man waiting for her. The whole awful thing was set to "Love Is All Around," the *Mary Tyler Moore Show* theme song.

When the voices sang "You're going to make it after all," I mouthed, "No, you're not." When the girl kissed her boyfriend, I muttered, "You whore."

"Our waitress was the prettiest girl in the world," Chris was saying. "I wanted to talk to her, but I was embarrassed."

"*You* were embarrassed?" I snorted. "She works at the Outback Steakhouse." On the scale of life's humiliations, it was hard to know exactly where living at home ranked, but I liked to think we were better off than the waitstaff at the Outback, who daily were subjected to uttering phrases like "Jackeroo chops" and "Kookaburra wings."

Chris wasn't convinced. "I know, but I live with my parents," he said.

In the spring, I got a job. The figure printed on my first paycheck should have made it clear that I would not, in fact, be "out of here by July." My parents knew it. They casually spoke of putting a door on the den, creating a more permanent space for me. But I scoffed at the idea and continued to store my clothes in a garbage bag. I refused even to start a magazine subscription because of the interruption in service that would occur when I switched mailing addresses. Of course, I did not date. Better to wait, I told myself, and start fresh when I moved.

I remember, sometime that first year, standing at a party, sweating and checking the time every three minutes. This was a night I had been dreading. The other guests were journalists, professional question-askers.

I had learned, since moving home, that there was only one question in the world: Where do you live? On any given day, there were many askers: a coworker breaking the silence of an elevator ride, an acquaintance from college whom I bumped into at 7-Eleven, the woman cutting my hair at the mall.

"Oh," I would lie, "I'm sort of nomadic right now. I pretty much just got back from Mexico. I was living there for a year." (I believed adding six months to my stay made it sound more impressive.) Then I rushed into a story about visiting graves heaped with marigolds during the Days of the Dead. Or shared a heartbreaking anecdote about the orphanage I volunteered at, or delivered my hilarious account of running out of toll money on a Mexican highway. I called this tactic Distract and Entertain; it usually worked. But I knew it would be tough to

pull off with reporters, trained diggers who understood the art of the follow-up question.

I'd arrived at the party early, hoping to be long gone by the time most people showed up. But my plan had backfired spectacularly. There were so few people—fewer than a dozen gathered in a bright studio apartment—that I couldn't hide. Everyone was sitting in a circle. Some of the guests were former colleagues whom I hadn't seen in a long time and who, I imagined, would be curious about my current situation. Jazz music was playing softly—no chance of that drowning out any conversations. How long did I have before someone asked the question and everyone looked over at me? How to get away?

Desperate, I requested a tour of the (one-room) apartment. Then I busied myself in the small kitchen area, pondering the drink offerings, fussing over the appetizers. I took frequent trips to the bathroom to think of topics I could raise in the group. I asked the questions, and they were inane: Whatever happened to so-and-so? Remember the case of such-and-such? Whatever happened with that? When someone made even the smallest joke, I laughed loud and long. While I laughed, I thought up more questions. After a few agonizing hours, I escaped into the cool night air, exhausted from the effort.

By that time, life at home had started to wear on me. I felt, as I had so often when I was a teenager, that there wasn't enough air in the house for the four of us; the walls were closing in. My quick temper, so successfully caged in recent years, loosed itself. I was angry when my mother left the door unlocked for me (did she think me incapable of using a key?). I was angry when she locked the door (did she really think, in this boring town, there was a need?). I was annoyed when, as I walked in the house after a long day at work, my father was already asking, "How was your day? How was your drive?" I was pissed that I had to stoop and hide behind the armchair in the den so that the neighbors didn't see me undress through the window. (I gave it up at last, and began to hope they were watching me, and started taking off my clothes with a flourish.) I was tired of rooting around in a garbage

bag every morning to find my underwear. I was upset that I could no longer remember the simple thrill of a man removing my underwear. I was damn sick of masturbating; I did it so often that my right forearm routinely cramped from elbow to hand and I sometimes had trouble gripping the steering wheel in the morning.

I saved a lot of my fury for myself because the only thing that made me feel better anymore was the same thing that had gotten me into the mess: spending money. Although I wrote my parents a check most months, the amount of that check varied greatly. I might pay them $1,500 one month and $150 the next. Sometimes it wasn't really my fault (dental work that wasn't covered by my insurance), but most of the time it was (a trip to Costa Rica; a $300 Nicole Miller dress; third-row tickets to a play).

I had also—this is hard to admit—started to furnish an imaginary apartment, beginning with small items (an area rug, throw pillows, artwork) and culminating, unbelievably, in the most psychotic purchase of all: a $500 pink armchair. I stored the chair, wrapped in plastic, in my parents' basement. At night, after everyone had fallen asleep, I sometimes went down and sat on it, trying hard to imagine a future me curled up on the chair with a phone pressed against her ear, talking to someone who loved her.

I spent to make up for the life I did not have and, in doing so, prevented myself from having that life. It was a pathetic cycle.

Through all this, my parents never nagged me for the money. They never asked me where I got off spending money on pillows and designer dresses when I owed them thousands of dollars. Perhaps they were letting me learn the lesson.

One of my mother's favorite sayings is "You dance, you pay the fiddler." Whenever she says it, I am reminded of "The Pied Piper of Hamelin." In that story, after the piper rid Hamelin of rats with his enchanted music, the town officials refused to pay the agreed-upon fee. So the piper played his magical flute, and all the town's children followed him, dancing out of Hamelin forever.

When I was a little girl, the idea of a man in tights who could lure

kids to follow him through a secret door inside a mountain, never to be seen again, terrified me. I used to think the story was about the separation of parent and child. I see it now, of course: "The Pied Piper" is about promises, debts that must be paid.

In April 2005, at the age of twenty-five, my younger sister moved out. But, to my parents' dismay, I refused to take over her vacant bedroom. "What's the point? I'm already set up out here," I said, shrugging. What held me back, really, was fear. I was scared that I would enter that bedroom, shut the door behind me, and come out thirty-five.

By this time, I was twenty-seven and had been sleeping on the couch for fifteen months. I'd finally moved my clothing and other belongings into plastic bins, which dominated the den. Looking at the clutter one day, my mother turned to me and said, "Someday we'll wonder how we did this. Living like this, in this cubicle."

One weekend that summer, I traveled to Washington, D.C., on a business trip. I was relieved to get away and marveled at my hotel room. My very own bathroom! A door! A lock! A sign that keeps people away! I kicked back with a few glasses of white wine to celebrate my freedom. Then I had a few more.

The next morning I awoke with a wicked hangover. I was due by eight A.M. to join serious people at a serious building for a daylong meeting. It was all I could do to shower and put on a suit and stockings, pausing several times to vomit (in my very own toilet!).

At the serious building, I stood unsteadily on line with a few coworkers, waiting to pass through security. As I handed over my license for inspection, a colleague, a higher-up, turned to me suddenly, as though seeing my license had jogged something in his memory. "I heard that you . . ." He paused, as though weighing whether a rumor so outrageous was worth mentioning.

"I heard that you live with your parents," he said. "That's not true . . . is it?"

I understood, I think for the first time, what it meant to reel, to be

reeling. The ground swayed, or I swayed. All I could see were the flags of the world hanging in the building lobby. I wondered if the people on line next to me were diplomats or foreign heads of state, if they had heard the question, if they knew the answer.

I heard myself begin to speak about Mexico, about being in between places. God, I was so fucking sick of saying it.

The man cut me off: "Time to get out, don't you think?"

In a sad effort to come to my aid, a female coworker chirped, "Well, it's the cheapest rent around!" We went upstairs to our meeting. At lunch, I excused myself to use the bathroom. Security was so tight that a chaperone had to accompany me; she waited outside as I retched in the toilet.

Later, I was trapped into accepting a ride home from the same man, who lived in Manhattan, and another colleague, who lived in Connecticut. I sat silent in the backseat, my teeth gritted with vomit, my mind racing. We would hit New Jersey first. There was no way in hell I was letting these people drop me off at home. What if my father was mowing the lawn, a sweaty red bandanna tied around his forehead, wearing his green jungle boots from Vietnam? What if my mother was standing at the window waiting for me? What if they came out to help me with my suitcase, meet my workmates? What would people at the office say?

"You can just drop me in Manhattan," I said as we barreled down the highway near my house.

"Are you sure?"

"Yes." We were passing my exit now.

"It seems odd to me," observed the man who had grilled me earlier, "for you to be in New Jersey and then go through Manhattan to get back to New Jersey." He was clearly either a sadist or some sort of ruthless undercover detective.

"Well, I'm actually not going home," I lied.

"Uh-oh! Party girl!" he teased. I forced the type of giggle that I imagined might come from a party girl.

When they asked where to drop me off, my brain wouldn't pro-

duce an answer; it had given up cooperating with this madness. "Any-where," I said again and again. Finally, I told them to drop me in Union Square, for no reason at all.

I unloaded my suitcase, thanked them, and walked off down the street. It was dark now, still sticky-hot, and the suitcase banged the back of my ankles as I hurried off nowhere to meet no one. I clunked down the subway stairs to the PATH train and then switched to the New Jersey Transit rail. The train slipped past the swamps of the Meadowlands, past the lights of the football stadium, all the way back home.

There is something—let's be honest—inherently perverse about living with your parents as an adult. I think this when I see the way my music library, set up on the family computer, has mixed in with my father's: his Ricky Nelson mingling with my Rickie Lee Jones, his Four Seasons with my Flaming Lips, our Bob Dylans overlapping.

I thought of this unnaturalness, too, when I saw the January 2005 *Time* magazine cover story about twixters. The cover headline screamed THEY JUST WON'T GROW UP. The photograph was of a grown man, or a man-child, sitting scrunched in a toddler's sandbox, his knees pressed against his chest.

I think of this especially now. The New York tabloids are full of breathless dispatches about a man they are calling the "Fake Fireman Perv." Dressed as a New York City firefighter, the man had set small fires outside a building in order to trick his way into the apartment of a thirty-four-year-old woman on Halloween night. Once inside, he knocked her out with a chloroform-soaked rag, tied her up, and sexually assaulted her for thirteen hours.

The suspect in the sickening attack, a former journalist, was on the run from cops. Every day the papers offered more evidence of his depravity. The *New York Post* told of "creepy passages" he'd underlined in books, his obsession with Edie Sedgwick, and the fact that, before going on the lam, the forty-one-year-old suspect had lived with his mother.

He'd lied about it, telling people that he lived in a "Manhattan penthouse with a wealthy woman who was an aspiring actress," the *Post* reported. A coworker recalled the time when she'd traced a phone call from the suspect back to his mother's apartment in Queens. "So I put it together that he was probably living in his mother's basement," she said. "So the joke after that is that he's George Costanza— a forty-year-old loser living in his mother's basement."

Reading the woman's comment, I wondered if this was what I had struggled so hard against. Was I scared that people would call me a loser if they knew I lived with my parents? Or consider my situation and, by extension me, sad and freakish? Or had the shame sprung from the fact that I thought these things myself?

My final check to my parents was pink and made out for $250. Handing it over did not make me feel unburdened, as I had once imagined it would. Instead, as savings for my own apartment accumulate now, I fret about reentering the world. How will I hang the curtains? I wonder helplessly. How will I sleep at night, knowing I am all alone?

I don't know how much longer I will live with my parents. In some ways, I am only just arriving. Not long ago, I packed up my things in the den. I carried them to the empty bedroom that had been my sister's and, before that, both of ours. I emptied the plastic bins, stacking up my books and slipping my clothes onto hangers. I hung a framed Loretta Lynn album cover in the center of the bare white wall. I sat down on the floor and said out loud, "You are here."

"Your hair is as dark as a handful of black pebbles held in moon-light," his mother says in Hmong. "It would be beautiful to the male eye!"

And he knows exactly what she, having borne no daughters, really means. It's his twenty-third birthday, so he's taken the day off from school for this haircut, a monthly tradition he and his brothers have shared with their mother for the last two decades. Ten dollars at a bar-bershop would've saved him the embarrassment that she still cuts his hair. He's never told anyone about these cuts, not even Stephen.

In the kitchen, the stove rattles. The bamboo steamer hisses as if they're cooking snakes for lunch. There are three cups of *mov ntshav*—literally translated as "blood rice," commonly known as sweet or sticky rice—steaming. His mother purchased a fifty-pound bag at the local Hmong market this morning after frisking through grocery bins for the freshest bundles of bok choy, Chinese broccoli, and a napa cabbage. The aroma has a buttery richness that is thick enough to drown the scent of green soaps and potpourri in their bath-room, where he is waiting for the buzz of the clippers.

"Your wife would envy such a dark and lovely shade," his mother compliments again, her index and middle fingers scooping through

his hair like chopsticks. "Look how thick it is! If only you were a daughter!"

"If only," he says, breathing in the sweet rice.

"Maybe your hair is too beautiful," she says, "that's why you don't have a girlfriend." She clicks the clippers on, the black cord twisting like a snake, and begins mowing the right side of his head.

Tiny hairs drop to his toes. He's not interested in anyone at the moment.

"I met an aunt at the market today. Her daughter is your age," his mother insists. She is always playing matchmaker.

He tells her he'll find someone on his own, to which she protests, "You'll only stay like this!"

"I'm only twenty-three," he says.

"Time passes faster than you think!" she bites. "You'll be thirty, then forty, and this beautiful hair will start to turn white, just like mine."

His father married her when she was fourteen; he was probably seventeen or eighteen then. In Laos, the old country, a person between the ages of fourteen and seventeen was considered mature enough to settle down, have six or seven children, and grow their own crops.

"Whatever you do in life," she says, as if ending a story with the moral to it, "you'll *need* a wife. Don't be like a Hmong man I once knew."

She wants him to ask her who the man is. How can he resist?

"Someone from the old country," she replies.

The man lived in one of the camps in the Xieng Khouang province during the secret war in Laos. He was tall, handsome, quiet, and kindhearted. Though he had never raised a rifle against a Pathet Lao or North Vietnamese Communist, he served the Hmong soldiers effortlessly as he cooked for them, washed their clothes, and tended their wounds day and night. It all seemed very patriotic for the victory of the people. Nothing out of the ordinary. But then the war progressed. And he grew older.

The men he knew began dying in battle and from diseases. Wives became widows. Sons dropped in fields clutching their fathers' rifles. One day he came back to his village to visit his parents. He was furious to discover that a wife—a village girl—had been purchased for him. At night he curled against the wall while the young wife wondered what she had gotten herself into, not that she had a choice, since her family was poor and needed the dowry money. Days turned into weeks of silence for the newlyweds. Their time together was fruitless. He could not make love to her through the long months. The war that had shaken the country outlasted their arranged marriage. Eventually, he returned the poor girl to her parents. He went back to the camp, never to return again. In the end, the villagers asked the young girl why she did not cry about his abrupt and unfathomable decision, to which she answered, "He was never a real man!"

His mother lets out a sigh. "It's all true," she says, nodding. She has not once mentioned the man's name during the story. He doesn't ask for it.

He lets her continue buzzing the back of his head and on to his left side. He is falling through the silence between them. The only sounds are from the steamer and the clippers. After all these years, it has become a kind of meditation. He closes his eyes. The vibration numbs his scalp, leading him into nostalgia. He is thinking of Stephen again. He hasn't held a hand in a long time, felt the simple warmth of two people.

In the few months they spent together, he told his family that Stephen was a colleague he had become buddies with. He'd met Stephen, unlike the men he chatted with on the Internet, through the school's teaching credential program. He wonders what his parents, especially his mother, would've done if they had discovered the truth. He imagines how the secret would have burned away their faces, their traditions and customs regarding marriage and family, their whole take on human morality. Since birth, he has never seen his parents holding

hands or hugging. Did they ever kiss while conceiving him? "Sex isn't talked about, it's a natural expectation," he had told Stephen once. The Hmong community isn't ready for their kind, let alone America.

So they kept it on the low. His mother didn't suspect anything, at least not until the night Stephen left his wallet in their living room after paying the delivery guy from Pizza Hut. The two had been working on a class project up into the evening, discussing student statistics in the Fresno Unified School District, when he told his mother not to cook for them. She was offended that her son had chosen delivery over her cooking, which he had loved all his life, which she always impressed her visitors with. He only wanted to keep his mother from having to rummage through the fridge for the sake of their bellies. He would have canceled the pizza.

The next morning she discovered Stephen's wallet by the lamp, and instead of placing it on top of the fireplace, she opened it. He wasn't there to witness the alarm in her eyes when she pulled a Polaroid cutout of a younger Stephen in the arms of his ex-boyfriend from the side pocket. It was a photo he never would've known Stephen still carried if his mother had not brought it to his attention. The next night she walked into his room and dropped the picture and the wallet on his desk. She didn't say anything. He was startled and hurt by his mother and the photo. So he acted surprised about his friend's sexual preference but not disgusted by it. He told his mother that Stephen was just a school colleague—that he was glad she had found out who the guy *really* was, but she should have respected the privacy of other people's belongings, especially something as personal as a wallet. She disagreed, saying it was her right to know about everything that went on under her roof, especially about people like Stephen.

There were several occasions after the wallet incident on which he had invited Stephen to join his family for dinner. While the family ate with silver utensils, his mother would give his friend an ugly red spoon he had never seen before.

"Why is my spoon different?" Stephen whispered at the table the first time it happened.

He lied that it was a guest privilege to eat with the red one. He doesn't remember if Stephen looked at his eyes. He was furious, but he didn't know what to say then, looking as surprised as Stephen at the spoon. The family kept their eyes down on their plates, but it wasn't their food they were looking at. He was angry at his mother for a long time, wondering if she had bought the red spoon from the local Hmong market, though he never confronted her about it. Besides the few dinners at his house, he and Stephen went to the movies, shared long conversations about their goals and common interests over quiet dinners at certain secluded restaurants, and parked in deserted parking lots. But the red spoon was always in the back of his mind, blooming like a drop of blood on white cloth, no matter what they were doing. Things began to fall apart between them. He became silent most of the time, not giving Stephen an honest answer whenever he was asked if something was wrong. At the end of five months, he let Stephen go, and the red spoon returned to the kitchen drawer.

His mother is halfway finished with the haircut. She sets down the clippers, then sweeps her fingers through his bangs like wind through grass. When she's pulled the right amount up toward the bathroom light, she snips off two inches with the scissors. She repeats that he shouldn't be alone anymore—that every Hmong man needs a wife before thirty, and that she wants a daughter-in-law, which will be the closest thing to having a daughter of her own. When she's finished with the top, she does her usual scrutinizing around his whole head for any hairs left sticking out longer than they should be. There are a few above the left sideburn, next to the ear. She chooses the scissors instead of the clippers. The metal is cold against his skin. The cut is quick, like lemongrass through flesh. Red grains drop from his ear. He swallows the cry, though the sting will stay forever.

After the haircut, he is bandaged. While he showers, she puts the

sweet rice into her bamboo basket and sets it on the kitchen table, where they will eat together. He's been drifting through six months of solitude. He hasn't entered a chat room in a long time. The water is hot on his face. The air is unbearable. He is standing in a womb again, eyes closed, thinking of the years ahead, men slipping out of his life like hair down the drain. He will come to know the silence of old age better than anyone else. He envies the widow's privilege. The son who will die in battle. He is the one who will return to his desolate camp empty of soldiers, sit white-haired like an old maid among rusty cookware and dry canteens, and listen to the wind cutting through tall grass.

When he enters the kitchen, she is already waiting at the table, quietly sipping a cup of ginseng tea. He joins her with a spoon from the drawer, though sweet rice is always eaten with fingers. He appreciates the silence at his end of the table.

"The red spoon is forbidden," his mother says, slightly lifting her eyes. "Family members should not use it."

The rice is sweeter than usual, stickier this time around. He eats with privilege.

THINK OUTSIDE THE BOX BUT STAY INSIDE THE GRID
FINDING THE BEAT YOU SHALL GO OUT WITH JOY AND BE
LED FORTH WITH PEACE THE IDIOT'S GUIDE TO YOUR PALM
SHEER DOMINANCE LIVE NUDE GIRL AN EVENING IN APRIL
CLICHÉ RAPE STORY ROCK MY NETWORK GOODBYE TO ALL THAT
ALL THE RIGHT ANSWERS WHY I HAD TO LEAVE IN-BETWEEN PLACES
A RED SPOON FOR THE NAMELESS **MY LITTLE COMMA** FIGHT ME
THE SECRET LIVES OF MY PARENTS MY ROARING TWENTIES
IN, FROM THE OUTSIDE THE MYSTERIES OF LIFE . . . REVEALED!
SO YOU SAY YOU WANT A REVOLUTION WORKING AT WENDY'S
JESS LACHER MARY BETH ELLIS BRONSON LEMER JENNIFER GLASER
RACHEL KEMPF JOHN FISCHER SHAHNAZ HABIB EMMA BLACK
ELI JAMES KYLE MINOR COLLEEN KINDER CHRISTOPHER POLING
KATHLEEN ROONEY RADHIYAH AYOBAMI MARISA McCARTHY
THEODORA STITES EULA BISS BRENDAN PARK LUKE MULLINS
MARY KATE FRANK BURLEE VANG **ELRENA EVANS**
MICLIVN FITZWATER KATE McGOVERN LAUREN MONROE

When I opened my eyes, I couldn't see. The light was harsh after the darkness I had plunged myself into for all of the five minutes it took to push my first baby out from my body and into the world. As the time had come to push, my midwife asked if I wanted to see, and, thoroughly disgusted by the thought (I had, after all, watched the movies in our prepared childbirth classes), I chose to shut my eyes. I was so intent on not seeing the miracle of birth, and on screaming to my husband not to look, that it came as a shock to hear the words "she's a girl!" and realize my daughter was here. We reached for each other, both blinking, both wet, both startled by our surroundings, and I heard my own voice crying, "she has red hair," just like my own. I collapsed against my husband as he wrapped his arms around his new family, and through the tears and the kisses, I looked at my daughter and knew she was, without question, the coolest thing I had ever done.

I am determined not to let my daughter get in the way of my studies. It looks so harsh, written out in black and white, but it is the truth, the hard truth I have to face as punishment for having a baby in graduate school. Most of my friends say I will never succeed, and I am determined to prove them wrong. A select few say of course I can do it,

a baby shouldn't stand in the way of a Ph.D., and I want them, desperately, to be right . . . at least sometimes I think I do. As a woman at the turn of the millennium, I can have it all: the husband, the child, the education, the career. But I stop to wonder, as I save my work and turn to pick up the baby, if I really want it all. If the legacy we have fought for as women is the ability to choose to do anything, what happens if I simply choose to be a wife and a mother? I couldn't do that; it would feel like a betrayal. I have a legacy to uphold, and now an example to set for my child. I nestle her against my chest as we rock, and I nurse her. I sing to her, talk to her, tell her stories of strong young women much like the woman she can grow up to be. And I read to my daughter. *Goodnight Moon. The Very Hungry Caterpillar. The Baby Goes Beep.* Then, with a nod to my studies, I read her *The Giver.* We walk into the kitchen and marvel at an apple.

My life has become a series of moments, an odd amalgamation of dirty dishes and thesis research, dirty laundry and comprehensive bibliographies. Added to this already complicated mix, my daughter now serves as the connective tissue linking fragments together, as my time is separated and divided, measured and spaced, by her constant needs. I write a paragraph and stop to change a diaper. I read a chapter of a book and stop to nurse. I revisit my paragraph, dismiss it as derivative, delete it, and change another diaper. I reread the chapter I didn't absorb the first time and stop again to nurse. These constant pauses give rhythm to my day and provide a cadence to my life. I begin to refer to my daughter as my little comma, the requisite pause at the end of every task. I type another sentence, delete it, then turn and pick her up once more. My comma. My caesura. My Selah.

I am in awe of my breasts. I've spent the bulk of my postpubescent life indifferent to them, these strange lumps that disfigure my clothing and serve as constant reminders of the end of my dream of dancing professionally. At best, they are toys I don't even play with; at worst, they are twin nuisances that must always be lifted, supported, and cov-

ered. But now I feel like my daughter is the Rosetta stone for the world of boobies. With her in my arms, I finally understand my breasts.

My determination to breast-feed was almost overpowered in the first few weeks of being a nursing mother. Her unrelenting need, the indescribable pain, and the realization that, although no one makes a nursing bra in a 34G, it is, in fact, a size (and I've got it), all combined to make me wonder if that pasty-looking gunk in the formula cans is really all that bad. But with help from a lactation consultant and a certain amount of personal grit, we stuck it out, and as she moved from the twenty-fifth percentile on the baby growth chart to the seventieth, the ninetieth, and then clear off the curve, I realized I had found a new passion. Nursies fix everything, my husband proclaims; my daughter nurses when she's hungry, nurses when she's tired, nurses when she's bored. We have good-morning nursies, good-night nursies, comfort nursies, silly nursies, marathon nursies. I am amazed by the contentment she finds at my breast. She pats my chest and plays with my hair, hums to herself while she eats, and occasionally laughs so hard my milk squirts out her nose. I am at a loss to see what's so funny, but I am glad I can provide such happiness for my daughter.

Through her eyes, I have new respect for my breasts. I discuss this with her as she eats. They aren't all bad, I tell her. They can get you dates. They can get you jobs. They can get you out of speeding tickets. And they mean the world to little babies. I pause when I see my husband shaking his head at me, then change my tune and tell her, don't you ever let me catch you using your breasts to get attention. God gave you a brain, and that will always be your best asset. I launch into more inspiring stories of intelligent women who have done great things until she falls asleep, milk dribbling everywhere, the picture of peace and contentment. I wonder if I believe the things I am telling her.

As we watch *Star Trek* together one afternoon (ignoring the American Academy of Pediatrics' recommendation that children not be allowed any television until the age of two, and wondering again if anyone in the American Academy of Pediatrics actually has children),

an ad for the *Sports Illustrated Swimsuit Special* comes on. I am disgusted and move to flick the channel, then spot my daughter. She is bouncing with glee, waving her arms and squealing as voluptuous women press their goods up into the camera. I laugh at her delight; to her, this must look like a smorgasbord. You would be disappointed if you met those ladies, I tell her. None of their nursies work, and half of them are plastic anyway. In a moment of revelation, I realize I am infinitely superior to the *Sports Illustrated* swimsuit models. And, at the moment, better endowed. I twirl with my daughter and we laugh, until I ask myself, why do I need to do anything else? Why am I in grad school again? The tagline from an Internet post rings through my head as we spin: "I make milk; what's your superpower?"

This morning, with only minor assistance from my husband, I managed to get the baby in the car seat, the car seat in the car, and the stroller in the trunk (with about a quarter inch of clearance on all sides) and transport a fed (twice), changed (once), dry (momentarily), rested (thankfully), bundled (under protest), happy (finally) twelve-week-old with me to campus for an eight A.M. meeting with my (male) advisor. To the list of triumphs I should also add figuring out how to both uncollapse and recollapse the stroller, attach and detach the car seat from its stay-in-car base, attach and detach said car seat from the stroller, and navigate my way from the parking lot clear to the other end of campus without having to use any of the many paths that involve stairs. I am also showered, fed, dressed, and wearing a modicum of makeup. Truly, I am superwoman.

As I navigate the stroller back to the car while the temperature plummets and it begins to sleet, I congratulate myself on being able to continue my studies and not succumb to the all-consuming nature of motherhood. I can do this, I am doing this, and all the people who doubted me, including myself . . . but I stop short. I have taken a wrong path and am about to push the stroller down a double flight of stairs. Undaunted, I turn around. We are now walking into the wind as the temperature continues to drop and I search for a place to safely

steer the stroller. My daughter begins to cry. She is hungry, tired, and cold; I have lost my way and cannot find a path that doesn't end in stairs. My daughter begins to cry louder, her piercing wails accelerating my heart rate as I frantically steer the stroller around another building in a vain attempt to get back to the parking lot. I am lost, my fingers are numb, and I can only imagine how my poor baby feels. There is nothing for it but to press on, and as I hurry I start to lose it. Soon I am crying along with my baby, the tears freezing on my cheeks after having smeared my mascara, clownlike, in streaks down my face.

The parking lot is at last in sight, and as I break into a run, I spot an old roommate walking toward me with her new husband. They are dressed immaculately, crisp suits and woolen trench coats whispering money as they clip across the barren ground. I make a vain attempt to pull myself together as my roommate prattles on about campus recruiting on behalf of the multibillion-dollar company she and her husband both work for. Then she asks to see the baby. I pull back the blanket, and my precious, chubby-cheeked, rosy-lipped baby has devolved into a purple ball of frozen, snot-covered misery. My roommate recoils, murmuring something about "how adorable" as she shudders. I try to explain, to say my daughter usually isn't like this, but my former roommate is already hurrying away, clinging tightly to her husband's arm in an attempt to ward off any possible contagion that might someday make her be like me. She is secure and confident in her choices; she is rich, warm, childless, and content. I am bawling along with my baby on a busy street in a college town, the balancing act I pulled off this morning crashing down around me. Who am I trying to fool, I ask myself as my daughter and I cry buckets of tears and snot. I can't do this.

Sometimes I wish I were Catholic. I find the idea of confessional strangely therapeutic, and I long for the catharsis of cleansing my soul through fessing up to a man of the cloth. I confess, I would say that not a single piece of clothing owned by any member of my family is currently folded in a drawer. I confess that I pretended to sleep

through the baby noise this morning in hopes that my husband would take her downstairs (which he did). I confess that I left my cat's throw-up on the rug on the off chance the other cat would eat it and I wouldn't have to deal with it. I confess that I let my baby sleep on her stomach. I confess that I want to drop out of school. I confess that before I call my (single, childless, six-figure-income) best friend, I make a list of things to talk about so I won't accidentally talk about the baby and thus become uninteresting. I confess that I really want to drop out of school. I confess that sometimes I want a new best friend, one who understands this strange new world I've fallen into where the right color poop means you are a Good Mother. After weeks of green, spinachy-looking poop, I would call her triumphantly and say, we are finally back to seedy and mustard-colored! She would congratulate me on my poop accomplishments and we would arrange to go out for a celebratory coffee (decaffeinated, of course, because my new best friend would also be breast-feeding). Then she would show up at my house in tears because she has no clean laundry and no way to do any, as her washing machine has gotten completely derailed by a baby sock sucked up into the hose. And I would scoop up her snot-nosed, crying, stomach-sleeping, seedy-mustard-colored-poop-leaking baby into my arms and console her. Then we would zap hot chocolate in the microwave and sit on the couch with our babies amid nursing pillows, baby blankets, spit-up cloths, and those stupid washing-machine-hose-clogging baby socks. We'd watch *Bridget Jones's Diary*. We'd laugh together over Bridget's foibles and smile, smug in our knowledge that, if nothing else, at least we went and got ourselves sprogged up before we were thirtysomething. Bless us, Father. For we have sinned. We had our babies before our careers. And we're loving every snotty, poopy minute of it.

The conference for which I'm trying to finish this piece is looming ever closer, and I'm scared to share what I write. I've spent the bulk of my writing career refusing to share, and it's become a habit I'm

comfortable in. I never submit anything, anywhere; with only one exception, I haven't since I was in high school. I jokingly tell my family that I can't submit my work, my pieces are my children, and being rejected would be like having someone tell me I have an ugly baby. (Which, thank God, and with apologies for being so shallow, I am thrilled to say I do not.)

But now the reticence is even stronger. My writing is not only my child, it is also, with increasing frequency, about my child—my real, flesh-and-blood, living, breathing, nursing baby. The thought of her somehow being rejected, or of my not being able to write well enough to represent her, makes it hurt to breathe.

My baby sits on the kitchen counter in the trendy, overpriced, ergonomic baby seat I swore I wouldn't buy because I didn't want to be one of "those mothers." She chortles to herself as I empty the dishwasher, and, out of curiosity, I hand her a soft plastic baby spoon. She immediately puts the spoon in her mouth, and I am elated. My infant daughter is the next Amelia Earhart, Pocahontas, Marie Curie. I have given birth to the first female president of the United States of America, until a baby's wail interrupts my reverie. The future president is now shoving a plastic baby spoon firmly into her right eye. She is not, in fact, the next Marie Curie. I scoop her up from her baby seat, and we go and have a comfort nursie.

I just got off the phone with my advisor, and if my daughter weren't watching me, I swear I would spit. The pressure is on, he admonishes me: finish your project or lose our funding. I wonder: if he knew how close I was to leaving, what he would say? I wonder what would happen if I left in the middle of the year, just scooped up my plump little baby and left. I wouldn't wait until the end of the semester to go, and I wouldn't leave everything tidied up behind me. I'd simply up and leave, tear myself out of the university and leave a gaping, jagged hole in my wake. My spine prickles guiltily at the thought. What a

lovely mess I would make. Part of me just wants to say "I don't care" and wait for the lion to eat me.

I am in love with my husband. I am in love with my child. And I want to leave the university. But could I do it? Could I turn my back on academia and spend my days just playing house and giving tummy kisses? More important, could I make myself stop there, or would that just be the first step on an inevitable slide into middle-aged suburbia, little chichi gardens, minivans, and scrapbooking? Could I go to a cocktail party, hold my head up high, and introduce myself as a stay-at-home mom? And who the heck is going to invite me to a cocktail party if I'm only a stay-at-home mom? I lean over to pick up my little one for one last nighttime nursie, and as she drifts back to sleep and we cuddle in the bed her chubby fingers stroke my hair, lying in a curl across my chest. My husband snores, rolls over, and reaches for me, and the three of us snuggle together for a moment. We are content.

And I know the answer to my question is yes. I can give it up; I don't need the university. I can be a stay-at-home mom and a wife to my husband and be perfectly content with my life. I can go to the party (if someone invites me) and proudly introduce myself as just a mother. I can do it, I really can. If I have my Ph.D.

Your elbow is the hardest part of your body.

I learned this in a self-defense workshop I went to at work one time. It was the company-sponsored kind where you take two hours from your job and do a bunch of yelling and getting in touch with your inner Wonder Woman, with muffins and juice at the end.

I am reminded of this fact when I run smack into a woman in my hotel lobby, jabbing my elbow into her shoulder. I wasn't looking where I was going. She seems peeved, but I am left wondering what her excuse is for having run into *me*. Amazingly, she doesn't say anything—I imagine she feels at least half responsible, which is correct. If she had gotten bitchy with me, I might have gotten snide, if not confrontational. I would have wanted to physically fight her, but I would have resisted. I have never been in a fight.

I have been spoiling for a brawl for some time now. Since before the self-defense workshop. It might have been part of why I took the course, although I am also very big on personal safety and would like to be prepared if anyone ever tried to attack me. I take the extra precautions. I carry pepper spray on my key chain, although I think it might damage my ignition. I also carry a personal alarm. I saw them at Rite Aid one time and, since there was a rebate, bought one for me and one for my sister. I have never had to use it. But I was in the bath-

room at a diner once—the diviest diner in my neighborhood—rooting through my purse for lipstick, and in this rooting around, I somehow knocked the pin out of my personal alarm. It was louder than I remembered and echoing off of tile and stainless steel, and I couldn't find the pin and my ears were starting to hurt, my heart bouncing around in my chest, absolutely certain that someone would come, blasting the door down in their haste, either prepared to rescue me from my attacker or ready to throw me out because I was causing a disturbance. I kept digging in my purse. It took me a full minute to find the pin. Still no one. Even when I emerged from the bathroom, I didn't get a single reaction. After this incident, I'm not sure I should depend on the personal alarm.

Yell "NO!" as loud as you can.

I often feel moved to fight other women. I know this is weird. I think I didn't get it all out of my system when I was a kid. I never fought, except with my sister, and generally, we were pretty tame. Slapping, maybe some biting, lots of yelling, and that was really it. I think there was a lot that I didn't get out of my system during childhood. I was too good a kid. My mom still laughs about how, when she told me to go sit in the corner, I'd go to the corner and stay, no questions asked.

Sometimes I go out downtown in Washington, D.C., and I run into these girls—you know the type, with perfectly flatironed hair and too-long pants, gold heels and silver eye shadow, drunkenly knocking into whoever has the misfortune of standing next to her while she totters, drink in hand, trying to fix the strap of her "Ooh! They're so sexy and strappy!" shoes. The girls who use their cell phones to call from the middle of the crowd at the front of the concert *during the performance* to their guy friend in the back to bring them more beer. The ones who think they can hit on your boyfriend just because you aren't in the room. Or even worse, the ones who hit on your boyfriend when you are standing right there and have already gone to great lengths to mark your territory. They want me to punch them. They really, really do. And so I imagine punching them. And, I think that if one of them gave me a good enough reason, I would do it. I'm still angry at myself that

I didn't go head-to-head with the girl who sang along with every single bit of music (even the guitar parts) at the Cake concert. I have to keep reminding myself that she had about fifty pounds on me.

My boyfriend, Shaun (whom I like to call my man friend, since it seems more appropriate for what we are: adults who live together), is a former bouncer and current "don't mess with me" man, and he says that this is all well and good, but the problems are twofold: 1) It absolutely sucks to be hit. So if you hit someone and he or she hits you back, it will suck. 2) He really doesn't want me to be in a fight.

Okay, I can get on board with number one. I'm hoping if I'm ever suitably driven to a brawl that it will be with one of those 105-pounders and I can knock her right off her excruciatingly pointy Steve Madden pumps with one blow, drink flying, purse spilling its contents on the hard checkerboard floor, her friends too shocked and now frightened of me to know what to do and, most important, finally struck dumb. Then I'll have a little bit of practice under my belt and can be better prepared to protect my probably glass jaw in the next altercation. If at all possible, one needs some practice hitting before one can practice being hit.

Now, number two is interesting. Shaun, adorable, progressive—"I'll raise our kids if you want to continue your fabulous career, oh talented you"—Shaun doesn't want to see me in a fight? On one hand, I can understand. I don't want to see him in a fight, either. And perhaps it ends there. But, of course, being a creative person and a writer and—dare I say it and feed the stereotypes—a woman, I want to overthink things. Perhaps this is deeper. Why is it okay, expected even, for men to fight? And why is it equally unexpected and not okay for women to fight? (Please let's abandon the "women fighting in Jell-O/mud/with pillows" mental scenario right now. I'm talking realistic situations.) At Shaun's house when he was growing up, there were four brothers who roughhoused so hard that the ambulance had to come out a number of times. If one of the older brothers hadn't been a member of the fire department, which I recently learned enabled the family to place free emergency calls, they might well have been sent to

the welfare office. This, to me, is like viewing clothing as purely utilitarian. This, to me, is like imagining that I could pee standing up. This, to me, is like the elevators in New York City that don't go to all the floors. Foreign concept.

Do not practice these moves on your boyfriend. A woman from a previous class broke her husband's nose. By accident, of course.

Fighting with men is something I'm not nearly as interested in. I do have the occasional wayward instinct to get into it with some jerky guy who says something way inappropriate or talks through a concert. But I don't fantasize about that situation the way I do about fighting with women. I have never made a boyfriend get into a fight because some guy pissed me off. I have, however, wrestled with boyfriends. I don't mean that "Oh, we're kind of making out, this could be construed as foreplay" way. I mean that "We're playing around and fighting and both sort of trying to win." I never win. I'm five-four and 130 pounds. Shaun, the current administration, has eight inches and a hundred pounds on me. I never even get close, although I do sometimes instinctually throw in some good maneuvers. But even if he hadn't (as it says on his résumé) "studied mixed martial arts in a full-contact setting," he could best me every time. I remember being in high school and going on one of my earliest dates, making out with a guy, a lacrosse player, and having a moment of realization. If he wanted to, he could pin me. He could easily best me physically. I've never forgotten that moment, and perhaps this is part of where my self-defense obsession comes from. I will not be the girl who is attacked and raped in the laundry room. I will be the girl who is attacked and seriously maims the guy who attacks me, forcing him to think twice about touching another girl again.

Go for the eyes.

Perhaps this has lots to do with being a female right now. We are staying single longer. We are supporting ourselves. We make our own car payments. We have more options than we've ever had before. This is an incredibly cool time for us. But simultaneously, we still feel constantly defenseless. We are more likely than men to be a target for sex

crimes and physical abuse. We still make less money than men do. Men are in control of our government. Men effectively run our world. Why are we still so vulnerable?

Make space between yourself and your assailant.

And there are these women—the ones I want to fight—who contribute to making all women more vulnerable. We hold each other back. We don't make it easy for each other to succeed. Any woman who's been to a party where she didn't know anybody and was ignored by all the girls knows exactly what I'm talking about. Any woman who didn't like her guy friend's girlfriend "just on principle" knows what it's like to feel threatened. Why do we feel so threatened by other women? Why do we want other women to fail so we can succeed? Why do we engage in constant competition with women we think are more attractive than we are? Why *do* we hold one another back?

And me, I want to fight these women. I want to fight women who play dumb to get attention, women who get too drunk to take care of themselves without a good support system, women who bail on their friends because they met some guy at a party, women who buy in to the stereotypes we're fed about how women should be, women who peddle these stereotypes. Oh, and women who personally piss me off.

Kicking is a very good thing.

I guess I, like many people, have pent-up anger without enough of an outlet. Maybe I should start exercising. I hear kickboxing is fun. Or I should call my girlfriends more. Or maybe I need to write more to try to change some opinions. Or, in the future, raise some strong little girls.

But for now I'm going to do as my mama taught me and keep my hands to myself.

On Election Day, I attend the first rehearsal for the first public reading of the first full-length play I have written as an adult. It is a moment of truth in my thus far only imagined life as a playwright, and I have a sense, emerging onto the sidewalk of Eighth Avenue and making my way to the uptown C train, that I am experiencing a new piece of real life for the first time. I have trouble controlling—find it impossible, in fact, to control—the grin that spreads across my face. I am laughing out loud, alone, on the train; people are staring. I am in love for the first time. I have never been in love before, but suddenly, at twenty-three, I fall hard.

My parents are waiting for the phone calls. They are at home in Cambridge, my childhood home of sloping floorboards and New England drafts, waiting to hear from me about the rehearsal, waiting to hear from my older brother about the results of his campaign for reelection to the Cambridge School Committee. My call comes first. As I flip a turkey burger over and over on the stove in the steamy galley kitchen of the apartment I share with two roommates, I give them the details. Because they are my parents, they are the only people who actually want all the details, and I am so high on this evening's events that all I want to do is talk, to explain and relive this awakening, this birth, that I have just experienced.

My brother calls. It's bad news. The election results are in, and he has been displaced by two new candidates. He is heartbroken. My brother has had a hard year. He needed this.

"The ecstasy and the devastation of our children," our father observes.

I have rarely heard either of my parents refer to my brothers and me as "their children." My three brothers, the children of my father's first marriage, ranged from ages thirteen to seventeen when I was born. We were seldom on the same page of childhood together. But there we are on Election Day. At twenty-three, I am a child in my euphoria; at thirty-six, my brother is still a child too, in his disappointment. And my parents hear us both, these adults in varying stages of adulthood who are, will always be, their children.

I am only beginning to see my parents as people. Perhaps this is because I am beginning to picture myself as a parent. My maternal instinct kicked in early, and though motherhood is distant in my real life, it is close in my imagined one. It is no longer the childhood game of playing house, stuffing a pillow under my shirt, breast-feeding a baby doll to a flat chest, but a set of palpable images, a future Technicolor reality of depth and certainty—the only fantasy, I found myself explaining to a group of friends over wine on a recent late night, that is absolute for me. In the selfish landscape of my twenties, there is only me at the end of the day to clothe and feed and satisfy, but down the road I can see life with marriage, parenthood, like the next space to collect rainbow cash on a Monopoly board. As these images sharpen, as what was always my bedroom becomes my childhood bedroom, as what was once practiced for pleasure becomes—secretly, piecemeal— a career, as I become an adult, my parents become people.

We begin growing up before we know what we are doing. Hints of our adulthood creep in stealthily: Sexuality bubbles up as unidentifiable stirrings, images of parenthood surface before the real possibility of procreation, imagined careers arise long before job interviews. When we are children, our pieces of adulthood are hidden, alive but invisible; over time, forcefully but intangibly, the child pieces and the

adult pieces trade places. A week shy of my twenty-fourth birthday, I have the outward shape of an adult. A young adult, to be sure, but nonetheless a woman, a petite woman of the kind whose age is hard to place; a woman who makes her living working with children and therefore asserting on a daily basis the legitimacy of her newfound adulthood. Rattling to work on the uptown 4, I catch a glimpse of my reflection in the window opposite. I am startled to see a grown-up there, a working woman, unaccompanied by a parent, off to clock some hours, get a paycheck, come home to a dinner I will make for myself, a glass of wine from a bottle I picked out. I have seen her before, I see her often now, but she surprises me every time.

Some milestones of this rising adulthood, my parents have witnessed; some I'm sure they have sensed intuitively; others they do not know about. My parents moved me into my college dorm freshman year, and when they left I cried for about a month; four years later and many pages read and written, friends made, boys kissed, I graduated and there they were, cheering through a downpour. They helped me settle into my first apartment in New York City, saw me begin to build a career. But they may or may not have noticed the subtle transitions that passed in the privacy of my body and mind. Arriving home for holidays, I have often wondered how I appear to those who never left, to the aunts and uncles and brothers and sisters-in-law and to my parents, how (or if) these changes register. Do they notice what I see in myself—how weight is redistributed, that my breasts have gotten smaller as I have lost all traces of baby fat, that my forehead reveals the first wrinkles of a woman who carries her worries in her brow. To my parents, I believe, I am nearly transparent; they are the only people who can wholly recognize in my voice and body both the child I have been and the adult I am becoming. How they reconcile these halves, I don't know, but that, I suspect, is the challenge and the heartache and probably the wonder of raising a person. And the more I begin to understand about the world—about work, family, sex, mortality, fear, about the vast courage required by love and marriage—the less I am able to hide from the fact that my parents are complex human patch-

works, too, people for whom being parents is only one piece of two complete lives with pasts, presents, and futures.

In the front of a book my father gave my mother for Christmas, I find an inscription: "When I met you at Shakespeare and Co. in Paris after being in the Pyrenees, you were the most beautiful thing I had ever seen." When my mother and father were teachers, they spent their summers traveling separately in Europe, and the Paris bookstore was their meeting place. I have long considered my parents' romanticism a cute fact of their middle age—holding hands at the movies, Friday-night dinners at the same local dive. But reading this note, I am faced with the inescapable truth of my parents' young love. The fact that I find their Parisian rendezvous more romantic than any Victorian fantasy leads me to believe that we might have more in common than I would have imagined.

My parents came of age in the sixties. It was an era of important unrest, of speeches and rallies and pervasive instability. Joan Didion wrote that things were falling apart, that the center could not hold, at least in California; my parents were East Coast babies, but things were falling apart there too, if in a more intellectualized, less sun-kissed way. Perhaps it is the sense that this is true again—that nothing can stick— that enables us to identify with our parents as we navigate adulthood in the twenty-first century. Did it feel to my parents, when they were my age, that the sky was falling? Did they, too, feel the urgency of a world unraveling, of natural disasters and bomb threats, of sour politics and impending epidemics? I suspect they did, and if so, it is possible that we have shared these experiences, decades apart. This may be a result of history repeating, as we know it does; we may have truly returned, forty years later and by no coincidence, to the place where the center cannot hold. But perhaps it has nothing to do with history. Perhaps this is simply what it is to grow up: to become aware, to carry, as one inevitably does in one's twenties, the weight of the world, and in so doing, to realize that others have done so before us.

This changes my view of my parents. My mother at my age was teaching English in Athens, living in the dorm with the little girls,

hitchhiking through Europe. She was sleeping on the roofs of white stucco houses on Crete, drinking tea in Istanbul, riding camels in Cairo. Did she already know how to cook without recipes and grow cherry tomatoes behind the garage? Did she already know how to love the way she does, without rules—this woman who was not much older than I am now when she fell for the father of three young boys?

I imagine that man, too, my young father. In sound bites, my father was the smart kid dealt the tough hand, the altar boy gone townie gone Ivy League graduate. He has told me the stories about sleeping on chairs pushed together, his father throwing the turkey at his mother on Thanksgiving, but these are difficult to reconcile with the father I know, my fly-fishing, saxophone-playing, meditating-every-morning, sentimental dad; my smart dad, from whom I learned about ice cream in the winter and gin and tonics in the summer, about silence and watching. My father at my age was already a parent; he had gotten through college on a full ride, served in the reserves, would soon be getting his master's. He was not going to Vietnam. Did he feel the guilt of this then, or did it set in later? Visiting the Wall on an eighth-grade class trip with my father as a chaperone, I accidentally uncovered this guilt, a glimpse into a life before me that I cannot know.

I can't, but I can try. In the pictures I have stolen from their albums of before I was born, my parents appear young, in love, overworked. My mother has long hair in these pictures. She had long hair until a few years after I was born. I remember hiding my face in my hands the day she cut it short—I must have been three or four. She has never grown it back, so the image of her with that glossy, pin-straight, almost-to-her-waist-stuck-in-the-seventies hair remains my idea of her before. Before I knew her, before she was the mother I know.

My father also has more hair in these pictures. He had not yet begun to go thin on top and so had not become taken with the idea of looking "squared away," as he calls it, reminiscent of his Marine Corps days—keeping his hair shorn as close to shaved as my mother will let him get away with. On the bulletin board in my parents' kitchen, for

years, was a drawing I made in early elementary school, a portrait of my father. I was not a particularly gifted fine artist, just as I was a terrible ice-skater—in the days when we do everything in order to determine what we might really do—and in this drawing, my father looks very much like a scary half-human pig. He has only four teeth in total, two top and two bottom, and he is grinning. He has a mass of brown hair, and his nose is a pink curlicue underlined by a bushy mustache.

For a long time, we made fun of this picture. I wondered why my parents left it up for so many years, but I see now: That was my childhood image of my father, and as creepy as the picture is, there is something lovely in it. I don't remember the workings of the child's mind that made this masterpiece, but I know it was created out of love, the complete, absolute, all-encompassing love of an only daughter for her daddy—created out of the purity with which a parent appears in a child's eyes. This is a picture by a child who sees her parents only as parents; he is not a person, he is Dad, he is all he needs to be.

But now I know that he is more, that they both are. My parents, it seems to me, have had at least nine lives each, but when and where did they experience these lives? Neither of my parents has traveled abroad since I was born. They have long since abandoned the pursuit of their own wild adventures in exchange for allowing me the possibility of exploring mine. My parents met as teachers. They are writers and educators, good ones, who have built careers that don't interest them much. They both write, read, edit, and educate for a living, but not in the ways they ever anticipated or desired. I wonder if their dreams linger. Do they inspire stabs of inevitable envy or at least moments of self-reflection when, say, my mother's brother publishes his first novel, or even when I call home to report that a close friend has just signed her first—and second—book deals? Or have the dreams been displaced by more pedestrian and probably more important joys—thirty years in love, owning a home with a backyard, becoming grandparents, releasing their only shared child into young womanhood?

I know what my parents will say to this: I am complicating the

issue, that raising me has never been an act of relinquishing. When I came to be, they will say, their world simply changed, and with it, their dreams. They will tell me that this is the part of parenthood I cannot imagine no matter how many pillows I have rolled under my shirt: Sacrifice is part of loving someone unconditionally, but in the act of loving so deeply, it becomes something other than sacrifice. They will tell me that I will not understand this until the moment I bring a child into life, that no love for a best friend or a spouse or even a parent is the same as a parent's love for a child. Somehow I know this already. They must have taught me. Still, I wonder: Will I, can I possibly, be as selfless a parent? And how can I honor my parents if I am not? I can't help but recognize that in growing up, in honoring the gift of life they have given me not once but countless times, I am also leaving them.

As I watch I-95 fly by through the window of a Greyhound between home in Cambridge and home in New York, I consider this. What is it to "go home for a weekend"? I step off the bus, full of stories, ready for home cooking, for sleeping late and free laundry, and then two days later, I pack up and leave again. It's not just that I have to leave, that I must return to my own responsibilities; it is that I am ready to leave. I am stuck between needing them and wanting not to need them. I snapped at my mother at dinner over a comment I took too personally. She asked about my writing, my most private insecurity, something vague about "where it was going." It was, at the time, not going anywhere—I had not written in months, was paralyzed and depressed and anxious, none of which she knew, and so how could she know that she was stepping into a minefield as she voiced the same questions I was afraid to ask myself. I have always been a private writer. She knows that. And perhaps because they are writers too, my parents have always given me this privacy. Even so, my mother was hurt by my response, and I was disappointed by it. These are my parents, they love me more than life; Christ, I thought, cut them some slack. Yet there was more than just lingering adolescent angst in my knee-jerk response, in the acidic tone I heard and hated in my voice. With this argument, I am telling them—telling myself—there are some

things I must do on my own now. If I am to be the adult you want me to be, I must do this on my own.

It must be a growing pain, this adult-onset homesickness, the simultaneous ache for what I cannot have anymore and for what I cannot have yet. My parents must choose when to carry me through it and when to release me. When I faced the choice of leaving a temp job that I felt was beginning to eat away at my insides, my parents refused to give me definitive advice. This was infuriating. I am still the Goody Two-shoes, the little girl who never broke the rules. I needed their approval, but they would not tell me what to do. I got a lot of "We think you should do whatever you think is right," which was maddening; it reeked of making my own mistakes and taking responsibility for my choices. But of course, they were right. It was my decision to quit, it was my struggle to find something new, and in the end, it was my triumph when I did. My parents must have held their breath the entire time, letting go of their child's two-wheeler and hoping she wouldn't crash.

And yet it is still my parents on the phone. It is still my mother talking me through the recipe, my father griping about the Red Sox game, my parents on speakerphone debating the tonal implications of a semicolon versus an em dash. Their role as touchstones, as first advocates, has not changed. When they have delivered me to adulthood, my parents must return in many ways to their lives before me: two of them together alone, still overworked, goofing off in the kitchen. The twenty-some-odd years they shaped for me are the backbone, the base from which I will build my own life, and now they have to let me, and I have to try. I hold them to a double standard. Will I answer their calls as an adult or as a child, will I be eager to share my life with them or will I shut them out; they have no way of predicting. Will I call just to say hi, will I call because I need something, will I not call at all? Will I fall in love with someone they can love too, will I give them grandchildren soon enough? Will I make enough money to help them into the retirement they have not saved for, opting instead to put me through school and fix my problem teeth without dental insurance? Some of

these are their questions and some, most, are mine. Some are their worries, some mine. Of course, theirs are of me alone and mine are of them, but such is family. Such is taking the risk to leave who you know, who you love, who you are made of, in order to become who you are. There is nothing to give back to my parents, nothing enough to repay them for what they give me; nothing to do, I suppose, except grow up.

FINDING THE BEAT YOU SHALL GO OUT WITH JOY AND BE
LED FORTH WITH PEACE THE IDIOT'S GUIDE TO YOUR PALM
SHEER DOMINANCE LIVE NUDE GIRL AN EVENING IN APRIL
CLICHÉ RAPE STORY ROCK MY NETWORK GOODBYE TO ALL THAT
ALL THE RIGHT ANSWERS WHY I HAD TO LEAVE IN-BETWEEN PLACES
A RED SPOON FOR THE NAMELESS MY LITTLE COMMA FIGHT ME
THE SECRET LIVES OF MY PARENTS MY ROARING TWENTIES
IN, FROM THE OUTSIDE THE MYSTERIES OF LIFE . . . REVEALED!
SO YOU SAY YOU WANT A REVOLUTION WORKING AT WENDY'S
JESS LACHER MARY BETH ELLIS BRONSON LEMER JENNIFER GLASER
RACHEL KEMPF JOHN FISCHER SHAHNAZ HABIB EMMA BLACK
ELI JAMES KYLE MINOR COLLEEN KINDER CHRISTOPHER POLING
KATHLEEN ROONEY RADHIYAH AYOBAMI MARISA McCARTHY
THEODORA STITES EULA BISS BRENDAN PARK LUKE MULLINS
MARY KATE FRANK BURLEE VANG ELRENA EVANS
MIELLYN FITZWATER KATE McGOVERN LAUREN MONROE
KATHERINE DYKSTRA TRAVIS SENTELL J. W. YOUNG JOEY FRANKLIN

I t must be Monday morning, because Marion is sitting at her desk eating scrambled eggs out of a plastic take-out container. Monday is egg day. The phone rings and rings, an incessant double jingle that is just the right tone to step up adrenaline production. Marion ignores it absolutely. She continues spooning the gelatinous egg into her equally soft jowls, said jowls flubbering into her dyed burgundy bob. Three lines ringing now. I'm on two lines at once, and Marion is in Eggsville. If I had a moment, I'd stop to admire her complete disregard. This is no run-of-the-mill insouciance. She's an indifference specialist. She's an award-winning apathy expert. She is *not* the office manager. We don't have an office manager. We have "job sharing." She writes "Office Manager" on her order forms, however.

Marion gives me a little half-wave, still chewing. I am tempted to scream, "Pick up the phone you dumb cow!" but then I stop and ask myself: What would Bettie Page do? Hell, everybody needs an archetype. At least mine is hot. So I give Marion a little half-wave back, sit daintily on my chair, cross my legs at the ankle, and purr into the phone:

"Good morning, ABC Realty, how may I help you? Please hold just one moment."

I intone this phrase hundreds, nay, thousands of times weekly. It is amazing how many nuances this one phrase can encompass, depend-

ing on the emphasis. Try it. It goes from perky and competent (*"Good* morning") to bitingly ironic (". . . how may I *help* you?" Grit your teeth slightly on that one, for added effect), even to seductive ("Good *morning . . ."*). Mostly I just say it rapidly, picking up one phone line after another, Administrative Assistant Me, at ABC Realty. "We're Number One in Sales in *Your* County!"

ABC Realty is home to forty real estate agents—all but three of them women—who work hard every day to keep us at the top. The top! The top of what, I am not sure. There are four of us admins: myself, Marion, Trish, and Louise. The Bosses call us the Secretarios, as if we are a barbershop quartet or a crunchy breakfast cereal. We are a team! We *love* teamwork! Well, technically there are six of us, if you count Anne and the other weekend girl, Kelly, which I do not. They only count for half a Secretario each, if anything. So call it an odd five.

Trish is mouthing at me over her headset, *Check the voice mail.* There's a message from The Bosses, our fearless leaders, the two multimillionaire women who own this fine establishment. They like to leave us little wisdom nuggets in the voice mail while they are off somewhere else, sipping margaritas or hiking in the Amazon. This one is a keeper.

"Good morning, agents and Secretarios! ABC Realty is number one in sales because we work hard and we play hard. We talk the talk and walk the walk. We are always professional. When you go out to meet a customer, you should never wear jeans or other casual clothing. When you are at the office, make sure that your shoes and your underwear hurt. That's how we know that we are working!"

End transmission. Thank you, O intrepid ones. I am enlightened.

I drink my free office coffee and answer phone calls. The beige phone stares at me with twelve blinking red eyes, twelve lines either ringing or on hold: hopeful young couples looking to buy their first homes, agents looking to seal the deal, or our clients asking for the umpteenth time why their house hasn't sold yet (*Um, have you tried removing the dog doo from the master bedroom?*). Hallelujah real estate! All hail low

mortgage rates! How may I HELP you? Three middle-aged women circle my desk, looking for a spot to land, holding out papers to be copied, faxed, stamped, and/or filed. The cold, harsh light of morning shimmies on the bags under my eyes, and I understand the truth. I am not a rock star. I am a mere Secretario, and I am firmly ensconced in the hole in the ground that is my life. I am twenty-four. My life tastes like a dead cat.

I picture Bettie Page sitting in the chair in front of me, lightly chewing on a strand of pearls, one eyebrow slightly arched. She's looking at me with not a little disdain. I can't even get a break in my daydreams. I stick my tongue out at Bettie and go back to work. Trish looks at me cross-eyed. I wiggle my eyebrows and roll my eyes at her until she laughs.

They say your twenties are supposed to be the best years of your life. "They who?" you ask. You know, Them. The People Who Say Stuff That Is Supposedly True About Life. Four out of five women named Beatrice, gynecologists, the judiciary branch of the government, fucking Hollywood. They all agree: You Should Do Stuff, such as go to college, get a job, get married, buy a house, have babies, exercise three times a week for twenty minutes, drink eight glasses of water a day, and refrain from dangerous and/or unhealthy and/or antisocial behavior. This may or may not include sex (of any kind), taking drugs (although alcohol or antidepressants or Valium are occasionally allowable—we must be realistic), swearing, wearing too much makeup or not enough makeup, and being an artist. Definitely, being an artist is the worst and most irresponsible thing one can do, if only because willfully committing the multitude of previously mentioned sins is actually required in order to be an artist. Essentially, I am completely screwed.

Ian asked me to marry him for the first time in the parking lot of Planned Parenthood. I had gone there to confirm the pregnancy test because I didn't have any medical insurance and they only charged a

few dollars for an exam. So we sat outside Planned Parenthood in his dad's fifteen-year-old Dodge truck, and he cried and asked me to marry him. I was twenty-two. We had been together for six weeks. I said no.

"But the baby," he said, his sleepy-looking eyes wide and a little frantic. He is a painter. A fantastic painter, actually. And he was cute in his painterly way when he asked me to marry him because of the baby, and I said no because it was the best thing I could have done.

"Having a baby is no reason to get married," I said.

He was stunned. He may have asked me if I was crazy. I think this was the first time (but not the last time) he told me that my heritage—Irish Italian—meant that I was mad as hell and angry about it. But I wasn't crazy. We hardly even knew each other carnally. How the hell were we going to be married?

He proposed again when I was seven and a half months huge. We went out for dinner. I had roasted duck with raspberry sauce. I knew he was going to ask me because he was fiddling with something in his pocket, his face having a spasm each time, a cross between an eye twitch and a strangled look. Assuming that he wasn't playing with himself in public, I deducted that it was a ring. After dinner we walked to the parking lot. Again, the parking lot. I guess he figured that if he needed to escape, it would be easier to flee. He asked me if I enjoyed dinner. I said that I had. He asked me if I was in a good mood. I said that I was. Then he asked me if I would please marry him. He gave me a very pretty ring, an antique from the twenties. The inscription said SWEETHEART, PAL, FRIEND. I loved it. I accepted his proposal. I haven't eaten duck with raspberry sauce since.

I didn't think we'd actually get married, I just figured we could tell his family that we were engaged and it would all be very pleasant, and then the baby wouldn't be a big scandal or whatever. I never wanted the whole Barbie Dream Wedding, but I couldn't imagine what kind of wedding we would have. My family is pretty poor. We often had potato chips and soda for dinner when I was growing up. So we tabled it for the time being, and everything was peachy.

A few weeks later, his great-great-whatever-ancient aunt was visit-

ing from Greece, and she insisted in broken English that we *had* to get married. I couldn't argue with her because I don't speak Greek. So instead, I said something to the effect of, "Yeah, you're so right, Thea-Whatever-Your-Name-Is! We *should* get married!" And apparently, other people within earshot wouldn't let me out of the statement, even after I protested that it was simply a matter of sarcasm, not being able to breech the language barrier. Later that night, Ian and I talked about it. We would elope. On my birthday. In jeans. I would wear my combat boots. It would be so *us,* so Zen and simple. We were so goddamned young.

It is nine o'clock at night, and my daughter is sleeping upstairs in her little pink room. She is four, her name is Eva, and she is funny and smart and beautiful. And that is not a mother's bias speaking.

Ian is still at work. He got a job at an advertising agency as a graphic artist. He's good at it. He gets paid well. We have insurance and our own little suburban town house. It is the nicest house I have ever lived in. We have a dining room with a hardwood table and a nice stained-glass lamp over it. I painted the walls a pale, cheery yellow. Dinner is cold for the second time tonight. He has to stay late. Again. He's sorry, he can't help it, he has to pay the mortgage, *Dammit, he's doing his best.* I make myself a plate of homemade vegetable-stuffed manicotti with my homemade sauce over it. I eat alone with Charlie Parker on the stereo for company. The candles I lit an hour ago are sputtering out. They cast a shadow of my silhouette on the wall. It is a phantom composition, a study of loneliness and empty space. My wine is salty with quiet tears.

When does my real life start? This is just a dress rehearsal, right? Waiter? Check, please.

———

It is nine-thirty, we've only been open for half an hour, we have probably already done three-quarters of a million dollars in deals this week, and it's only Wednesday. It is freezing in here. I am the only one

who's cold because I am also the only one who isn't menopausal. I keep a black sweater on the back of my chair, my official secretarial sweater, a cardigan with buttons down the front that goes with everything. It has been here for months, and I haven't washed it. It smells vaguely like stale cigarette smoke. I guess that's a little gross, but I wonder: If these women are making millions of dollars, and I, in fact, do most of their work, then why can't I afford a new sweater? This kind of question plagues me in the lulls between phone calls. I suppose I could wash the sweater, but it's my tiny revenge. Revenge on whom, I'm not quite sure, since I'm the only one who actually smells the thing.

"Good afternoon, ABC Realty, how may I help you?" This is my mantra. I am one with the Universe. Om.

"Yeah, this is Chris from Yadda Yadda Realty calling for Heidi. She there?" The voice on the other end is male and, I can tell, stupid. One gets a sense for these things after a couple of years in the trenches.

"Heidi is on another line. Would you like to hold, or shall I transfer you to her voice mail?" I am a competent, perky Secretario. Om.

"*No,* I don't want her friggin' voice mail, I'll wait." Petulant *and* stupid. A winning combination.

"Certainly," I say, and click off. Page Heidi over the intercom.

She yells from behind the half-wall that separates the agents' corral and the admins' pen. *"I'm on the frickin' phone, whaddaya want?"*

I push the intercom button again, tell her Chris from Yadda Yadda is on the phone.

"Tell him to go in my voice mail, I'm busy."

I stab the intercom, inform her that he wants to hold.

"Well, he's gonna have to hold for a few minutes, then, because I'm frickin' busy over here."

One more time on the intercom: "Alrighty, sounds good, I'll tell him." Fuck you very much, have a great day. Did I say that out loud? She's probably just jealous of my estrogen. Om. Iamonewiththeuniverse. Om.

Meanwhile, I notice out of the corner of my eye that there is someone standing to the left of my desk. Someone tall, I ascertain. A man-

shaped tall person. I plaster on my best secretarial mask and point my face in his general direction, preparing to mouth *Be with you in just a moment.* The phone is tucked under my chin. As I begin the patented Secretarial Head Tilt, I see his face for the first time. He. Is. Hot.

The phone starts to slide out from under my chin, and I get as far as "Be with—" before it clunks down into my lap. I recover quickly, thank you very much, and laugh a little (*giggling covers a multitude of sins.* Oh, Bettie, you are *so* right), give Random Hot Guy a little nod and waggle my index finger, which means "Just a second, I am experiencing technical idiocy."

"Oh, no prob," Random Hot Guy says, "I'm here to see Heidi." There's just enough of a wrinkle around his eye to say that he's appreciating the floor show.

"Oh, okay," I reply. "Feel free to have a seat anywhere, she'll be right with you." Please, please, please do not sit in the chair directly across from me. He does. Damn. It is too early for this. *Mmmmm, cute boy,* says Inner Bettie. I picture her curled up in the seat next to him, ridiculous-yet-hot stilettos tucked under her curvy little bottom. *Could you loosen the pearls around my wrist just a wee bit, sweetie? They're lovely, but they're starting to chafe.* Pipe down, I mentally hiss at her. And this is the best conversation I've had all week.

I sneak looks at him from behind my monitor: Wavy brown hair. I hate wavy hair; it's insipid. Is it straight? Is it curly? No. It can't decide. (*Hmmm, it looks thick, wonder what it would feel like . . .*), dark brown eyes, dark jeans (*mmmm, nice*—wow, shut up!), and loafers. Loafers? No way, I hate loafer-wearing guys, and he probably doesn't have a single tattoo, and he probably drinks Budweiser (*well, gee, it would be fun to find out*). No, back off, you hussy! And he's probably into classic rock or something. So forget it.

An agent comes over to my desk, asks me to make fifty copies of something.

"Sure," I say. "No problem." Even though you know how to use the copier and I have twenty other things to do. Sure. No problem. Om.

Damn. I have to walk past him to get to the copier. *Smile.* I am al-

ready smiling, so there. *Talk to him!* Oh, please. And say what? I mean, what am I going to do, ask the guy out? And then explain how I'm technically married but I'm not really married because I sleep on the couch and have for months? Right. I'm sure that would go over big. *Take off that sweater, it's terrible and it smells like a saloon.* Damn it, knock it off! Who cares?

I take off the sweater. He's watching me walk. When was the last time someone checked out my legs? *They are rather nice legs, you know. You may want to give them a little stretch every now and again.* I mentally stick a gag on Bettie. She doesn't seem to mind. It's part of her job, after all.

I enter "50" into the copier and wait. I stretch my legs out a little as I stand next to the machine (and you can just wipe that smirk off your face, Bettie, I'm getting a cramp is all). And here he comes, he's walking toward me, he's smiling, he's . . . walking out the door with Heidi. And the copier is jammed. Now I have to negotiate with its mechanical innards to give me my goddamned papers back. Bettie shakes her phantom head at me. Sometimes I wish I could fire her.

———

When was the last time you thought about your gallbladder? Have you ever thought about it? The next time you are considering eating a marzipan cookie—you know, the rainbow kind with chocolate on the outside—please, consider your gallbladder first. If you don't practice proper gallbladder maintenance, this handy little organ can and will make its displeasure known to you in less-than-subtle ways. Appreciate your gallbladder, and it will be good to you. Ignore it, and it will rise up against you like a fascist military coup: sudden, painful, incontrovertible, and ugly as a mofo.

Willy-nilly consumption of foodstuffs with any kind of fat (this includes avocados, nuts, and other "healthy," nonmeat fats, my dear vegetarian gallbladder owners), combined with shite genes and/or crap luck, can cause little pieces of evil to form in your gallbladder, commonly known as gallstones, but more accurately described as little pieces of evil.

Normally, the gallbladder sits around in your abdominal cavity storing bile for you, which you may not think you need or like, but trust me, you do. You like bile when it's in its proper place, doing its happy fat-breakdown dance. You may not, however, like bile at twelve-thirty A.M. when you're projectile vomiting it in between begging any god who's listening to please, please help you or let you die, because it feels like someone dropped a ball of burning lead mixed with glass into your gullet, shot you twice in the shoulder, and then proceeded to do the flamenco on your bleeding innards. That is the first three minutes of a gallbladder attack.

The next forty-five minutes may include the following: grunting instructions to your husband to please call 911 and not to let them put you on any goddamned machines, because you're sure you're having a goddamned heart attack; lying flat on your stomach like a homicide chalk outline, drooling and recounting all the things you didn't do that you aren't going to get to do now because you are surely going to die in five minutes; listening to said husband tell you that he's not going to call the ambulance because he doesn't want to wake the baby, you're probably just exaggerating, you probably just have food poisoning; and even though you cannot move, speak, or breathe properly, having just enough life left in you to hate the sight of his back as it disappears up the stairs. All this just from eating an innocent-looking rainbow marzipan cookie. Forewarned is forearmed.

I lie down on the couch and watch my brain's projections reel across the ceiling. My organs are declaring mutiny. Well, one organ, anyway. I picture them packing their bags (do they look like sausage casings?), leaving me a note that says: Off to happier climates, see ya never, sucker. Bettie is here somewhere, tied to an ottoman. The ghost of my high school boyfriend provides the sound track, beating his guitar and shouting *Don't be a sellout, punk rock kids don't give a damn about fancy houses; it's all about the passion and integrity.* My mom floats by, shaking her head over the unkempt state of my kitchen. And here comes a cavorting little cartoon monster, green and black and globby, saying *Smoke, smoke, all you want to do is smoke, nicotine,*

aaaarrrrgggghh. I imagine that The Bosses would leave me a pithy voice mail extolling the virtues of a high-colonic cleansing followed by margaritas and a motivational video. The thought of their hypermoxie blather makes me nauseous all over again. I am not going into the god-damn office tomorrow, no matter what those capitalistic mavens of blah blah say. I cannot stomach their mercenary sales-pitch sputum. I wish gallstones were fatal.

It is late at night a week after the gallbladder insurrection, and I pack my bags silently. We have been fighting for hours. Ian wants to fight some more. I do not. I am going to my mother's house, tonight. I rented a little log cabin, and I'll stay with my mother until I can move in. He looks sad. I guess I am, too. But I can't do this anymore; I can't live like a shadow anymore, and I have to go. I have to figure out how I can make myself into a real person with a real life. It's not anybody's fault, I tell him. It was just a bad match. It was just bad timing. We just weren't ready, I tell him. He doesn't buy it. It's probably all your fault, he says. I don't have the energy to dissuade him. I take all of my clothes, my shoes, and my laptop. This is all that I will need. My daughter is excited to have a sleepover at her granny's house. I feel terrible for my daughter. This is not her fault, this is not her mistake, and all I can do is hope that she will not have to pay for it in some way.

———

I fantasize constantly about quitting, about packing my bags, about being anything else but this, anywhere else but here. In between answering the phone, I imagine how it will go down. I always return to this, my favorite reverie:

I will stand up on top of my desk and start doing the Funky Chicken, kicking over sales reports and gyrating around the computer, singing "Ding Dong! the Witch Is Dead" while Trish laughs hysterically, her slightly gap-toothed mouth roaring as I kick the mouse off its mouse pad and watch it die. Marion will stare at this spectacle, slack-jawed, her burgundy waves plastered to her little moon face, her vacant

forehead protruding and moist. I will scream, "Hey, *Marion!* Pick up the phone, Marion! Customer service is our number one priority!"

Even in my daydreams, she won't pick up the phone. So I pick it up, one last time, for old time's sake.

"Good afternoon, A Buncha Cunts Realty, how may I help you?"

"Um, hello?" The customer will be confused by my usage of the word "cunt" and won't know if he heard correctly. I will savor this moment of surprise and then press on.

"Yeah! Spit it out, aspiring Colonial homeowner," I will say. I am sure he will be looking for a Colonial home. They always are.

"Um, is this ABC Realty?" he will ask, because as I said, he won't be sure at this point, due to the use of the c-word.

"Hell yeah, it is. Speak your piece, filthy renter," I will spit out. Renters are the lowest form of life in a real estate office. They should be made aware of this salient fact.

"Um, I was wondering if you could help me," my victim will say, clearly in dire need of some real estate.

"That depends," I will reply. "What's your goddamned credit rating, bra size, and personal highest aspiration?" These things are important when you are buying a home. Again, I feel that it is my duty to make these poor slobs aware of their situation. Customer service is my number one priority.

"Um, I just wanted to inquire about the three-bedroom Colonial you have listed for $500,000?" He will want it, but will be unsure if his bra size is large enough. I doubt it.

"Yeah," I will respond. "It's fucking mint! Mint! Mint! It's spectacular! It will change your godforsaken life! Hallelujah!"

"Um, where is it, exactly?" Now I will have used the f-word, so he will probably get the idea that I'm being smarmy, but he's invested too much at this point. He has to know where that elusive house is.

"Have you looked up your arse?" I doubt he has, but I think that is where the builders might have to cram it in this raging overdeveloped suburban sprawl, so I will ask.

Then Marion will have overcome her temporary paralysis, and she'll come at me like a dislodged Ferris wheel in a nightmare, her tapered-leg pants making her huge ass look positively epidemic, rolling toward me, ever faster.

"Hold just one moment, please, my dense-as-cement coworker will help you. She is *not* the damned office manager, though. We have job sharing here. Her name is Marion. Just a sec," I will say, handing the phone to Marion. "Help the customer, Marion. Customer service is our Number One Priority. Number one, Marion." And as she stands there, turning various shades of red that will clash with her hair, I will Watusi my still-slender, still kind of hot ass out the door, humming with sweet, sweet freedom.

Reality, however, is a cup of cold coffee and the insectile hum of ailing fluorescent lights. "Fly Me to the Moon" is streaming on Marion's computer. She is wearing hot-pink lipstick today. Her ample cleavage is swinging as she bops along to Frank Sinatra and, I am somehow sure, visions of her youth. Maybe she wasn't always a complete ninny. Maybe she used to be hot in her 1950s kind of way. Maybe she wanted more from life than sitting in this dingy office, too. I surreptitiously focus on her and squint my eyes, softening the hard edges, looking for her real aura, reducing her to energy waves. Still repulsive. Am I hurtling toward Marionhood? Is this an immutable fact?

The phone is practically vibrating off the desk, with all twelve lines lit up, some of the lines doing the extra-special double-ring that means they have been on hold for more than a minute, the red lights blink-blink-blinking fast enough to cause epileptic seizures. I sneak a look over at Marion, thinking at her with all my might, *pick up the phone or die, pick it up, or die, die, DIE.* Trish and I pick up call after call, relentless in our pursuit of secretarial excellence. I am an eight-armed goddess of administrative assistance. I brandish my mouse and click and swivel with amazing secretarial speed. Om. Marion is playing

Party Poker. She does not pick up the phone. She does not die, either. My powers are useless against her.

Just as suddenly as the rush started, it stops. My caffeine levels have dropped to a dangerous low.

"More coffee?" I ask Trish.

She is still on the phone. She grabs her throat with one hand, sticks her tongue out, rolls her eyes back like she's choking, and says, "I'll get right back to you with that information."

I mime jamming a pen repeatedly into my eye, get up, and make us fresh coffees. I put Trish's cup on her desk and walk around to mine. The phone rings just as I sit down; I pick it up and scream, suddenly hurtling backward. The chair has completely collapsed, and I am reduced to a heap on top of the rubble. The phone is swinging from the end of my desk, a voice on the other end saying from far away, "Hello? Hello? Is anybody there?"

Trish is yelling, "Hang on! She fell down!" in the general direction of the headset. She grabs my arm and pulls. I am covered in Rainforest Nut coffee and shame. Marion is trying hard to suppress a smirk, her doughy face nigh quivering with the effort. I stare at her as I run a hand over my torso and squeegee off most of the coffee, purse my lips in a pinup girl pucker, and retrieve the dangling headset. With one foot firmly planted atop the wreckage that was my chair and the other hoisted up behind me in a classic Bettie cheesecake pose, with boobies defiantly outthrust, I reach deep into my eternal wellspring of secretarial snazziness.

"Good afternoon, ABC Realty. How may I help you? Pardon me? Oh, that. Yes, my chair unexpectedly exploded into hundreds of pieces. Yes, I fell down, but I'm fine now, thank you. Um. Sorry about the screaming. Yes, I can get right back to you with that information. Please hold just one moment."

The day I left for the St. Regis Hotel, I hid my suitcase in a broom closet so it wouldn't elicit any questions from the students. Once, when I left on a trip directly from PACT, the nonprofit after-school program in Harlem where I tutored in the afternoons, one of the twins stopped me just before I reached the door. "Miss Katie, you going on a trip?"

"I am."

"Where to?" I could feel the attention in the classroom shift: Pencils stopped scratching, side conversations halted, eyes came up.

"Colorado to visit some friends."

"Nuh-uh!"

"Yuh-huh."

"Tonight?"

"Yup. But I'll be back on Monday."

"Nuh-uh!"

"Yuh-huh."

"Nuh-uh!" she said, throwing her eyebrows skyward in disbelief.

The idea that I could take a flight from New York to Denver on a Friday and return on a Sunday was unfathomable. And why not? Many of my students, for whom traveling meant taking the subway south of Ninety-sixth Street, had never seen the inside of a plane. My

cheeks hot, I smiled, nodded, and quickly made my way out of the room, cursing myself for calling attention to just one more thing that separated me from them.

Sheets of rain engulfed the cab as it pulled up to the hotel, lit up like a Broadway stage on an otherwise darkened Fifty-fifth Street. I didn't hear the bellman open the car door over the windshield wipers' furious work, but once I paid the cabbie, there the bellman was, having already wrested my luggage from the trunk and staving the rain with an umbrella big enough for the beach.

"Does this look like everything?" he said.

"Uh-huh."

"May I ask your name?"

"Katie. Katherine Dykstra."

I climbed out of the cab and went to take my suitcase, but he whisked it out of my reach, beckoning me up a short flight of red-carpeted stairs and through a set of grand brass revolving doors. When we spilled out on the other side, I found myself in the warm glow of the lobby, under vaulted ceilings, and surrounded by St. Regis staff.

"We've been waiting for you."

"We thought you were arriving earlier."

"Your room is ready."

"Can we take you upstairs?"

They waited for me to speak. Confused and suddenly self-conscious, I stammered, "Uh, yes, the *Post,* I'm Katie." I felt my face flush, convinced they were judging me in my pilled coat and worn boots, the same clothes I felt overdressed in at PACT.

The St. Regis was one of seven New York City hotels that had recently renovated to incorporate condo units: "the ultimate in luxury living." My stay constituted research for a story I was writing for the *New York Post*'s Home section on the phenomena.

"There's really *no* way for you to understand the level of service unless you stay there." This I'd heard from the St. Regis PR woman in some form or another during every conversation I'd had with her

over the course of my research. Of course, I believed her and desperately wanted to take her up on her offer, but I just couldn't find any reason to.

"You're not thinking hard enough," complained a friend.

He was right. When would I, Katie Dykstra, of neither old nor new money, ever have an opportunity to stay in a suite at the St. Regis again? This was, I realized, the story. My editor loved it: middle-class midwestern girl who struggles to live in New York at all, tosses herself in with the city's elite and reports the details. It will, he said, be hilarious.

"Miss Dykstra, may I take you to your room?" asked a flagpole of a woman with an Eastern European accent.

I turned to follow her, but halfway to the elevator bank realized I hadn't tipped the bellman. I reached into my pocket and, extracting a couple of ones, moved toward the man, who was still standing where we had left him, but as I did, I thought: What if he's the same guy who'll bring my bags to my room? I should just tip him then. I pocketed the money as I looked him square in the eye, then turned to follow the woman upstairs. The man who delivered my luggage turned out not to be the same one I neglected in the lobby, but a new one whom I would also neglect, since he left while I was busy watching the butler put away my clothes.

Alone in my suite, I yelped and took a quick tour. The living room had an oak armoire, a dressed breakfast table, a chandelier dripping with crystal. Antique-looking furniture that I couldn't identify surrounded a brass and glass coffee table. The walls were sunshine-yellow silk, the elaborate molding done in white. The bathrooms were both marble, with double sinks and great big soaking tubs outfitted with expensive Italian soaps. The kitchenette boasted a dishwasher, a silver plate covered with glassware, and a tea tray on which stood a ramekin of tea bags, a plateful of honey sticks, a cream pitcher, and four flowered cups. In the bedroom, the carpet was the color of butter and

sprinkled with blushing pink roses that reminded me of the wallpaper from my childhood bedroom. There were oak-and-glass end tables, a dresser built into the wall, an enormous television. Even the radiators, sheathed in wrought iron and embossed with a cursive SR, were ornate.

I got up to look through the curtains that billowed around the bedroom windows. Outside was Fifth Avenue, St. Patrick's Cathedral, the Peninsula Hotel. The suite cost $1,800 a night; for me it came compliments of the St. Regis. The rent at my two-bedroom Upper East Side apartment was $1,850 a month. I split that with a roommate.

I leaped on top of the king-size bed and fell onto my back. Staring up at crystal chandelier number two, I called my mother. "You will not believe where I am."

PACT's classrooms are located exactly fifty blocks north of the St. Regis, at Fifth Avenue and 105th Street, deep in the musty basement of the Museo del Barrio. My apartment building sits at Eighty-eighth and First Avenue, halfway between.

Fluorescent-lit and concrete, the room where I work has two windows that, if they weren't covered in plastic to keep out the cold, would open to a view of the grates in the sidewalk above. There are three folding tables that wobble and squeak when touched and are surrounded by chairs whose padded guts spill out over their sides if they aren't missing altogether. Our program coordinator decided—optimistically, I thought—instead of replacing the chairs, to teach the kids to reupholster them, since they were the ones who destroyed them. Though months passed before the project commenced, I recently entered our classroom to find four of our chairs neatly recovered in thick green plastic. We also have a bookcase full of donated books, text- and otherwise, a shelf of games, a myriad of brightly colored inspirational and educational posters that cling to the walls, and two computers, which, for as long as I've been employed there, have never both worked at the same time.

The day I started at PACT, I stood in front of fifty kids, all black or

Latino, all from Harlem, and I was certain I'd made a mistake. Nervous, I bumbled through my introduction, stuttering as I explained that I was a journalist there to help them with their writing. They stared at me, curious but doubtful. Some snickered; others ignored me altogether, choosing instead to whisper to their friends.

In the days that followed, I tried to reach out, mention a musician I thought surely they'd like or a video game I'd seen advertised on TV. They'd giggle or shake their heads and turn away.

I assumed they thought I was too different from them to understand what got them excited, made them angry, or made them cry. And on many levels that was true. When the twins asked me to swing the rope so they could skip double Dutch, I didn't know how. When I inquired about the reason one girl was so melancholy, I was told that she'd been born HIV-positive. While helping another girl memorize the states and their capitals, I naively asked her about the boy whose picture was taped inside her binder, assuming it was her boyfriend. "That's my brother. He's dead," she said. I found out later that he'd been killed in a drive-by shooting earlier that month. All I could think to say was "Wow, I'm sorry. That must be really hard." I had taken the job because I thought kids were a kick, because I thought maybe this job could be parlayed into a real teaching position, because no matter how confused I was about what I was doing with my own life, there was no way working with underprivileged kids could ever be the wrong decision. But as I struggled to ingratiate myself, I wondered whether I had anything to offer.

As time wore on, I figured out that though I might not have had the same life experience as my students, I did know how it felt to be thirteen; I'd been picked on, had a crush, hated school, been passed over for a team. And slowly, a small following of kids began to sit with me at lunch, come to me with questions: "Miss Katie, will you help me study for my Global test? Miss Katie, can I ask your advice? Miss Katie, you like my new shoes?"

The teachers I worked with were harder. Miss M—a heavy Nigerian

whose accent was like a lullaby and whose knowledge of numbers bordered on genius—was nice enough, but we couldn't seem to alight on a topic that interested us both. And Miss O, a *Mother Jones*–reading kindergarten teacher with an intimidating streak of realism, had taken it upon herself to inform me of my place. "You really think you can help him? Honey, you're lucky he hasn't stolen your wallet" were the words she offered when I tried to reach out to a boy whom I hadn't seen pick up a book since I'd started. And when I discovered one of our thirteen-year-olds was illiterate and, concerned, shared it with Miss O—"She can't read!"—her response was a simple "Duh." But I didn't really care whether or not the teachers liked me. It was the kids whose affection I was after.

When I was a young girl, I desperately wanted to be rich. At night I would dream of sprawling houses on grounds blanketed in flower beds and etched with winding paths. Inside, there were rooms so big I couldn't see their ends, filled with indoor pools, tennis courts, and lots and lots of stuff. I would wander from room to room and discover secret alcoves overflowing with pillows, special tile and glass rooms made for hot tubs, dining tables dressed with china and stretching into eternity. In those dreams, I was always alone but completely content. When my alarm clock summoned me back into reality, I'd fight to stay with my riches, squeezing my eyes shut and willing myself to fall back into the dream. Occasionally, I was able. But usually, the illusion was gone, the blissful feeling just beyond my grasp.

In reality, my family lived in a two-story home on a tree-lined street. We had four bedrooms, two and a half baths, two cars in our garage. A perfectly nice home. A big home, even, except when I compared it to what I found around me. Our neighborhood lay thirty minutes south of Kansas City on the Kansas side. The surrounding suburbs, which had sprung up in the years since my family moved in, were stuffed with multimillion-dollar homes and manicured lawns, country clubs and four-car garages. My suburb, Leawood South, was

the oldest development in the neighborhood, one that, as we got older, my friends and I sarcastically dubbed "the slums of Leawood."

I learned early on that what I had wasn't enough. In fourth grade, one girl called me out in front of the class when the teacher stepped away from the room.

"Katie Dykstra wears the exact same thing every day," she'd said to the other students' snickers. "Why do you wear the exact same thing every day, Katie? Don't your parents have any money at all?"

I looked down at the Mickey Mouse sweatshirt my mother had bought for me in Orlando and flushed. I loved that sweatshirt and wore it not because it was the only thing I owned but because I thought it was cool. But under the class's reproachful gaze, I decided that she was right, of course I wore the shirt too often, of course they'd think we were poor, and thereafter eliminated the shirt from my lineup. The irony, which I can see only now, is that that girl's family also lived in a smaller home in Leawood South; they couldn't have had any more money than we did.

Leawood Middle School teemed with girls who carried Louis Vuitton bags and vacationed in Barbados. Their parents drove Lexuses and owned summer homes at the lake where they Jet Skied and suntanned from the decks of their speedboats. These were the girls whose friendship I longed for. Girls on the drill team, girls who threw parties, girls who had the attention of boys. I just knew that our differences lay in money, that if I had the same things they did, they would make room for me at their lunch table, invite me to the lake for the weekend. So I took note of the brands they wore, the places they went, and then begged my mother to give me the same. But she rolled her eyes at my requests—"*I've* never owned a hundred-dollar handbag, and *I'm* thirty-nine"—and instead my family took trips to the Ozarks and stayed in motels, drove Datsuns, and shopped at the Jones Store.

When I complained, my parents shook their heads and explained that they had chosen our house, which was "*way* out of their price

range," so that my brother and I could benefit from the school system. It was "one of the best in the country." They'd explain to me that I was being ungrateful, that I was better off than 95 percent of the world. But I didn't know the rest of the world. I didn't know anything except Leawood. And in Leawood, I might as well have been destitute.

By high school, I loathed all displays of wealth as the rest of the people I knew embraced them. Our class T-shirt had AMOR PECUNIA (love money) emblazoned on the front. On the back were the top ten reasons to attend Blue Valley North High School, which included Perrier water in the drinking fountains, signing bonuses for athletes, and valet parking. I found it nauseating. I had decided I hated all that I couldn't have.

During my junior year, I began volunteering. Every Saturday I drove to a church in downtown Kansas City and spent a few hours setting up, doling out, and cleaning up food for the city's homeless. I did this not out of generosity but because philanthropy was required to maintain my National Honor Society status. Many of the people who showed up those Saturday mornings frightened me—the bag lady whose bird-nested hair was so unkempt I couldn't tell if it was her own or some sort of hairpiece; the little person whose cheeks were caked in bright red rouge, her vacant eyes smeared with blue eye shadow and rimmed with spidery mascara-coated lashes; the Vietnam vet who came in raving about buying rocket parts; the pair of paraplegics who shared a wheelchair, one on the lap of the other, and laughed hysterically, nonstop—and some made me sad: the children, the people who wouldn't look me in the eye, and those who said thank you.

As that fall wore on, I began to understand what my parents had been trying to tell me: I was a "have." At sixteen, for me it was an epiphany. I easily adopted the plight of the underprivileged, railing against the government for the dearth of adequate social programs to anyone who would listen. I denounced the upper classes for the blind eye they turned toward the impoverished. I even complained about those who having no money to give didn't donate their time. And I be-

lieved what I said, I still do, but I also know that the realization that there were people worse off than I helped me reconcile my hatred for my own situation.

Somewhere along the line—probably during college, when I divorced myself from Leawood—I lost some of that passion. I still believed in being socially active, but I felt less righteous, less personally offended by blatant displays of wealth. I volunteered a little, but not much, and instead concentrated on school, partying, friends. When I moved to New York, I was at first frightened and then repulsed by the homeless who lived in the shadows of everyday life—the streets, the subway, the stoops in front of churches. I gave homeless men a wide berth when I passed them on the street, holding my breath so as not to inhale their stench. On the subway, when they'd walk through the cars, give their spiel, hold out their cup, I looked down at my magazine, pretending I couldn't see or hear them. And as I tried to become myself, I found myself once again looking at women with nice things, wishing I could afford to go to the theater at night, wear Marc Jacobs, own a pair of Manolos. Not that I ever let on. To say that I wanted these things was an affront to who I thought I was. I believed in people, not things, or so I said.

One afternoon, not long after I landed in New York, I found myself standing outside a boutique off Prince Street in Soho. I had been freelancing at Andy Warhol's *Interview* magazine, which was a lot like sitting in on a fashion show every day of the week. The fashion editor cruised the loft in clothes made for runways, and designers like Dolce & Gabbana made regular appearances in the office. I would stare in shame at my own outfit, inevitably from the Gap; my shirt might as well have had Mickey Mouse stretched across its front. In a desperate attempt to fit in, I went shopping.

With the exception of mega-labels like Prada and Gucci, I knew nothing of fashion or designers, so I wasn't able to choose a store on name alone, but I found some general rules held true. Namely: The smaller the store and the more outrageous the clothes in the display windows, the higher the prices.

The store I stood in front of, sprawling with modest clothes on display, passed both tests, so I figured it was safe. I was wrong, said the three-hundred-dollar price tag I found on a cotton T-shirt near the window. My pride, however, kept me from making an about-face. Instead I made a leisurely circle, every once in a while fingering the material on a pair of pants or holding a dress up to myself as if I could afford it.

I was just steps from the front door when a swishy salesman sidled up to me. "May I help you?" he said, his eyes starting at my sneakers and slowly working upward to khakis and barn jacket. His tone went straight to my core; unable to absorb the insult, I said, as a matter of fact, yes.

"I'm actually looking for something to wear to an event."

"What sort of event?" he said, cocking his head.

"A premiere and a party. I'm an editor at *Interview* magazine." I squared my shoulders to him and pointed up the cobblestone street for effect. This was partially true. *Interview* was hosting a premiere that weekend. That I was merely an assistant, freelance at that, and wasn't invited bore no relevance at the moment.

"Oh, well, we can certainly find something for you here," he said, and pulled me into a dressing room. "Take off your clothes."

As in some twisted Julia Roberts film, the following hour saw me in nearly everything the store had—including but not limited to floor-length silk skirts, low-brimmed hats, and unwieldy shawls. By the end, I stood staring at myself in a three-panel mirror, a most average-looking girl dressed head to toe in purple: heels, pants, shirt, and a big violet shawl that might or might not have been a cape. I was draped in the most expensive clothes my body will ever see, and I looked just like a grape.

"Fabulous," shrieked the man. "That's it."

It wasn't until I was at the register with my credit card out and the register flashing three thousand dollars that I snapped to. "You know? I have a couple other errands to run before I go home. Would you mind holding these until I get back? It'll take thirty minutes, tops."

I looked him in the eye. "Just so I don't have to drag all this around with me."

His tight-lipped smile told me he knew that I was a fraud. I wondered if he had known from the beginning. Embarrassed, I skulked from the store.

On my third night at the St. Regis, I allowed myself two hours to dress before meeting friends downstairs at the King Cole Bar. I soaked in a frothy bubble bath until I pruned; I padded from the walk-in closet to the dressing table to the armoire in St. Regis slippers and a downy robe; I listened to classical music piped over speakers I couldn't see, though the music reached every corner of the suite.

I was sitting at the vanity, my makeup spread out before me, when the doorbell rang. I jogged down the chandeliered hallway over the Oriental runner to the front door, outside of which I found a round-shouldered woman in a black-and-white housekeeping uniform. Her wiry hair was pulled into a messy bun and topped with a white cap. I smiled and leaned against the door.

"Oh, I am so sorry. I am here for your turndown service. I will come back," she said quietly and began to back away.

"Oh. Yes. No. Actually, I'm just on my way out. But I don't need a turndown; you don't need to come back," I said, waving my hand dismissively and shaking my head as I began to close the door. But then I had a second thought. "Oh, but could you help me out? The bar downstairs? Is it right or left when I come out of the elevator bank?"

"The bar?" She looked confused.

I assumed she hadn't understood my question and so turned to the right and acted it out: "If I come out of the elevator bank this way"—I stepped forward—"is the King Cole Bar right or left?" I motioned with my hands

She shook her head. "I am sorry, I don't know. I have a separate entrance. I do not know the main floor."

I stared at her in disbelief. A service entrance? It sounded so archaic, so upstairs/downstairs, so wrong. When I turned back to my suite, everything felt sordid. I loathed classism, and at that moment I loathed myself for loving the St. Regis.

Night number five: I invited some editors and colleagues from the *Post* over so I could show off my suite. I proudly gave the tour as each arrived, pointing out the dishwasher, the walk-in closet, the sprawling guest bathroom, as if I had paid for or in some way earned the room myself. Once everyone had arrived, I asked the butler to deliver a cheese tray, some french fries, and a bottle of red wine, which came to nearly a hundred dollars, my daily budget from the *Post.*

"So what'll the butler do?" asked my editor.

"Oh, you know, pretty much anything, iron your clothes, bring you coffee in the morning, do your laundry."

"Have you done any of that?"

"He unpacked for me."

"Anything else?"

"Not really."

"Well, you have to ask for more for the piece. And see if the concierge can get you last-minute reservations at some hard-to-get-into restaurant, maybe one of Mario Batali's."

"You should have them draw you a bath before you get back from work," said the photo editor.

"I know, you should make a bunch of celebrity-like requests," said a designer. "You know, like make them sort out the green M&M's." Everyone laughed.

"I couldn't," I said.

"Why not?"

"I don't know. I just couldn't."

"Whatever. It's research."

"You know," I said, "it's been kind of a head trip going back and forth from PACT to here."

"I know, I know, you probably want to bring like twenty homeless people back here with you," said my editor.

"No, I want to give twenty homeless people the eighteen hundred dollars it costs for me to stay here for one night."

This was true. Sort of. It made me sick to think what that money—or, worse, $10,800, what my six-night stay would cost—could do for the PACT program. But I couldn't deny that I was enjoying myself. I liked waking up to *The New York Times* and fresh-pressed coffee. I liked stepping into slippers after climbing out of a bed bigger than my bedroom and living high enough for sunlight to spill into my room.

One afternoon not long after I'd started at PACT, when the sidewalks were heaped with snow and the temperature was subzero, one of my students caught up with me on my way home. We shouted over the wind and squinted as snowflakes pelted our faces. My shoes were soaked through, and I cursed their thin leather.

"You know what I'm going to do tonight?" I said to her. "I'm going right to a shoe store to buy some winter boots; this is ridiculous, look at my feet." I held up one of my sopping shoes, hoping to make her laugh.

But instead of giggling, she said, "You're rich, aren't you, Miss Katie?"

I stopped and turned to her. "You think I'm rich? No, honey, I'm not rich."

She looked at me skeptically, and in that moment I had no idea whether I was telling the truth. I wasn't rich. I'd started out in this city sharing a bed with a friend from college in a room so small that in the morning she had to ask me to lift up my legs, which hung off the foot of the bed, just so she could pass, and most months I live paycheck to paycheck. Except, when I needed new boots, I bought them. And if I couldn't afford them, I could always call my parents. I knew nothing about the financial situation of this girl's family. She was always clean, well dressed, as was her sister. Their mother worked in the post office downtown, which likely paid more than my writing, but she had five kids to care for, and to my knowledge, the father was absent. So where

did that leave us? I had no idea. Perhaps it didn't matter. All I knew was that I didn't want her to associate me with the rich. I feared that if she did, she would forget the trust we'd gained, resent me the way I resented those who were better off than I was. Then again, maybe I was only projecting my own ambivalence onto her. I was repulsed by the excess and exclusionary culture of the rich, even as I wanted to be a part of it. I thought the wealthy were selfish, shallow, and so I thought she must too.

I kept the St. Regis from the people at PACT the entire time I was there. I reasoned that I hadn't told the concierge about my students, so why would I tell them about the St. Regis? Really, I felt guilty for partaking in such extravagance when I considered myself a champion for the lower classes. But that didn't stop me from taking advantage of the perks. I had my shoes shined, some dry cleaning done. I dressed up to walk through the lobby, pretending I belonged, and took pleasure in what I perceived as people's confusion about me. The *Post* had me pose for photos in the lobby, under the awning, stepping out of a Bentley. Passersby stopped to stare, wonder who I was and what was going on. I loved it.

At the end of the week, I checked out of the St. Regis, and my life went back to normal. I climbed four flights of stairs to reach my apartment, washed my dishes by hand, brewed my own coffee, read the *Times* online, and cursed my radiator, which sporadically sprayed me with scalding water while I slept. And it felt good. There's just something, I would say to people, about being around your stuff.

The Wednesday after my story came out in the *Post,* a few weeks after I'd returned to my apartment, I picked up a few copies for my clip book on my way up to PACT. During announcements, D. reported the Knicks score, M. gave a three-word review of *Be Cool*—"It was fine"—and Ms. O informed the kids that state tests were rapidly approaching, which meant they would have to start staying late for test prep.

"Anyone else?" said our program coordinator. "Staff?"

I hadn't planned on speaking, but suddenly, my right arm was up, my left scrounging in my bag for the clip. When I found it, I felt my face flush. "Um, so you all know how I write for the *Post* in the mornings, right? Well, not long ago, I stayed in this hotel downtown for a story, and they printed my picture in the paper with it." I held up the clip, which pictured me smiling from just inside the doorway of my suite.

"You did what?" said one kid.

"Lemme see," said another. As the story went around the room, I answered questions: "No, my picture doesn't go with every piece I write"; "Yes, I came up with the idea myself"; "No, I didn't have to pay for the room"; "Yes, I invited my friends over to see it"; "No, we didn't have a raging party." A couple of the kids read the story, but most just looked at my picture and passed it on. One girl told me she'd thought about being a journalist, and I nodded. "Good idea," I said. "It's fun, but you'll never make a lot of money."

Then the room got loud, kids shifted in their seats, talked to their friends. And one kid remembered he'd just done well on a test, which made other kids remember that they, too, had done well on tests, or even not so well, and on and on.

Fact #1: The first miracle I ever saw was being sold on eBay.

The winning bid, I believe, was in the neighborhood of $28,000.

If holiness exists anywhere in modern society, this would surely be a small price to pay for it, but I never entertained the possibility of raising the money. I didn't need to hold it or own it—all I wanted was to see it, to verify its existence. Booting up my computer, blinds drawn and lights off, I felt like some middle-aged voyeur of holy pornography. I couldn't pinpoint precisely which commandment I was breaking, or whether it would qualify as a venial sin, but when the Web page loaded, I felt a shudder course through my body. The screen went blinding white, and then . . . there she was.

The Virgin Mary.

Encased in grilled cheese.

The bidding war seemed as blasphemous to me as the congealed cheddar next to her eye, and I stared for a long moment, committing the sight to memory.

The days that followed provided the bedrock upon which all future theological discussions would sit. I quote, verbatim:

"It's not a sign from God."

And my retort: "Did you see it?"

"Yeah, so?"

"It looks exactly like the Virgin Mary."

"Yeah, that's the whole point."

"Well?"

"Well, what? God doesn't speak through grilled cheese!"

And there it was. Because I wasn't sure if He did or not. Forget the veracity of this one miracle, or the chances of a face arising by accident, or any kind of scientific explanation. Could God speak through someone's lunch? Of course. But *would* He?

My inability to decide immobilized me, and for weeks I debated the pros and cons of burning bushes versus overcooked sandwiches. The crux of my inner debate stays with me to this day: Where would God speak if not through the culinary flaws of a desperate housewife? Would He take over the airwaves? Project His voice through the heavens? Possess Britney Spears? No matter how hard I thought, I couldn't come up with a method of communication that wouldn't be written off as a hoax or, worse, a fluke. A talking burning bush today would most likely be a can of lighter fluid and a midget with a megaphone, and there isn't a single trick in the Bible that couldn't be replicated by David Blaine. How could God be God in a society where every available medium is inherently profane? How could He possibly show Himself in a way that wouldn't be ridiculed? Is a grilled cheese really that far-fetched? Because manifesting as a waterspout or a cloud wouldn't be that much better. And as the notion of God's communication slid further and further from my realm of possibility, I suppose the notion of His existence went with it.

Fact #2: I lost my virginity while listening to a man with Down syndrome sing a cover of "California Dreamin'."

Mind you, I'm not proud of this, but it's the sexual cross I will always bear. I've since rationalized the experience to provide some sort of post hoc intentionality, but I suspect the truth is that it was nothing more than an accident, a random twist of fate. To this day, my defining sexual moment sits in my memory as both a beacon of individuality and a gross bastardization of something beautiful.

It started innocently enough. My girlfriend and I had recently discovered that the actor Chris Burke (Corky, from *Life Goes On*) had a thriving side career as a recording artist. We had also just discovered Napster. This combination of events somehow became a sexual catalyst, and bam, the deed was done. For the record, I don't think this is much worse than losing your virginity to "How Deep Is Your Love" or a Teddy Pendergrass song; at least I have originality on my side. And these days being "original" seems to have gone the way of the bald eagle—protected by a few left-wing nutcases and mocked by everybody else. In the past, it seemed like everyone's first time was special. But when you've seen twelve television episodes, four Hollywood blockbusters, and a Lifetime special about losing your virginity, avoiding a derivative experience becomes more important than your actual performance. I would rather be unique than romantic. I would rather be different than right. But if there's one thing that modern twentysomethings understand, it's that there is very little we can do that is truly original.

Considered separately, these stories are merely embarrassing. Taken together, they represent, for me, the dissolution of the most important concepts in modern society:

Sex and Religion.

Two things I've spent my whole life searching for.

Two things historically known for promising experiences they can't quite deliver.

Two things absolutely dependent on mystery for their success.

And consequently, two things that have been ruined for me.

It's a new development rooted in an ancient conflict. In my mind, America has always been a society teetering on the brink of intense cognitive dissonance. Founded by Puritans but encouraging free trade, America has been doomed since its inception to be a nation of people who use two-pronged dildos while counting rosary beads and crying with shame. Our free market encourages self-satisfaction of the highest degree, while our religious underpinnings encourage austere, monastic repentance. This disparity never bothered me much until recently. It seemed a finely tuned, carefully balanced schizophrenia. It seemed to work.

I've always tried to construct my life on these two pillars—the sacred and the profane, the spiritual and the hedonistic. If one broke down, I found solace in the other, seeking comfort in an afterlife when my corporeal existence wasn't going so well, and ignoring my eternal soul when I aced a test or got asked to the Sadie Hawkins dance. As long as I had one or the other to fall back on, I was fine. This mélange of existential solutions worked well until *both* ends of my world began to misfire, leaving me anxious, alone, and stuck in the middle. These two pillars, I began to suspect, were crumbling for the same underlying reason.

Like a good David Copperfield show, both sex and religion rely heavily on atmosphere and prevailing expectations. As such, they are dependent on a keenly developed sense of mystery for their visceral impact. Without mystery, they strike with all the force of an unloaded cap gun.

This is where I began to feel cheated.

In the past, children were taught to revere the cosmos as a repository of unanswerable questions, as the home of the gods, as a vast expanse of hope. I was taught about the *Challenger* and the fact that the nearest star is over forty trillion kilometers away. My parents got acts of God, miracles, and angels. I get global warming, stage magicians who reveal their secrets, and psychotic hallucinations. Our grandpar-

ents had the secrets of life embedded in their own bodies. I know that over 50 percent of my behavior comes from genetic material. It used to be Freemasons and the Kabbalah and the Illuminati. Now it's Google. There is no hidden knowledge, there is nothing I can't know, there is no information that can't be obtained instantaneously—or within minutes if my DSL is down. My mind thirsts for nothing, and I fear it has learned not to drink. Knowledge is a universal good, I understand that. But, I argue, a keenly developed sense of the mysterious is also a universal good—one that I have not been afforded.

There is no enemy, there is no concerted attack; there are only advancement and progress. I understand that, but I wouldn't be a good twentysomething if I didn't kvetch about the media. After all, if you can't pinpoint the message, pinpoint the medium. And growing up ensconced in a world of bright lights and overstimulation, I found it extremely difficult to hold on to a sense of quiet mystery.

I suspect I'm not alone in this.

The process begins early in our lives, as we are continually stripped of the simple, everyday awe-inspiring acts. We experience everything visually before we experience it viscerally, and as a result, we never really experience anything at all. I knew what marijuana was like and was disappointed when it wasn't. I knew how senior prom was going to be and was crushed by the reality. I knew what the Eiffel Tower looked like and found out it's not that tall. I knew what cynicism felt like. And thanks to *MacGyver,* I knew how to turn a pinecone into a bomb, but that didn't work either. Media is not new, but its utter dominance over our mental landscape is. In a twenty-four-hour news world, mysteries are systemically eradicated, leaving sex and religion to dry up like water droplets under a burning sun. And since those are all I've ever had and all I've ever wanted, I am left scorched, thirsty, and pissed off.

Let's look at them one at a time.

First, religion.

Every society has some concept of it, most modern conflicts have some relation to it. And it's changing. As science has crept up, organized religion has slowly relinquished its hold on absolute knowledge.

Once the repository of all global inquiry, austere bodies like the Catholic Church have ceded much of their intellectual territory to other branches of thought. However, while doing this, they have tightened their grip on the one area where they maintain complete dominance: the realm of the unknowable. One of the primary purposes of religion has always been to provide answers to the existential questions. Where do we go after we die? Where did we come from? What is our purpose on earth? These answers, though provided with confidence, are rooted in esoteric knowledge, revelations from the mouth of God, and the mysteries of the ages. To put it another way, they are based in faith—in a belief that does not rest on logical proof. Consequently, the individuals best prepared for a strong religious faith as adults are those who have grown up maintaining belief in things beyond the rational. The media have stripped us of our childhood beliefs and, as a result, have unintentionally stripped us of our adult beliefs. At least that's what happened to me.

What are the hallmarks of childhood faith? Santa Claus. The Easter Bunny. Parental infallibility. The government. The inherent goodness of mankind. I, for one, found out that Santa Claus wasn't real while watching an episode of *Cheers* with my parents. I watched movies with crumbling buildings, bumbling adults, and sinking ships. I read newspaper articles mocking the government and disproving the Shroud of Turin. Everywhere I turned, I saw blanket refutations of magic, ghosts, goblins, and fairies. Even cartoons today are more likely to be sardonic than uplifting.

Don't get me wrong, I applaud the rise of rationalism and reason as much as the next guy. I even subscribe to *Skeptical Inquirer* magazine. But I also support the idea that if you remove a person's belief system, you should be prepared to replace it with something. We all thought that hard science would be an acceptable surrogate for misty religiosity. Maybe it's not. There are certain things we'll likely never have unequivocal answers to—life after death, the existence of a God, etc. And maybe, just maybe, maintaining innocuous areas of myth in our society is a small price to pay for developing a deeper sense of

wonder and mystery. After all, that's the only way to deal with the big questions later on in life.

What I'm saying is this: If you have the Tooth Fairy as a child, you might not need the grilled cheese as an adult.

If you grow up losing your awe of the universe and awe of yourself, if you lose your fairy tales and ghost stories and your belief in angels, then what exactly is supposed to translate into a mature belief in the sublime? If you know about red blood cell transport and what causes lightning and earthquakes, if you know why the sky is blue and precisely how humans evolved from apes, why would you ever knowingly seek out mysteries? If you've never had to wonder about something for longer than thirty seconds, how do you ever become comfortable simply not knowing? We are the first generation to encounter this problem—the recipients of a great social experiment perpetrated by our predecessors. It's beyond the rise of rationalism our forefathers had to confront; it's the rise of visualism. Fast answers and easy explanations, presented in convenient, graphically designed packages. Logos have become the Word.

A twenty-four-hour-news society needs to move quickly, but metaphor and deep cognition take time. Pictures are worth a thousand words, moving billboards are worth at least a novella, and movies are worth a lifetime.

By trimming down our attention span and lessening our capacity for complex discussion, the media have (at least tacitly) encouraged people to search for ready-made solutions to life's difficult problems. Sadly, true religion cannot exist in a world of empty pictures. It is a deeper concept, one that requires words, stories, and metaphors for its transmission and comprehension. Twentysomethings today are confronted with the rise of visual religions—complete, packaged ideologies that require no discussion, thought, or analysis. If you spend your entire life being taught that there is a solution to every problem, it's a relief to have a body that provides answers to the unknowable.

By stripping away mysteries and keeping us unprepared for the big questions in life, the media may have pushed millions toward the

warm blanket of organized religion. But in the same breath, the media may have also seriously damaged religion, perhaps irreparably. In a world where the idols of Christianity can be contained by cheese and bread, there is not much room for God to manifest His awesome power.

If the sacred in our society can be diminished by a dearth of mystery, it's easy to believe that the profane can be as well. If something as powerful and complex as religious belief rests upon the unknowable, perhaps our most basic evolutionary urge is similarly dependent.

Let's talk about sex.

In a world dominated by Cinemax, *Real Sex 1-47,* and *elimiDATE,* there is not much room for healthy sexual development. Information is the enemy of mystery, and mystery is the bedfellow of sexual arousal. The largest sexual organ in the body (contrary to popular belief) is the brain, and a certain amount of societal eroticism primes us for the leap into the sack. The mysteries of the human body, of romance, and of sex propel young minds to heights of wild fantasy. Or they used to. I saw at least a hundred breasts in 2D before I came close to exploring them with my other senses. It's sad when a teenage boy is no longer dreaming of what breasts look like but rather what they taste or smell like. We know how we're supposed to kiss, so we never enjoy the wonder of exploring it. We know what we're supposed to say, what we're supposed to do, how long it's supposed to last, and exactly what types of dirty talk are okay (thank you, *Seinfeld* and *Taxicab Confessions*).

To a large extent, the media help define modern sexuality. For evidence, look to cultural anthropology. If women in a culture expose their breasts but cover their legs and feet, what elements of the body do you think become sexualized? And you can't even get a good silicone foot implant these days.

Put succinctly, the question is this: How does a generation with absolute knowledge of felching, donkey punching, and the dirty sanchez maintain healthy sex lives?

Answer: We don't.

Forget oil. Forget diamond reserves. Just leave us something to explore, for Christ's sake.

I wasn't left much. Growing up, during moments of intimacy, I would find myself comparing and contrasting rather than experiencing. "This isn't quite like Joey and Dawson" or "This isn't nearly as good as Mikey's first kiss in *The Goonies*." Every pair of breasts I saw was compared to Shannon Tweed's, and every pair of legs had to live up to Cindy Crawford's, which just meant I was constantly disappointed by the things I'd been waiting my whole life to experience. By showing us what to expect from our sexual encounters, and by sensationalizing these very private experiences, the media have managed to strip sexuality of its mystery. And without mystery, sex is just one more thing we have to fit into our schedule. It's a sad state of affairs when, just to make a sexual experience special and unique, you have to resort to downloading bad covers of bad songs sung by out-of-work television actors.

So what do we do?

Devoid of mystery and sick of reality, what options do we have?

Where do we go when we're stripped of the sacred, bored of the profane, and stuck squarely in the middle?

I see two possible answers that are, not surprisingly, at opposite poles. One solution, fame, is provided by the media, while the other solution, individualism, is (ironically) provided by the masses. Both are worth examining.

Let's look at the media solution first, since it's both basic and pervasive: When you lose the unknown, make the known hyperreal. Fame. Ultra-bright with full-time coverage of Ben and Jen, Brad and Angelina, Paris and Anyone. Watch the shadows on the wall so you don't have to turn around, because really, that's just a bummer. By creating a culture full of immediacy and accessibility, the media has provided the two things that mystery doesn't. If we focus on the now, now, now, we will never be in doubt, because the present is the one time in our lives that is never, ever mysterious. You can't regret losing something you never have time to miss.

We are even given stewards to guide us through this shift toward instant gratification. Modern celebrities seem to be merely temporary guides to handle the little things in life—what to wear, where to go, how to speak, what to think. We are given overt social clues to follow because the more solutions we're provided, the less we have to seek. Stated another way, if globalization and mass media provide answers to all of life's big questions, they had better provide answers to the small ones.

The end result is that people are elevated not necessarily because they deserve to be but because that is where they are *needed*. Often modern fame isn't about talent as much as it is about the ability to live one's life in the public sphere. It's a necessary job that requires no résumé—it reeks of ease and luck, and it sounds as simple as being yourself for a living. Which makes us all crave it.

At least it makes me crave it. And if there is one overarching lesson my generation has absorbed, it's that individual stories always resonate with the culture at large. We are the generation of memoirs and reality television, and that gives me and everyone else the right to speak for our peers. In fact, we are expected to.

We can all become celebrities. We can all guide the nation through the valley of the shadow of death. What I ate for breakfast this morning is interesting and of worth. My blog should be popular. We are pushed to admire actuality over potential, because hopes, wishes, and dreams require that which has been stolen from us. Because the unknown has become rare and frightening, we are taught to admire taut skin over wrinkled brains. The average age of our American Idols is twenty-two.

Wisdom and talent take time, but fame is immediate, since there are no requirements. It's accessible to everyone. There are no genetic boundaries, no societal boundaries, no gender or race boundaries. Born poor? Perfect. We can market that. Nelly. 50 Cent. Born rich? Perfect. We can market that. Paris Hilton. Nicole Richie. Born into fame? Good. Gwyneth Paltrow. Not born into fame? Even better. How about Tom Cruise? Born attractive and untalented? That's fine. Try Heather Graham. Born the other way around? Perfect. Steve Buscemi.

Fame has no boundaries. It gives the illusion, and who says it's an illusion, that everyone could and should be royalty. That everyone should be immortal. That everyone deserves his or her fifteen minutes, talent, looks, money, fame, or morality aside.

Persuasive, isn't it? Now imagine if I presented it with neon signs and dancing girls . . . verrry hard to resist.

That's where they get us—we admire it because we want it. I certainly do. The thought of Kevin Federline being more famous than I am is the cruelest form of torture this side of slow evisceration. We all want it because without mystery in our lives, we can't aspire to some hazy and vague reward. We have to want what is here and now. We have to want something we can see, touch, and believe, as we don't know how to trust anything that isn't tangible.

We admire the newly minted bourgeoisie because we're paying dues toward our own future fame. We support it because we aspire to it. It's like Social Security. If I support the system today by buying an Ashlee Simpson CD or a copy of *Us Weekly,* I get to be on a game show in twenty years. Everybody wins. Because fame can come at any time, to anyone.

And, of course, to paraphrase *The Incredibles* (and Ayn Rand): If everyone is famous, then that means no one is. If you remove the top and the bottom of a society—the base and the elevated, the sacred and the profane—you end up stuck in the middle, homogenized.

It's a vicious cycle: The more information we are shown, the fewer mysteries remain. The less mystery is in our lives, the more we turn to the media.

Fame is the solution provided by our mass-media culture. Our personal answer is a little more devious and a little more combative.

Individualism.

This is the struggle of modern youth—how to find isolation in a connected world. How to find the unknown in a sea of information. How to be an individual when we know from day one that it's a virtual impossibility.

This is *our* answer to losing our religion. *Our* solution to losing our

sexuality. It is human nature to rebel against categorization and to defy reductionism. We are large. We contain multitudes.

It's safe to say one of the enjoyable attributes of mystery is that we're uncertain of the outcome. As a result of media proliferation and the gradual removal of mysteries from our public and private lives, our generation has pursued the notion of individuality with a ferocity matched only by the manner in which our grandparents pursued conformity. In an age of global connectivity, the notion of doing something unique is a pipe dream that spirals further and further away, the longer you live. The notion that someone else is having the same sexual encounter at the same time—or the idea that there are others communing with the divine with identical results—is anathema. These are private activities and unique activities, and they are intentionally kept separate from public consumption. But precisely because they are private, unique, and therefore entertaining, the media puts them at the forefront of our consciousness.

And so we rebel.

We strive to be different because it's the only way we know to rediscover mystery.

The X Games are less an adrenaline rush than a societal existential crisis.

Bondage is less a sexual deviance than losing the virginity that was stolen from us.

Self-mutilation is less angst-ridden conformity than knowing we are individuals who contain pain, love, and sadness in one corporeal body.

The media struggles against this counterattack, but still we fight to maintain the one truth we are born with and die with: that We. Are. Different.

Our generation knows attempts at independence. You know angsty Nine Inch Nails and Tori Amos, cutting yourself in your room, tattooing yourself, piercing your body and dyeing your hair to institute some of your own permanence instead of having it forced upon you by institutions that were outdated the day they were born. You know that

the worst feeling in the world isn't loss or heartbreak or searing fire—it's thinking your whole life that you're original and then finding out in one dark, crushing moment that you're not. It never crosses your mind that statistically, you can't be an individual. It never crosses your mind that Tori Amos is a multiplatinum artist or that there are thousands of tattoo parlors. It never crosses your mind that this pain that feels so real and deep and unique might be part of a worldwide trend or part of a future marketing campaign. The quickest way to kill innermost thoughts is to assume that someone, somewhere, is thinking the exact same thing at the exact same time. We know that if all pain is relative, then what we feel cannot be pain. We know that if all love is relative, then our lives must be devoid of passion. Our experience rarely competes with the devastation of a tsunami or the romance of Casanova.

And yet we struggle on.

Fame versus individuality.

Media versus person.

Mystery versus the known.

Where are twentysomethings today? Confronting our cognitive dissonance head-on. Knowing we aren't different but struggling desperately to appear that way. Knowing that the world is filled with pain and suffering but trying to live our lives nonetheless. Knowing fame is fleeting but feeling that it's all we have.

You take the good, you take the bad, you take them both, and there you have . . .

Us.

A generation caught in the middle because both sides have been destroyed.

A generation whose only mystery is how we got here.

A generation anxious to teach our children about Santa Claus and about God and about a time when man stared at a shooting star and thought about his soul.

My good friend The Poet wants to start a Revolution, but he can't because his wife is watching HGTV. A few days ago, he tells us as we sit at The Café, he found her in front of the television. After he lumbered down from his attic study where he'd locked himself in for twelve hours to write and read, he said to her, "The Khmer Rouge. Those people suffered." This last word caused his eyes to shut, his fist to clench. His wife was glazed over, watching Martha Stewart teach everyone how to fold napkins into the shape of a Thanksgiving turkey. She handed The Poet the piece of paper on which she'd scrawled a menu. "I'm thinking of making grilled salmon with an avocado-lime sauce for dinner."

The Poet recounts all of this to us with a straight face, his blood rising to his neck and ears. We're all frustrated with our lives. It's me, twirling my hair, my Fiancé, rubbing his hands, and our Writer Friend, who constantly adjusts her shirt cuffs. We're all smoking, politely listening to one another's grievances, and halfheartedly mocking the Saturday-afternoon shoppers combing the square in their semi-designer shoes.

"Look at that girl. Could she kill another sheep for her coat?" Writer Friend points with the lit cigarette between her fingers. We all

turn toward the girl, who has heard Writer Friend and is trying to ignore us by ducking into another shop. We all scowl.

"Maybe your wife's depressed," Writer Friend offers. "That's what happens sometimes. You get stuck in a job you hate . . ."

The Poet is not satisfied. "We used to have great conversations," he says. "That's why I married her. She's the most intelligent person I know, next to me." He laughs self-consciously when he says this. "Now there's just nothing there. Just home-decorating shows."

I'm watching the girl with the sheepskin coat through the shop-windows. She's browsing the racks, trying to see if we're still staring at her. I'm tempted to point to the boutique's other door and mouth, "Escape." Instead, I turn to The Poet and say, "Yes, it sounds like depression to me. I mean, I've been watching television a lot more since we moved."

Fiancé nods without looking at anyone.

It's true. I've been suffering since we started our New Life. We recently moved two states away from The Poet and Writer Friend so I could take a teaching job. It was supposed to allow me to not forget that the most important thing in my life is Writing. I'm making a decent wage, we have a better apartment, better food, and can afford haircuts at the local salon. But it's been two months and I haven't put pen to paper. Nor have I had a decent conversation with anyone but my cats since we left The Café, The Poet, and Writer Friend. So we're here for a visit and to revive our hopes for The Revolution.

Fiancé and I are two months shy of our wedding, and lately, the only thing keeping me from jumping headfirst into the depression pool is the stupid wedding gown in the closet. I put it on and parade around the house, pretending my cats are bridesmaids holding up the train, until they pounce on it and snag the delicate fabric only my mother knows the name of. I sometimes find myself saying things like "I just can't wait to be married" to women in the supermarket who comment on my engagement ring. Little details like monogrammed

cocktail napkins take up hours of my day. I find myself staring at my reflection in the bathroom mirror, wondering who the hell I am and what has become of the person I was in my early twenties—that dumb kid who was overconfident and sipped bourbon with her college professors before classes. What has become of my Old Life? In the New Life, I'm not even the shadow of the person I thought I would become—the writer with the book deal and a summer house in Oregon. I'm just a Fiancée, a Teacher, a Wage Earner.

And those wages aren't enough for two. Fiancé hasn't found a fulltime job, and this grates on my nerves. At a dinner party hosted by my new coworkers, a woman told me, "Make sure you keep separate bank accounts. That way—" She made her fingers into scissors and moved them through the air. "You know?"

I nodded. But no, I didn't know. We'd just opened a joint account, and secretly, I was looking forward to sharing my debts. I'd said to Fiancé something like "You take care of the checkbook and just tell me when I can spend some money." Again I stood in front of the mirror for an hour, wondering if, during the move into the New Life, I'd forgotten my brain in the Old one. I frantically searched the boxes in our attic for some lost bill, a relic of my single days, to remind me I wasn't always a joint account, a corecipient of important mail. I found a student loan package addressed only to me, at an address I'd forgotten, and held it to my chest as if it were a doll.

I think The Poet's Wife is experiencing the same frantic strain. She's working four days a week at a tiny community college, teaching public speaking. I point out to The Poet that this may be the reason behind the HGTV binge. "But she wanted that job," he says. "I told her not to take it."

I have no doubt he did. "It's slave labor, what they pay you in those places," I can almost hear him saying. "It will dull your mind." And now, faced with his fulfilled prophecy, what might be bothering him is the fact that no one has told him how right he was to begin with. So I turn to him and say, "Okay, you were right, now what?" He shrugs me off, taking a drag from his cigarette and readjusting his black sports

jacket. We've all given up smoking, but here we are, dumping out packs of cigarettes onto our table and divvying them up among us. We'll quit again once we scatter back into our lives.

But The Poet is not as quick to dismiss his wife's job as he used to be. He knows how hard it is to find a job worth taking. He spent over a year looking for one, looking for a place that would hire a Revolutionary Poet. No one was biting. And I can imagine his wife becoming frantic, wondering what they would do for money.

"And don't forget," I say, "you've got the Baby, and I'm sure she's worrying about that, too."

"*I* watch the Baby when she's teaching," he says.

There's nothing I can say to this. He is, by most accounts, a laudable father. The Baby has given him a broader perspective on the world, has opened his poetic gaze from the holocaust and tombs to burps and giggles. As he points out, "I'm preparing the next generation for The Revolution."

In graduate school we all decided the mainstream would kill you. We'd meet each week at The Café to discuss our writing, but what we were really doing was voicing our views against popular politics, conventional religion, circus media, and fashion trends. We spent hours discussing how most people are ignorant when it comes to good literature. We were all so full of self-righteousness that we audibly condemned people wearing any colors other than black, brown, and gray. We smoked our cigarettes, huddled over our cups, and prepared for The Revolution.

At first The Poet's Wife believed as we all did. But now she seems to be taking up domesticity, and this doesn't gel well with The Revolution. The Poet says, "I mean, when I tell her I'll do my own laundry, she makes me out to be the bastard. Shouldn't that be good, that I want us to be equals?"

I shrug. Writer Friend is quiet. Fiancé looks between his shoes for the answer and finds it. "Maybe she's going through a phase," he offers.

He should know about this, too. I have moments of cleanliness. I vacuum sporadically, scrub the toilet, do all of the laundry in one day.

This domestic behavior has increased in the New Life. Not knowing anyone, attempting a new routine, forces me to face my home. I look around and don't like what I see. If I can't change the world, at least I can change the bedsheets.

This depression about the New Life started before we left the Old Life. It was as if Fiancé and I were mourning the upcoming death of someone we knew very well. We were reluctant to talk about what would happen once our Old Life was over, or what to expect in our New Life, so we spent hours with the PlayStation he'd gotten as an engagement present. I was between careers with nothing to do but pack for our move, and he'd just finished a summer job. It was acceptable to spend fourteen hours a day on one level of Metal Gear Solid as long as we didn't spend too much time looking at the boxes piling up like coffins in our apartment.

We declined farewell-dinner-party invitations so we could stay home, connected to the television. Entire conversations went something like this:

"You hungry?"

"Didn't we eat?"

"That was on level seven. It's almost nine."

"We should eat."

"What are you fixing?"

"I'm not cooking. Food was your idea."

Consequently, we dined on takeout, playing a game of Gran Turismo to determine who'd have to pick up the food.

In the New Life, the PlayStation stayed hidden for two days. After all, we had things to unpack, joint bank accounts to open. We had a brave new future to worry about. We joined the local gym and started swimming.

Then I came home one afternoon to find Madden NFL 2004 had once again invaded the living room.

"What're you doing?" I said.

"Relaxing."

"Relaxing from what?" While Fiancé claims to be spending his

time writing or reading, I can't testify to seeing either thing done without the television on.

"I'm trying to read," he said, book splayed next to him on the couch, red controller in his hand.

I put my bag down and kicked off my shoes. "What's for dinner?" The cats came clamoring out of their naps and were hungry, too. "You feed them?" I asked, although I knew the answer. I went to the kitchen and opened their food. For a second I considered that Fiancé might be just as depressed as I was, might understand me through what I wasn't saying and come into the kitchen and give me some sign of reassurance. But when the television snapped off and he came huffing into the kitchen, he only asked, "What's wrong with you?"

I didn't know how to tell him I hate the woman I'm becoming in this New Life, so I said, "I was thinking about making tacos tonight."

There was a twitch over his left eye, a moment when I thought he might give me the comfort I needed. He took a step forward, opened the fridge, and said, "I'll grate the cheese."

This depression has caused me to fall away from the rational world. I find myself thinking more than one time during the day, If I lived in Italy, I wouldn't need a husband, just a series of lovers and a sports car. I've never been to Italy, but I see myself there with windblown hair and a maid I call Chee-Chee because I can't speak Italian. I imagine myself as a Bond girl in one of the early movies. Better yet, as Miss Moneypenny. Someone caught up in nothing more than lust, whose job it is to fantasize about one man over and over again.

I frequently watch Court TV on the days I'm not teaching. I set up mock court in the living room, placing my cats on opposite sides of the couch and saying, "So, Doc, you are the plaintiff, and you're suing Tinkerbell for damages that occurred on the night of September twenty-fourth. Could you explain to me the circumstances surrounding the disappearance of your fuzzy mouse?" I sentence both of them to life in prison for running from the courtroom.

I don't share any of this with The Poet. It's too embarrassing and

Unrevolutionary. But I can't help but feel that his wife and I are sharing a room in the same void. Here we are, educated women, and neither of us can get over what's expected of us on HGTV. While I'm sitting drinking my tea and smoking myself into a headache, I look around the place I've left. The Café used to be my outlet in the Old Life. I had a weekly appointment, a place to be on Wednesday afternoons, and a reason to wash my hair. It was the place where things like "I'm a socialist" were said without anyone raising an eyebrow. A place where The Poet once warned me, "Hitler had more compassion for animals than humans. Be careful how much you love your cats." We'd discuss apartheid, consumer ignorance, global warming caused by SUVs. Now these thoughts are slowly turning to mush, and it's scaring me.

Explaining how difficult it is in the New Life to form a new café group is not as hard a concept, though. I say, "We have a café, but everyone works as much as everyone else. It's hard to find a good time to meet. And no one's really serious about it."

"Just come out here once a month," The Poet says. "We could have marathon meetings."

"Or e-mail stuff," Writer Friend suggests.

These are good ideas but aren't what I want. I miss the womblike atmosphere at The Café, our great society. I miss The Revolution and waiting for change. It's not easy for The Poet and Writer Friend to understand this—they see each other on a regular basis and are still wearing shades of gray and brown. They openly condemn me for buying pink Puma tennis shoes. "You might as well have just killed a kid on the street, wearing those," The Poet says. Fiancé squeezes my hand, and somehow I feel this is the first loving gesture in the New Life.

"Drank any coffee lately?" I say, pointing to The Poet's cup. "Is it Free Trade? You know how many farmers lost their lives last year because of Folgers?" Fiancé squeezes again, and I smile.

"Touché," The Poet says.

I smoke another cigarette, and we move on. Writer Friend is looking through the boutique windows for the girl in the sheepskin coat.

"What a chicken," Writer Friend says. "She was too afraid to come out here and defend her slaughter."

The Poet scoffs and begins to tell us about a system he's devised that will distribute the country's wealth based on hard work, not social status. "This is *not* communism," he emphasizes. He hasn't given up, and I can't help but wonder if I have. Or if I ever knew what I was waiting for.

Lest you forget, this lovely book you hold in your hands is the product of a national contest, and, as with all contests, there had to be a winner. Clearly, this was an agonizing decision to make—all the essays in this collection are practically perfect in every way, and we could have easily made the case for giving any of them the grand prize. In the end, though, one simply grabbed us. Scratch that: It took us by the arm, looked us squarely in the eye, and kissed us hard on the mouth. That's right, we've fallen in love with "Working at Wendy's" by Joey Franklin, and we don't care who knows. Incisive, wry, warm, and cinematic, it is unique as a deeply personal, socially astute account of American twentysomethingness. But enough about what we think. Read for yourself.

t's 8:45 P.M., and I am standing in front of the counter at Wendy's. It smells of french fries and mop water. In my right hand I hold my résumé. I don't know if I need a résumé to apply for the Wendy's night shift, but I bring it anyway. It anchors me as I drift toward the sixteen-year-old kid behind the counter and ask to speak to his manager.

"One mandarin orange salad?" the boy asks.

"Uh, no. Actually, I'd like to speak to the *manager.*" As the cashier retreats to the back of the store, I recognize a large kid with curly hair working the fryer—he used to play football with some of the members of my Boy Scout troop. He looks up at me, and I avert my eyes. Part of me wants to turn around and leave before the manager comes out. A couple in their twenties walks into the restaurant behind me. I step away from the counter and pretend to read the menu, holding my résumé close to my chest. The urge to leave increases. Just then the manager comes out and asks, "You here about the night shift?"

As I hand the manager my résumé, I realize it is a mistake. He doesn't want to know my service experience, or my academic references, or my GPA. All he wants to know is if I can spell my name correctly.

"Er, the application is over there," the manager says, handing me back my résumé and pointing to a file folder mounted on the wall next

to the counter. I take the application to an empty table in the corner of the restaurant and hunch over it, wishing I had a drink, or a hamburger, or something to put on the table beside me.

The next day I go for an interview with the hiring manager. I sit down at a table in the lobby and answer two questions: "What hours do you want to work?" and "When can you start?"

When he was sixteen, my brother, Josh, got his first job at McDonald's. He lasted two weeks before deciding the greasy uniform and salty mop water weren't worth $5.25 an hour. His manager used to show off rejected applications to the other employees in the back of the store. Most were high school dropouts looking for spending money, but a few had college degrees. One application was from a doctor who had recently left his practice because he "couldn't handle the mortality rate."

I think about that doctor now as I sit in a small back room at Wendy's. I have just watched thirty minutes of training videos about customer service, floor mopping, heavy lifting, and armed robbery. Chelsea, the training manager, hands me two neatly folded uniforms and a brand-new hat. Holding the hat in my hand, I look out into the kitchen at my new coworkers. At the fryer is the large high school kid I remember from the night before. A skinny brown-haired Asian-looking boy who must be about nineteen years old is washing dishes. Two girls are at the front of the store taking orders, and the manager is on the phone with an angry customer. "Can I do this?" I ask myself, and put on my hat.

Chelsea is pregnant. During our training session, I guess she is about six months along. It turns out she is due in three days. "This is my last week on the day shift," she says. "After the baby is born, I'll be back on nights." This is her first child, she explains, and says she is looking forward to being a mom. She smiles as she pats her stomach and asks about my son.

"Eighteen months," I tell her, "a real handful." I explain that I want to work nights so I can take care of my son during the day while my wife finishes her last semester of college. I ask about the pay, but I already know her answer. "We start at five-seventy-five," she says, "but the night guys get six." I ask her what she thinks about $7. She says she'll see what she can do.

Chelsea trains me on Tuesday and goes into labor on Wednesday. I don't see her again for three weeks.

Kris Livingston's mom ran the register at the Taco Bell on the corner of Lombard Street and Allen Boulevard in a poorer section of Beaverton, Oregon. Her name was Dawn. She was divorced and had three boys. She shared a three-bedroom apartment with another single mom and her own five children. They listened to Snoop Dogg and Ice-T, drank forty-ounce malt liquors, and walked over two miles round-trip every Saturday to watch the neighborhood boys play basketball at Schiffler Park.

On welfare-check days, Dawn went grocery shopping and brought home twelve-packs of Pepsi, stacks of frozen steaks, crinkly bags of potato chips, several gallons of 2-percent milk, and bag after bag of Malt-O-Meal cereal. The week before welfare checks came, they ate eggs and instant ramen—lots of ramen.

Her son Kris was my best friend in sixth grade. We often walked to Taco Bell together to visit his mother. She usually bought us a taco while we sat in a booth in the corner of the store and talked about bicycles, girls, and football. Once, on the way home from visiting his mom, Kris said, "She used to sell drugs, you know. We had plenty of money, and nobody thought she was a bad mom then."

My first night on the job, I work with Dave. He is seventeen years old, five-ten, and keeps his hair short, like a soldier. He goes to an alternative high school if he wakes up in time and is looking forward to enlisting in the military when he turns eighteen. His dad, who re-

cently remarried and moved, told Dave he would have to find his own place to live. When Dave isn't sleeping on his friends' couches, he lives in his car, a 1982 Volkswagen Rabbit with a hole in the floor just beneath the gas pedal.

Dave works with me a few nights a week and knows the business well. He's quick with a mop, can make all the sandwiches blindfolded, and has the entire computer memorized. When he's not working, he hangs out in the restaurant lobby trying to steal Frosties and old fries when no one is looking. The manager says she will give him food if he needs it and asks that he not steal anymore. "Asking gets you nowhere," he says, and keeps stealing.

Because I live just two blocks from the store, I recognize a disproportionate number of the late-night drive-through customers. Mostly, I see parents of the scouts I work with, or other scout leaders, and occasionally a friend from school. When they pull up to the window and see me in the Wendy's hat and headphones, the following conversation ensues:

"Joey, I didn't know you worked here! How's it going?"

"Good, good. Just flipping burgers."

"Hey, you've got to do what you've got to do."

Then I explain the job is temporary, and it's the only job in town that allows me to work at night so I can watch my son during the day while my wife finishes school. I tell them in another month I'll be back in school and working at a better-paying, less humiliating campus job.

One evening a fellow scout leader comes through, and after an exchange similar to the one described above, he says, "Hey, more power to ya. I know a lot of people who think they're above that." He thanks me as I hand him his triple cheeseburger, and he drives around the corner and out of sight.

At 250 pounds, Danny really fills out his uniform. He played varsity football for the local high school, has earned his Eagle Scout award, and knows his way around a car engine. On several occasions he has

changed spark plugs, jumped batteries, and even replaced brakes on the cars of fellow employees, usually right in the store parking lot.

Wendy's is the first job Danny has ever had. With six months' experience, he is the senior employee and is being considered for a management position. He brings in about $1,000 a month, much of which he gives to his grandmother. At closing, he always saves the good salads for me and talks the manager into letting me go home early. He likes listening to Metallica, working on his Trans Am, and talking with Tonya, a high school junior who also works at the store.

While I'm washing my hands in the bathroom at work, a well-groomed twentysomething man standing at the sink next to me starts a conversation. "Do you like working the night shift?" he asks.

"It's not bad," I say, shaking my wet hands over the sink.

"How long have you worked here?"

"Two weeks."

"Have you ever thought about college?" he asks. I want to tell him I'm in the top 5 percent of students at my college, that I am two semesters away from graduating, and that I'm on my way to grad school to get a Ph.D. in English literature. Instead, I shrug and tell him the same line I tell everyone: "Oh yeah, I'm just working here until my wife finishes." He doesn't believe me. To him, I look like another wasted life, another victim. He thinks I got my girlfriend pregnant, that I never graduated from high school, that I can't do any better than flip burgers at two in the morning. He feels sorry for my kids.

"I only applied here because I knew I would get hired," says Sara the first night I work with her. She is a nineteen-year-old single mother with a sixteen-month-old boy. She is very tall and wears her long brown hair in a ponytail pulled through the hole in the back of her Wendy's hat. I ask her why she needed a job so bad.

"I had to get one," she tells me. "My parole officer said it was the only way to stay out of jail." I start at this and then ask, "Why were you in jail?"

"Drugs," she says, and pauses, testing me. "I was wearing my boyfriend's jacket, and the cops found a heroin pipe in the pocket." I ask how long she was in jail. "One year," she tells me. "I just got out a month ago."

When I was in fifth grade, my dad got a job delivering pizza. As an eleven-year-old, pivoting on that blurry edge between boyhood and adolescence, I found myself bragging to my friends about the prospect of free pizza and then wishing I hadn't told them anything about my father's job. He worked a few nights a week, and when he came home, his uniform smelled like steaming cardboard and burnt cheese, but he always brought home pizza.

Oren is nineteen years old and works at Wendy's to pay for a cell-phone bill and to get out of the house. His parents are devout Mormons and think he is a disgrace to their entire family. He wants to sell marijuana because he believes he can do nothing else. "I don't do anything well," he tells me one night while washing dishes. "I don't know what I want to do with my life." He asks Sara to find some pot for him to sell.

Oren's mother is Japanese, born and raised, and speaks to her children in her native tongue. That means Oren speaks Japanese and has family connections in Japan.

Oren also owns an AK-47 and likes to go up into the canyons and shoot jackrabbits. He showed me a picture once of a rabbit carcass out in the desert, its innards all blown out and dangling for the camera.

Tonight, while working the grill, Danny tells me he has never been on a date. "Girls don't like me," he says as he flips a row of sizzling, square quarter-pound patties. I can tell he believes it. Danny, by his own admission, is the kind of guy whom girls like for support. He is a gentleman, he asks thoughtful questions, and he's always willing to talk. He thinks his weight and his scruff turn girls off. He tells me he is going to ask Tonya to a movie this weekend but isn't sure she'll say yes. Later, Tonya comes into the store, and Danny disap-

pears with her for a few minutes out in the lobby. He comes back with a large smile on his face and says, "I've got a date this weekend, can you work for me?"

I don't like when Dave works the front line with me. I can't make sandwiches very fast yet, and he gets tired of waiting. More than once he pushes me aside to finish an order. If he sees me hesitate on a step, he barks at me, "Red, green, red, green! Ketchup, pickle, tomato, lettuce! Come on, Joe, it's not that hard."

Later, while I'm mopping the floor at closing, Dave comes by and takes the mop from my hand. "Like this," he says, scrubbing the tile vigorously. He thrusts the mop back in my hands and walks away, rolling his eyes.

Chelsea is back at work tonight for the first time since having her baby. She appears fairly happy, and I am surprised at how well adjusted she seems to being a working mom. The phone rings several times, and Chelsea takes the calls in her office. She tells me her husband has lots of questions about putting the baby to bed. After the lobby closes, Chelsea disappears into the bathroom for nearly half an hour. This happens every time I work with her. I wonder if she is sick. Then I notice the breast pump in a case on her desk. Another employee tells me Chelsea has been expressing milk in one of the bathroom stalls on her breaks.

Danny and Tonya have been dating for two weeks. He shows up for his shift an hour early to see her before she gets off. They sit in the lobby holding hands and talking for almost the entire hour. When they're not in the store together, she sends text messages to his phone, which I catch him reading while he stands at the grill.

Tonight Danny approaches me while I'm opening boxes of french fries. He wants advice on how to ask Tonya to her junior prom. "I want to do something romantic," he says. I suggest Shakespeare's eighteenth sonnet. He has never heard of it. " 'Shall I compare thee to a summer's day . . .' " I recite. "She'll love it." I print off the sonnet at home and

bring it to work for him the next day. He writes it in a card and delivers it with flowers. Two weeks later, in a rented tux at Tonya's junior prom, Danny gets his first kiss.

I call my dad tonight. He asks about school, about my son, and about work. I tell him about Wendy's.

"What? Who?" he says.

"Me. I got a job at Wendy's." Long pause. "I needed a job I could do at night." More silence. "It's not so bad." Still silence. "I work from nine P.M. to one A.M. a few nights a week."

Just when I think the line must be disconnected, Dad clears his throat and asks, "What happened to your computer job?"

"The guy ran out of work for me."

"Oh." More silence. I imagine he looks around the room to make sure no one is listening before he says, "Wendy's? When did that happen?" I want to tell him that it didn't *happen,* that it wasn't an accident, but I am stuck wondering how to make him understand, and at the same time wondering why I should have to explain anything at all. I wonder what his reaction would be if I had chosen to get more student loans instead of the part-time job. I choose to say nothing. Then I offer him my employee discount on fries next time he is in town. He says he'll take me up on it.

When I come into the store tonight, Dave is talking loudly to some employees gathered in the lobby. I ask what all the laughing is about. They tell me that last night Dave and Oren siphoned all the gas out of Dave's stepmother's four-wheeler, and then they urinated on her car handles.

Everyone dreads working with Chelsea. When she is not in her office counting the till or on the phone with her husband, she sits on the front counter and complains about her mother-in-law. She does very little to help prep the store for closing, and we rarely get out before two A.M.

Tonight she tells me about her mother-in-law's most recent visit. "I cleaned the house for hours before she came," Chelsea says, nursing a Diet Coke. "And the first thing she says when she gets there is how disgusting the place looks. She won't even eat my cooking." According to Chelsea, her mother-in-law has hated her ever since she got engaged. She wouldn't even visit except that Chelsea has a baby now, and the mother-in-law feels obligated. Chelsea's mother-in-law is disappointed that she is still working. "A mother's place is in the home," she says to Chelsea. "Your kids will be ruined."

Tonight Waymon Hamilton comes through the drive-up window with his family. Waymon lives around the corner from me, and his three sons are in my scout troop, but they spend most of their free time traveling around the state playing premier Little League baseball. They order a few value meals, some drinks, and they ask how I'm doing. There is no hint of concern or condolence in their voices, and I appreciate it.

I hand them their food and watch them drive away. Most people know Waymon the way I know him, as a dedicated father who works hard at a thankless job to provide for his family. His unassuming nature and warm smile are what I see when I think about him. Few people know him as the fleet-footed running back who helped Brigham Young University win Holiday Bowls in 1981 and 1983. Few people know he holds several BYU scoring records, including second place for touchdowns in a season, third in career touchdowns, and fifth for both season and career points scored. I didn't even know he played college football until someone mentioned it at a scout meeting. I once worked all day with Waymon, putting in a new driveway for a neighbor, and he never mentioned his football days once. He told me about his boys, about teaching public school in California, and about pouring lots of concrete.

After the store closes, I come home, take off my uniform, and climb into bed with my wife. She rolls over, tells me she loves me, and murmurs something about the smell of french fries. I kiss her on the

cheek and close my eyes. It is winter, but the house is warm. My son is asleep in the next room. There is food in the fridge, and I have a job that pays an honest wage. In the morning I will make breakfast and send my wife off to school. And then, after the dishes are done, if the weather permits, my son and I will take a walk to the park.

RADHIYAH AYOBAMI holds a certificate in poetics from the Bowery Arts and Science Center, New York. She is a finalist for the 2004 Hurston-Wright College Writers Award and a Cave Canem Fellow. She has also been published in *South Loop Review* and is currently working on her first novel. She lives in Brooklyn.

EULA BISS is the author of *The Balloonists*. She teaches nonfiction writing at Northwestern University. Her essays have recently appeared in *Columbia, Ninth Letter,* the *Seneca Review,* the *North American Review,* and *Harper's.* She lives in Chicago.

EMMA BLACK graduated from Oglethorpe University with a double major in English and education. Emma won the Anne Rivers Siddons Prize for Short Fiction (2004) and has been published in *Ophelia Speaks* (2000) and various other local publications. She lives in Birmingham, Alabama, where she still teaches third grade.

KATHERINE DYKSTRA is the senior editor at *The Independent: Film and Video Monthly,* a contributor for the *New York Post*'s Home section, a frequent freelancer, and a writer of personal essays. She is also a recent graduate of the New School University's MFA program. She lives in Manhattan.

Proud aunt **MARY BETH ELLIS** is a freelance writer masquerading as a college professor in central Florida. A native of Cincinnati, Ohio, she obtained her undergraduate degree at Saint Mary's College and was the first SMC student invited to read at her brother school's marquee literary event, the University of Notre Dame's Sophomore Literary Festival. Her vast and frightening array of day jobs after completing an MFA in nonfiction writing at Bennington College has included bodyguarding Jimmy Buffett, working in education at the Kennedy Space Center, and sports-reporting for the Thoroughbred racing industry. She currently writes for BlondeChampagne.com, a kinda daily updated humor site.

ELRENA EVANS holds an MFA in creative writing from Pennsylvania State University where, she regrets to say, she was not offered classes in truly important subjects such as Typing with One Hand While Nursing. She is currently working on a Ph.D. in education. In her free time, she likes to write proposals to major clothing manufacturers asking them to design and carry nursingwear.

JOHN FISCHER is an advertising wonk on the long road to recovery. Born and raised in scenic Long Island, John majored in music composition at Vassar College before discovering that he needed a real job. He currently lives in Brooklyn with a hairy roommate.

MIELLYN FITZWATER writes and produces television promos for TLC and, in her unpaid time, writes, designs some of her own clothes, and goes to too many concerts. The daughter of a novelist and a computer scientist, and the sister of a pop-culture professor, she has an awful lot to say. She lives in Washington, D.C., with her brilliant man friend and their three plants.

MARY KATE FRANK was born and raised in New Jersey. She has a master's in journalism from NYU. She and her pink armchair currently reside in New York City.

JOEY FRANKLIN is an English major at Brigham Young University in Provo, Utah. Outside of class, he spends much of his time helping his wife, Melissa, chase around their two-year-old son, Callan. He plans to study creative writing and literature in graduate school in fall 2007. He no longer works at Wendy's.

At present, **JENNIFER GLASER** lives the nomadic life fantastic, trekking between Philadelphia, where she is a graduate student studying American Jewish literature and intellectual history in the comparative literature program at the University of Pennsylvania, and New York City and Boston, where she engages in more clandestine writerly pursuits. She has written for the *Columbia Journalism Review* and Beliefnet, and has a chapter on Bernard Malamud and an essay on the Lower East Side forthcoming in other anthologies. She plans to expand her essay on Neil's death into a full-length memoir.

SHAHNAZ HABIB is not good at writing bios. She is Indian, Muslim, a woman, a writer, and addicted to coffee and the Internet. Everything else is in a state of flux.

ELI JAMES lives in New York City, where he plies his trade as an actor, writer, and musician. He was a writer/performer in the sketch comedy group Quiet Library and the front man for the adolescent pop group Eli and the Indoor Boys. His plays have been produced in festivals around the country, and for five years he did silly voices on a British TV show called *So Graham Norton*. "Finding the Beat" is Part One of his upcoming serial, "The East Side Diaries." Visit his website at www.elisongs.com.

RACHEL KEMPF recently graduated with a BA in English from Truman State University. She has had her plays, *Projections* and *Just Like the Ones I Used to Know,* professionally performed in Chicago, Bloomington, and Kirksville.

COLLEEN KINDER was born and raised in Buffalo, New York. After graduating from Yale, she spent a year in Cuba on a fellowship. She is the author of *Delaying the Real World: A Twentysomething's Guide to Seeking Adventure* (www.delayingtherealworld.com) and co-editor of *Confessions of a Word Nerd.* She is currently living in Iowa City, where she is getting her MFA and has found a new palm reader named Spirit Wolf.

JESS LACHER is a Northwestern graduate whose plays have been performed in Chicago, New York, and Los Angeles. In addition to writing, Jess builds puppets for the New York children's theater company the Striking Viking Story Pirates; she also performs improv and sketch comedy. She has just moved to New York City to work with the Delicious Theater Group, of which she is cofounder. She is of strong midwestern stock.

BRONSON LEMER was born and raised in Harvey, North Dakota. He spent six years with the North Dakota Army National Guard, including deployments to Kosovo and Iraq. He is currently an MFA candidate at Minnesota State University, Mankato. He still can't grow a mustache.

MARISA McCARTHY is the only child of Thomas and Cathleen McCarthy. Marisa was born and raised in San Francisco. She studied English at Boston College, graduating with a BA in 2003. Marisa currently lives and works in Manhattan. This is Marisa's first published work. She plans to continue writing and hopes her next piece will be something her entire family can read and enjoy.

KATE McGOVERN, a native of Cambridge, MA, is spending her twenties in New York City, where she writes, performs, and works as a middle school language arts specialist. She has performed her solo show, *Dreaming of Kitchens,* at several venues around town. Kate received her BA from Yale in 2003.

KYLE MINOR's fiction, essays, and reviews have appeared in the *Carolina Quarterly, Mid-American Review, Quarterly West, River Teeth, The Antioch Review,* and many other magazines and journals. He placed second in the 2004 Atlantic Monthly Student Writing Contest for non-fiction and was awarded honorable mentions in the same contest in 2005 for both fiction and poetry. He lives in Columbus, Ohio, where he is completing a book-length memoir for which "You Shall Go Out with Joy and Be Led Forth with Peace" is the first chapter.

LAUREN MONROE can sense her thirtieth birthday looming ominously, but she feels all right about it. She lives in suburban New York with her daughter, lover, two cats, and a collection of old Polaroid cameras. Asparagus, magenta, and the guitar stylings of Django Reinhardt keep her going.

LUKE MULLINS graduated from Boston College in 2000, spent two years in the Peace Corps in Mauritania, West Africa, before spending eighteen months in the Dominican Republic working as a baseball coach at an elementary school. He then earned a master's degree in journalism at Syracuse University. He now lives in Washington, D.C., where he grew up, working as a reporter at a financial daily paper and as a freelance writer.

BRENDAN PARK was born in 1979 and has spent his twentysome-odd years since, in chronological order, pursuing higher education, working minimum-wage jobs, traveling, and inventing creative ways to avoid responsibility, always delighted simply to be a part of the magic.

CHRISTOPHER POLING is a twenty-five-year-old second-year law student and an aspiring screenwriter who lives in California. He played football for three years at UCLA, where he picked up his BA in political science. In addition, he worked at a gym for a year, was Jay Hernandez's stunt double in the movie *Friday Night Lights,* and scored four touchdowns in a single game in high school (in honor of Al Bundy).

Christopher gets annoyed when middle-aged white guys try to pick up chicks by mixing Spanish and English (e.g.: "I'm looking for a gorgeous señorita!").

KATHLEEN ROONEY's first book, *Reading with Oprah,* was published by the University of Arkansas Press in 2005. A winner of a Ruth Lilly Fellowship from *Poetry* magazine, she has published poems in *Crab Orchard Review, Smartish Pace,* and *Passages North.*

TRAVIS SENTELL holds degrees in religion/philosophy and psychology from Emory University, and an MLitt in creative writing from St. Andrews University in Scotland. He currently resides in Los Angeles, California.

THEODORA STITES grew up in Connecticut and the Florida Keys. After attending boarding school at Northfield Mount Hermon, she studied anthropology at Connecticut College. She lives in New York City and works in advertising. Her blog is www.zoogomza.blogspot.com.

BURLEE VANG is currently pursuing an MFA in poetry at California State University, Fresno. He is working on a memoir and facilitates biweekly creative writing workshops for Hmong college students on the weekends.

Antelope Valley native **J. W. YOUNG** earned her MFA in fiction from the University of Mississippi in 2003. She is an assistant professor at Middle Georgia College and is currently at work on her first novel, set in the Southern California desert.

MATT KELLOGG and **JILLIAN QUINT** are proud twentysomethings and indentured servants, er, assistants in the Random House editorial department. They both own iPods and have never seen an episode of *Welcome Back, Kotter.*